# Social Context and Social Location
# in the Sociology of Law

# Social Context and Social Location in the Sociology of Law

edited by Gayle M. MacDonald

broadview press

NATIONAL LIBRARY OF CANADA CATALOGUING IN PUBLICATION DATA

MacDonald, Gayle Michelle 1957–
    Social context and social location in the sociology of law

Includes bibliographical references and index
ISBN 1-55111-370-8

1. Sociological jurisprudence. I. Title.

K370.M32 2001                340'.115                C2001-901570-4

BROADVIEW PRESS, LTD.
is an independent, international publishing house, incorporated in 1985.

| | |
|---|---|
| *North America* | *United Kingdom* |
| Post Office Box 1243, | Thomas Lyster, Ltd. |
| Peterborough, Ontario, | Unit 9, Ormskirk Industrial Park |
| Canada K9J 7H5 | Old Boundary Way, Burscough Rd. |
| Tel: (705) 743-8990 | Ormskirk, Lancashire L39 2YW |
| Fax: (705) 743-8353 | Tel: (01695) 575112 |
| | Fax: (01695) 570120 |
| 3576 California Road, | *books@tlyster.co.uk* |
| Orchard Park, New York | |
| USA 14127 | *Australia* |
| | St. Clair Press |
| *customerservice@broadviewpress.com* | P.O. Box 287, Rozelle, NSW 2039 |
| *www.broadviewpress.com* | Tel: (612) 818-1942 |
| | Fax: (612) 418-1923 |

Broadview Press gratefully acknowledges the financial support
of the Book Publishing Industry Development Program,
Ministry of Canadian Heritage, Government of Canada.

Cover design by Zack Taylor. Typeset by Zack Taylor.

*Printed in Canada*

# Contents

## Part III: Social Location and the Application of Law

## Part IV: Social Location and Resistance to Law

# Acknowledgements

As with any collaborative work, the compiling of a reader takes time, energy, and, most of all, patience. I would first like to acknowledge the contributors to this volume. Many thought it would never see the light of day, and it is a testament to their patience, as well as to their scholarship, that this book is finally realized.

This book has had many lives. The germ of the idea I owe to a kitchen table session about eight years ago with Dawn Currie, who was very encouraging of the original concept. Thanks also to the colleagues I had at Queen's University: Christine Overall, who said "just do a book, it's the only thing the guys will understand"; Mary Morton, who was supportive of just about any idea I had; and Roberta Lamb for her kind and sustaining friendship.

Of my colleagues here at St. Thomas University, I owe my greatest debt to Peter MacDonald. He gave sympathetic and critical readings of many versions of the early chapters, as well as acting as an "in-house" reviewer for others, when needed. To Chris McCormick, thanks for all the research talks and tips.

Others that need thanks include Lori Beaman, for some fine editing and encouragement; Brian Henderson, for supporting the original concept; and Michael Harrison, Barbara Conolly, and Judith Earnshaw of Broadview Press, who helped realize the final product. To Jason Doherty, research assistant extraordinaire, my heartfelt thanks, and to Anita Saunders, secretary extraordinaire, many thanks also.

A final tribute to my family, both to my partner Jonathan and to the two most interesting interruptions a book could ever have, Eris and Breagh, without whom the book could have been completed earlier, but it would not have been nearly so much fun.

Gayle MacDonald
Fredericton, New Brunswick

# Preface

The sociology of law in the 1990s encountered uncertain terrain. The certainties of race, class, and gender that gave stability to the discipline's discourses over the past 30 years were decentred, disrupted, and divided in that decade. Global economic politics, restless divisions within both nation and state, and increasing demand from the marginalized have nearly paralysed these discourses in their attempt to address the very real and serious problems faced by increasing numbers of the population.

As we move into the next century, it has also become apparent that the needs of various disenfranchised groups are being pitted against one another, for example, legal aid costs against social assistance costs, sustenance needs of "racialized" communities against land claims. The needs of the disenfranchised are also pitted against those of the powerful, the needs of a victim against the needs of a professional association to protect itself, the downsizing of the corporate market against the needs of the worker,[1] the needs of children against the need for the state to protect its policies. What is clear from these struggles is the lack of theory to explain these frictions. What are the options for critical work? Other than pitting an analysis of politics and economy (as Marx does) against analyses of power and discourse (as Foucault does), perhaps it is more important to examine how critical theory needs to move with this decentring. Feminist critical theory has been moving, globally, toward analysing the fractionalized subject.[2] However, critical theory in the sociology of law needs to address the fracturing, intersection, and disruption of the very social services that claim to support the needs of the victim, the poor, and the child. The fact, for example, that apathy and despair have replaced activism

9

around "community" and that survival has replaced service as the economic motif from which we are expected to construct our lives is a serious problem in the social world, and one that the sociology of law is just beginning to understand.

The strength of a critical sociology of law is its ability to map the realities of social issues of the day, in direct contrast to the inability of law to do the same. New challenges to the authority of law and newly disenfranchised groups created by law itself all call on critical theory to encompass, challenge, and critique the dominant social structure that creates and perpetuates such social injustices. Public relations machinery of the corporate world force us as academics to document more effectively the nature and patterns of the life worlds of the people we study. How do we account for the fact that all of us live, work, and reproduce in social contexts that we name differently, depending on how we intersect with others? How do we rescue "family" from both corporate marketing and the rhetoric of the right? How do we define the "homeplace" in a world that fractures our sense of public and private? How do we name the body marked by poverty and despair in a social ordering that sends more and more people to the "ineligibility" line of legal service? How do we name the victim in a social world increasingly bored with the concept?

A critical sociology of law has to document, displace and disrupt normative understandings of the "social facts" of a world that is no longer cohesive, but racked by conflicts, not all of which may be entirely understood using conventional sociology. Conventional sociologies are challenged by these quests for new explanations, challenged by what the next century might bring as we lumber into it with antiquated law intact. The work in this text represents an evolving body of critical work around law and its social context. It is my hope, and the hope of the other authors in this reader, that the way we present critical work here will both aid in the understanding of the socio-legal world, and invite others to do the same.

## Notes

1. Buzz Hargrove with Wayne Skene. *Labour of Love: The fight to create a more humane Canada.* Toronto: MacFarlane Walter & Ross, 1998.

2. A recent conference (June 1998) held at Keele University in Stoke-on-Trent, England, entitled "Gender, Law and Sexuality," had fully one-third to one-half of the 100 presentations from academics around the world concentrating on concepts of identity and the subject, both in literary terms and in terms of their applicability to social sciences and law.

# PART I

*Theorizing the Struggles:*
*New Challenges, New Directions*

# 1

# Theory and the Canon:
# How the Sociology of Law is Organized

GAYLE M. MACDONALD

## Sociology and Law

Sociology has much to offer to the study of law, as sociology is, by definition, the critiquing discipline. Sociology examines from a critical standpoint the institutions, the social processes, and the organization of work, family and gender relations that exist in the social world. As a discipline that critiques everyday social practices, sociology thus enables students to see how what they come to take for granted in the social world — or what they think they know — is neither without precedent nor inevitable but definitely predictable. To do this in a classroom is to empower the sociology student to question "the way things are." In order to do this well, students need to learn to discern an urban myth from a social reality. To unravel social process from urban myth, to uncover social organization rather than simply accepting "the way things are," sociologists engage in the research exercise. How a sociologist does his or her research or how research questions are asked determines the types of answer that can be unearthed.

Sociologists conduct their research from a number of theoretical and methodological traditions. Which tradition one chooses for the study of socio-legal issues can have different implications for the nature of legal research. For example, we might realize through the study of sociology of law that access to law, a legal right in Canada, can be tempered by race, class or gender. We might also observe that the institution of law, in the same manner as any institution, can be changed, challenged, and reformed. As a result, law may not be the institution that we know today just a few short years from now. That shaping, reforming, and re-organization of law comprise a social process that is of interest to sociologists, as it reveals the effects that law has on the social world. Studying law without a sociological analysis is to learn how to practise it, to learn its language or discourse, to learn its "canon" — but not to learn its effects. A lawyer may easily be able to relay to a sociologist the socio-legal problems in the area of law in which she practises, but can do little either to analyse why these problems arise with such regularity or to suggest remedies for prevention. One may make a similar argument about physicians, who may know a great deal about medicine and about health care in general, but far less about disease prevention.

In other words, sociology, as the study of social organizations and social processes, can tell us more about how law operates in certain contexts than can law itself. Why is this the case? One of the strengths of law is also its weakness: law is completely self-referential. Furthermore, legal research is often self-referential, that is, it rarely considers systems of thought or ideas outside of the canon of law. Law represents a dialogue of ideas, each speaking to itself. The conversation is widened, includes more standpoints,[1] and is more inclusive of all groups within society when sociology enters that dialogue. It is for this reason that a sociology of law is useful.

Law has particular canons, or bodies of literature from which certain traditions evolve. These traditions are applied in cases, and when this happens, precedents are set. For example, common law or case law evolves from particular cases, using specific rules for interpretation. The burden of proof or onus in common law is not as great as that of criminal law. In common law, one only has to prove a case within a balance of probabilities: the likelihood that A did x is greater than the likelihood that B did x. Criminal law represents another separate canon, with very rigorous rules of evidence and interpretation.[2] Criminal law still represents the arena in which the most serious crimes are tried, as it contains an exacting burden of proof, which means that a prosecutor needs to prove that A, rather than B did x, and that proof needs to be assured beyond a reasonable doubt.[3] Other areas of law, including family law, tax law, and law governing land claims often rely on past case decisions which set the standards (or precedents) by which law is followed to establish claims, proofs, and rules about how to proceed in similar cases in the future. We will examine, in this text, examples of each of these types of law, through particular issues.

How, then, does one "do" sociology of law? To answer that question, it is necessary to understand the traditions within sociological work.

## Old Paradigms, New Problems: Old Problems, New Directions

Theoretical work in the sociology of law has followed two distinctive paths over the years, broadly defined as consensus and conflict theory. Accompanying those traditions have been two other tendencies in the work of sociology, that is, the micro and macro traditions of inductive and deductive reasoning.

### CONSENSUS THEORY

The premise of this paradigm is that there is agreement on norms and values within a given society or culture, and that how we determine what is lawful or not is based primarily on an understanding of social order as a necessary aspect of the functioning of the social world. Known as structural functionalism, the concept of law and order has primary importance in this paradigm. The work of Emile Durkheim, a classical theorist associated with the paradigm, involved the idea of a collective conscience, a group ordering that for him occurred naturally in human society, but was influenced and changed by the organization of labour. For Durkheim, such ordering was developed in tandem with the industrial organization of society and its corresponding need for functions and specified roles within institutions as social groupings, for example. In Durkheimian analyses, the more developed a society is in terms of industry, the more complex its rules and regulations and the more restitutive law becomes. Durkheim held that professional associations (such as a medical or law society) have just as much to do with the upholding of a social and legal order as do statutes or law itself. For Durkheim, the ordering of a social group holds an implicitly moral character, one that has been most recently emphasized in writings around the concept of "rule of law." Such ordering is based on agreed-upon social norms for social life, that is, we fundamentally agree on values, which are then reflected in law. Family law, for example, can be seen as one canon of law that adopts this premise.

### CONFLICT

The conflict paradigm is based primarily on the writings of Karl Marx, and centres on the premise that any order within a social group, legal or otherwise, involves a collection of specific and narrowly focussed interests, and that conflict between dominant and subordinate interests is a fundamental characteristic of human nature in social groups. For Marx, conflict was exacerbated, by further industrial development, but also by the nature of competitive, corporate capital. Conflict arises naturally, for Marx, when humans in social groups are stratified according to some separate, pre-determined valuing system, like a salary scale. For Marx, law is an instrument of the dominant groups, and is such as employers or owners of production, structurally designed to benefit these dominant groups. Analyses that use the conflict paradigm generally agree that conflict is the basis of the social world, and that law is merely a reflection of or reaction to the nature of that conflict. Furthermore, law in some instances can actually replicate the dominant/subordinate conflict, for instance in legal forums, especially when even participating in such forums can require large sums of money. Corporate law, for example, can fit into this premise, as well as the oft-cited statistics that fully 80 per cent of the legal canon is concerned with property.

## The Theory/Method Dialogue

We observed earlier that law appears to be a self-referential dialogue. Within sociology there are a few dialogues as well, a few traditions from which different ideas or standpoints arise. One tradition focusses on the *theoretical* implications that issues create, or the "why" of a social problem. The other tradition focusses on *methodological* implications that social issues create, or "how" such a social problem comes to be.

Theoretical explanation can be a rigorous elaboration of a specific set of social phenomena. In terms of the physical world, this differs from law, as we usually use law in the context of unchangeable phenomena, such as the "law" of gravity. Theory can be described as law that remains to be proved; however, it can also operate as a useful framework with which to analyse observable social phenomena. We might, for example, observe that sexual assault cases seem to be handled differently under criminal law than are other violent criminal offences. There are particular theories that might help us better explain that. We might observe that access to legal process may have class, race or gender components that appear to favour certain groups over others in terms of accessibility to law. There are theories that help explain that phenomena. This type of explanation is often considered a *deductive* form of reasoning; that is, the explanation is fairly strong and general, and examples or evidence for its proof are deduced in the research process.

On the other hand, we might observe that there are patterns of resistance in First Nations peoples' abilities to make certain and consistent their claims to lands and other rights within Canadian law; or we might observe that workers' compensation packages have a particular bureaucracy that may disadvantage particular workers. Both of these social issues can be analysed using specific traditions or explanations within the sociology of law. This type of reasoning appears to be *inductive*; that is, a close examination of the "data," evidence of the social issue or problem reveals a trend that can be traced back to certain traditions and even reproduced in other, seemingly unrelated contexts. For example, Sandra Wachholz analyses in her chapter the legal concept of child neglect, arguing that it is not the character of the mother that is problematic in determining child neglect, but rather the quality of the economic life of the family. Consensus or traditional theory would simply brand the family as dysfunctional and apportion blame to a mother for a child who falls asleep at school due to hunger. Wachholz ends with an appeal for peace-making as a way forward in policy analysis.

To illustrate: as indicated earlier, one usually finds theoretical frameworks such as structural functionalism in discussions on land disputes involving First Nations and government. Usually the history of oppression is couched in a liberal pluralist rendition or a more sophisticated rendering of social control.[4] However, in her chapter on Listuguj, Melinda Martin presents a historical understanding of protest at Listuguj, which she writes as a historical view of resistance: resistance that unifies community. Indeed, the resistance documented here continues beyond resource industry land disputes. The latest battle, for example, has been over the custody of the children of a status woman and a white man.

## Sociology of Law and Liberal Democracy

A tradition within the sociology of law that is often assumed to be implicit, but is rarely made explicit, is that of liberal democracy. Within this tradition, law is explained by its adherence to or departure from traditions of liberal democracy. The overarching premise of work in this area is that of liberalism as a core foundation of the principles upon which democracy is based, and by inference to legal frameworks as well. Liberal democrats find fault with law when it does not adhere to the basic principles of liberalist philosophy: equity, justice, and fairness. These principles, first enshrined by the likes of Jean-Jacques Rousseau during the French

Revolution, would appear to be values upon which all would agree. The translation of these values into codified law, for Canada, is enshrined in our *Charter of Rights and Freedoms*, a document of legally enforceable human rights that has been the centrepiece of Canadian contributions to law in the industrialized world. However, this tradition does not come to us unproblematically, largely due to the influence of our neighbours to the south, where individual rights have not only become enshrined, but actually permit hatred to exist, legally and constitutionally. The inherent tension is one that exists not only between the United States and Canada, with differences on fundamental concepts such as free speech, but also within Canada itself, partly as a result of the differing traditions that Canada has inherited through its history of colonization. To explain further: the concept of free speech in the American tradition, because of its legal location within their constitution, is considered an absolute right. Such interpretations allow for the existence of groups such as the Ku Klux Klan, their racist and anti-Semitic discourse permissible under the free speech provision. In Canada, similar pronouncements would be considered hate crimes under the Canadian Criminal Code, as our right to freedom of speech is accompanied by the social and legal norms of responsibility. The legal norm of responsibility comes to us, in part, from the British system of responsible government, through which representatives are elected to be responsible for and to their constituents. Freedom of speech in Canada, therefore, is not absolute.

Where we encounter tensions within the Canadian legal framework, however, is around our application of this principle. In fact, wherever concepts of free speech arise, such as in the debates around pornography we can see how a liberal democratic sociology of law might explain this. For example, one explanation of the use of free speech may come to represent how much or what type of pornography one has the "right" to own or control. This is not an unsubtle distinction, as this conceptual blending of rights and property is a unique one under liberal democracy. Such conceptual blurring leads to a tendency to overestimate the power of individual rights as having precedent over, or emphasis with, legal concepts of property. One might argue that debates around gun ownership in Canada, a legal "right" in the United States, often centre around individual property rights, and therefore are considered unassailable rights in law. This is where one sees what I call "creeping liberalism," an interpretation of liberalism as a supremacist form of individual right that would deny the existence of a collective right, however defined.

The denial of collective rights in favour of individual ones has been documented in a critique of the *Charter*, as in the comprehensive work of Michael Mandel or in the critique of free speech in censorship over pornography, as in the work of June Callwood. Similarly, the right to carry a firearm, often considered an individual right, can suddenly become confused with the state's right to control and license arms. Such thinking, although useful for debate and work in the sociology of law, never takes us past the liberal democratic framework, to new possibilities and critiques waiting just outside its conceptual boundaries. Too often, because liberal democracy is taken for granted as "this is just the way things are," students and academics alike accept its approach as the only one possible and that working "within the system" is the only way to change. Critics argue that this keeps us solely focussed on reform rather than radical refashioning, debate rather than revolution, exclusion rather than inclusion, and measured effects rather than as a narrative method of explanation. Such thinking is ultimately self-referential, as it never moves beyond the paradigm in order to explain it more fully. Such thinking is often referred to within the discipline as *hegemonic thinking*. Critical theorists, therefore, like to implode hegemonic thinking in order to expose its inherent ideological core.

## Patterns within the Sociological Traditions

Any explanation of sociology would be incomplete without an outline of the micro/macro distinctions framed within inductive and deductive reasoning. Micro/macro distinctions usually indicate size or scale, which is probably an accurate description of how sociological theories operate. Macro theories involve explanations of how large structures or organizations operate to influence the social world. Included in this group are political economic explanations, structural functionalist explanations, and some feminist explanations of social processes. Micro theories, on the other hand, explain smaller, more intimate social interactions that influence social process in different ways. Such theories include interpretive, and social constructionist theories. Broadly speaking, the micro/macro distinction can be understood as a contrast between inductive and deductive reasoning. Inductive reasoning tends to be more intuitive, leading to conclusions only after patterns have been determined. Inductive work tends to be more inquiry-based, letting the data lead the researcher to observations and tendencies, rather than to conclusions. Deductive reasoning, on the other hand, follows a certain logic of an established theory or method. Deductive reasoning is applied in situations where the evidence matches or proves the established theory or method application. Micro traditions, then, follow a more inductive reasoning path, whereas macro traditions tend to be more deductive in logical progression.

Both of these contrasts or distinctions within sociology have different theoretical or methodological traditions which reflect different orientations in the explanation of social problems. For example, one macro theory, political economy, is concerned with the division of labour, in terms of who owns production, who sells their labour or time to those owners, and the social organization of work that results. The processes involved in corporate capital, their corresponding fallout effects for workers within the corporate structure, and the consequences for political economic structuring in the future are primary concerns of a political economist. A macro theory such as this begins with certain assumptions, for example, that what governs corporate structure policies and procedures is surplus or profit, rather than concern for the workers it employs. There is an inherent assumption in political economy that political and economic structures are inextricably bound to each other, and that changes or influences in one will be experienced by the other. A political economist might be particularly interested in, for example, how corporate mergers and takeovers have an impact upon the social processes of work, how the conditions of work are changed, and how the worker fares in the process. This approach seeks to confirm or deny particular patterns of theory, thus employing deductive reasoning as a mode of explanation.

Susan Machum's chapter on farm wives captures this tradition. In order to conduct a study using this theory, one begins with the assumptions of the theory and tests it in certain contexts, much as Machum does with marital property questions on farms. She notes that different types of farms create different production problems and that when productivity is measured in terms of actual financial gains, farm wives are often left out of the picture. Machum's work, is thus an example of macro theorizing from the political economy tradition.

Micro theorists, on the other hand, are interested in more interactional social processes. For example, a micro theorist might be interested in mapping how the everyday intimacies that occur between family members can reveal patterns that extend to the social organization of work. Or the micro theorist might be interested in how the social relations between co-workers lead to changing the face of the economy. Researchers in this tradition tend, as mentioned above, to use more inductive rather than deductive reasoning, and tend also to favour the primacy and authenticity of fieldwork over grand theorizing.[5] Scholars in this tradition let the "data speak to them," to quote an often repeated description of this tradition. Subjects in a study are permitted to talk for long periods of time, and are often revisited by the researcher to affirm or deny patterns or pictures that emerge from earlier interviews. This type of work can inform theory, but creating theory is not necessarily the goal of such research. Documenting and tracking social relations are fundamental to the process of learning in this tradition, and its greatest strength is in its ability to create data banks that invite comparative situations. For example, women going through bereavement may actually have patterns of grief and recovery similar to abuse victims, and so on. Work that uses this tradition in the text can be seen in Lori Beaman's piece on legal access. It is the stories of women under the auspices of legal aid that help the author piece together the pattern presented by their problems with access.

Other work in this text, such as Chris Doran's on workers' compensation, uses the social constructionist approach of Michel Foucault, with the work of feminists Dorothy Smith and Carol Smart, to demonstrate how workers' compensation can be denied systematically to workers who demonstrate the symptoms required. The author successfully weaves together complex ideas of Foucault with the "everyday, mundane" analysis offered by the feminisms of Smith and Smart, and in so doing he creates a tight, analytical vehicle that tempts the reader to use it again, in other areas of law, as explanation of denial of benefit. What is unique about Doran's work is that it eschews the usual explanations of denial of benefit presented by liberal or consensus theorizing on the status of law, and the conflict explanations outlined so clearly by political economy. In this way, the author manages to situate his work in an area designated as "critical" examinations of theorizing.[6]

The traditions described above are typical of the subdiscipline of the sociology of law. In the next chapter I will outline the history and currency of critical traditions in the field, and provide a theoretical foundation from which to read the rest of the book.

# Notes

1. The concept of standpoint comes to us from the work of Dorothy Smith. Smith's argument is that much of the organization of the social world, its work, documents and institutions, constitute a particular standpoint, that of men. In her work, she explores the possibilities of what a world constructed from a woman's standpoint might look like.

2. In criminal law the presence of both *mens rea* or intent and *actus reus* or the guilty act is necessary to establish full culpability as charged.

3. This is why defence lawyers try to raise instances of reasonable doubt, as any such doubt is more likely to be in their client's favour.

4. See Russell Smandych and Gloria Lee, "Explaining law and colonialism: toward an Amerindian autohistorical perspective on legal change, colonization, gender and resistance" *Post-Critical Criminology*, ed. Thomas O'Reilly-Fleming (Toronto: Prentice-Hall, 1996).

5. One method that attempts to blur the distinction between the macro and the micro involves institutional ethnography, or the ways in which textually mediated forms of social control, exercised by professionals, for example, actually influence or determine social structure. Examples of this appear in this text: see, for example, Beamen, Chapter Four, "Legal Discourse and Domestic Legal Aid"; Johnson, Chapter Eleven, "The Persuasive Cartographer"; Doran, Chapter Seven, "Medico-legal Expertise and Industrial Disease Compensation."

6. This "critical" designation is not to be confused with Critical Legal Studies or CLS, a movement spawned largely by Unger and others in an attempt to create an explanation for trends in legal curriculum. Heralded by many as a breakthrough in legal thinking, which indeed it was in jurisprudence circles, it has indeed reformed thinking around legal curriculum, which was long overdue and may have radical implications for future lawyers, but it has failed in providing the critical stance needed to examine social problems created by law itself. Indeed, the CLS movement can be seen to be trapped within the self-referential property of the study of law. See chapter two for an expanded discussion of these points.

# 2

## Critical Theory and the Sociology of Law: Contradiction and Currency

GAYLE M. MACDONALD

### Sociology of Law

An overarching theme for the collection of readings in this book can be outlined as follows: the readings all apply critical theory to the study of the sociology of law. Although these chapters address radically different social conflicts in law, and even vastly different time frames, they do have one coherent, unifying pattern, which is often a unique blend of theory, method, and socio-legal struggle. This is the very strength of critical theory: its ability to shift between both the theoretical paradigms and method traditions within sociology.

In this book, readers will find that the "expected" theoretical explanation, or method used, is usually not the case. In fact, many of the chapters address unconventional issues with predictable theoretical explanations, or, conversely, predictable scenarios with an unpredictable use of theory or method. For example, Susan Machum's chapter on the inequitable distribution of property for farm wives upon the death of a spouse or dissolution of marriage, commonly addressed by feminist theory, is rooted firmly in a critical assessment of the social reorganization of work and property which agribusiness creates. The chapter by Patricia Hughes addresses timeless issues, such as the sexual assault of women, but does so within a unusual context; that is, the victims are patients of abusive physicians. Hughes argues that the old debates around victim vs. consenting adult that appear in so much of the literature on violence against women should be addressed as a new struggle in law for women.

Similarly, the denial of rightful benefits is hardly a new struggle in law, but the analysis Chris Doran presents offers new hope for injured mine workers. He argues, using a new blend of both feminist and discourse analysis, how one can actually trace oppressive patterns of benefit denial through worker compensation decisions. Audrey Sprenger, in her fascinating account of the "industrial forest," argues that the blurring of our usual categories of race, class, and gender are needed to explain, in her words, "the native wearing the company jacket who refuses to tip the white female waitress for coffee, as a form of protest."[1] Political economy can explain the presence of the company, feminist theory can explain the situation of the female worker, but what can explain the First Nation worker's antagonism toward the white female waitress, someone who probably makes far less money than he does? Structural functionalists would have us believe that it is "reverse racism." Critical thinkers know that such situations are far more complex, and that such euphemisms do not always describe what is occurring on a social level. Critical theory can help untangle such seemingly problematic theoretical conundrums.

To explain how critical theory works in these chapters, and what traditions are simultaneously embraced and excluded as analytical tools within the sociology of law, I will examine the theoretical foundations of critical sociology.

## Critical Traditions within Sociology of Law

In this section I will outline some of the legacies of critical legal theory, all of which the sociology of law has inherited as part of its tradition. Although the sociology of law is very much influenced by its mother discipline, sociology, it is also clear that developments in jurisprudence have also been an undercurrent in the formation of what is currently considered its mode of analysis. As sociology-of-law adherents come from both fields, law and sociology, this influence is not surprising.

### MARXISM

Probably the longest-standing influence of critical thought in sociology has been the persistence of Marxism, and there have been many fine Canadian scholars who have used Marxism or socialism as a tool to analyse socio-legal relations — Elizabeth Comack, Steve Brickey, Brian Maclean, John McMullan, Bob Ratner, and Susan Boyd, to name just a few.[2]

The Marxist tradition in law, initially, was not strong. Marx left a woefully inadequate analysis that pales in comparison to his analysis of politics and economy. Some speculate that this was the result of his father's pressure for him to become a lawyer, an idea which the young Karl rejected wholeheartedly. It became the task of other scholars to apply the genius of Marx to an analysis of socio-legal relations, a task which at times was at odds with itself. Marxist thought has been most influential in arguing for an examination of the use of law as an instrument of ruling and as a structure of oppression. It is this dualism around law that has been both useful and somewhat lacking as a point of analytical departure. Analyses that merely point to the use of law as an instrument of the ruling class, although itself an important insight, do not address the capacity of agency or change around law that lobbying, even by grass-roots organizations, can have on the status quo. Undoubtedly, many laws are enacted by and for the ruling, but its circumstances and actors can shift and change at any given time. Law can sometimes be created for reasons of public pressure alone, and there is the capacity for ordinary people to have great impact on how legislation is formed, via their electorate. However, there is little doubt that, by and large, parliamentarians represent the privileged classes, and that business and corporate interests completely drive some governments (Mike Harris' Ontario provincial government comes to mind, or Ralph Klein's Alberta government). But law can sometimes surprise us. Recent Supreme Court decisions such as *R. v. Marshall* can actually upset the status quo in ways that may appear quite revolutionary to some. Further, it is unclear how law can operate as an "instrument" when it appears that it is the process by which it operates, rather than by which it is formulated, that appears to be at issue.

The second half of the analysis, that of structure, has appealed to many more scholars for a longer period of time. It is quite plausible to see that the organization of the law, the manner through which it is structured, can reveal the three tenets of Marxist analysis — ideology, politics, and the economy — as all are relevant to the structuring of law and the maintenance of bourgeois interest. But this structure can also create some checks and balances that ensure that control by the bourgeois is not completely intact or static. However, it is Marx's labour theory of value and commodification ideas that actually prove more interesting in legal analysis than the original instrument/structuralism thesis might allow.[3]

The labour theory of value rests on the premise that labour represents an abstract, historically contextual and materialist value for capitalism generally.

This value is abstracted from the labour itself, or put more simply, the cost of a pair of shoes reflects not so much the labour of their creation, as it does the marketing of the middle manager (the petit-bourgeois, as Marx would claim) and the markup by the store owner. The shoemaker is abstracted from the process of making shoes (they are now made in factories), and the cost of the shoes does not reflect the cost of materials, production or distribution, as all are done very, very cheaply. The difference between the actual value of the shoes and the stated value equals the concept of profit, which although real in its impact if you are the buyer of the shoes, is simply a concept, reflecting nothing. This can explain, for example, why that number can be lowered or raised depending on a great number of factors, or why the price of a similar pair of shoes at a completely different store, can be much the same despite the claims of capitalism to competition. It is this necessary condition of the economic to the political that makes the study of commodification, and its connection to law, so potentially interesting, for some have argued that fully 80 per cent of law is concerned with boundaries of property, transaction, and contract. In other words, is it the interests of the middle to upper classes that are protected by law's structure rather than the "interests of us all"? Those examining law through a Marxist lens could argue that it is the property rights of the landlord that are protected by such laws as tenancy, which is supposedly designed to protect the non-property owner. Similarly, as Doran argues in his chapter, even worker compensation legislation supposedly designed to protect the worker can serve to protect the interests of the employer, by rendering bureaucratic and legal structure so complex that denial of benefit is a certain result.

### FRANKFURT SCHOOL

This section addresses, albeit briefly, the influence of the Frankfurt School on critical thought in sociology. Although the school did not specifically address socio-legal problems, it influenced many thinkers who did, including Michel Foucault in the 1970s. Its legacy to the intellectual theoretical development of sociology today is legendary. Not without its detractors,[4] and despite our re-examination now of its influence, it is clear that the Frankfurt School became the viable political and critical theory of its time.

It is difficult to summarize succinctly a school of thought as vast and as varied as that which has come to be known as the "Frankfurt School," or its offspring, "critical theory," which has come to be considered as somewhat synonymous. Critical theory is no less easy to capture in a definition.[5] What follows is the best I've found:

> Critical theory has been variously characterized as a radical social theory (or sociology), a sophisticated form of cultural criticism combining Freudian and Marxist ideas, and a utopian style of philosophical speculation deeply rooted in Jewish and German idealism. (Ingram and Simon-Ingram, 1992:ix)

Born as a reaction to repressive politics of the early twentieth century in Europe, particularly in Germany, the Frankfurt School brought together a series of intellectual ideas and debates that have loosely become known as "critical theory." It is also not insignificant to note at this time that the leading intellectuals of the day (and of this school) were Jews. In *Die Frankfurter schule* (1994), a most engaging and comprehensive compendium on this period, Rolf Wiggershaus traces the history of the Frankfurt School from its early inception in 1923 through to the late 1960s and early 1970s. Wiggershaus traces the personal lives of the founding members of the School, and the political struggles of their time, as they crossed the Atlantic and fertilized theoretical debate at whichever university or city where they happened to be writing. Encompassing the work of Theodor Adorno, Max Horkheimer, Herbert Marcuse, and Jurgen Habermas, and due both to the diversity of writings of its founders and to their travels from one university home to another, the Frankfurt School became influential on schools of social science on both sides of the Atlantic.

The origins of the Frankfurt School are ironic, to say the least. It was founded by a wealthy part-time scholar, Felix Weil, and at the beginning of his book Wiggershaus notes Weil's original intention: "Felix Weil, son of a millionaire, founds an Institute for Marxism, hoping one day to hand it over to a victorious German soviet state" (9). Weil was determined to discover an enriched and intellectual environment for Marxism, which for him had political, rather than academic, outcomes. The influence of the political on the intellectual never changed, although the school hardly became an instrument of the German state. Indeed, as many of its leading proponents were intellectual Jews, it became a critical bastion for intellectuals who found capitalism abhorrent, but fascism equally intolerable.

The label "critical theory," according to Wiggershaus, was originally a thin disguise for Marxism, which became the basis of much of the thinking of the founders. Yet as the above definition suggests, there were many strands of both influence and theoretical difference, the greatest of which can be represented by two of the most influential founders, Adorno and Horkheimer. Adorno's work is seen as the beginning of institutional ethnography, a theory that is influenced by social psychology, or the beginning of cultural theory, depending on how one reads his work. What is certain, however, is that his work is theoretically critical of the status quo and revolutionary for its time. For Adorno, a critical social theory can only seek to explain social process, social production, indeed society itself, by understanding those who live in it (Ingram and Simon-Ingram, 1992:xxiii). He was especially critical of the dominant theoretical explanations of the social of his time, which he claimed were both uncritical and based on false premises. As the following indicates, Adorno was unafraid to critique the doctrine of positivism, claiming that the theory itself is a social construction:

> What is wrong with positivist theory is that it accepts the division of labour between the sciences, as it is socially enforced, as a standard of truth itself, admitting no theory in which the division of labour itself merges clearly as being derived, an epiphenomenon the authority of which is falsely assumed (cited in Ingram and Simon-Ingram, 1992:25)

In other works, Adorno challenged the authority of prevailing wisdom in another way, by critiquing the use of mass media for ideological purposes. He saw such use as having profound effects on culture. Adorno was particularly critical of visual mass media, especially its attempts to "channelize audience reaction":

> This falls in line with the suspicion widely shared, though hard to corroborate by exact data, that the majority of televison shows today aim at producing or at least reproducing the very smugness, intellectual passivity and gullibility that seem to fit in with what totalitarianism creates even if the explicit surface message of these shows may be antitotalitarian. (Ingram and Simon Ingram, 1992:74)

His interest in propaganda, how television quickly became a medium for propaganda, and what types of assumptions about human nature were made to use television in this way, are further exemplified in his "Freudian theory and the pattern of fascist propaganda" (1951). In this work he weaves socio-psychological theories to develop further his critical theory of the social, which begins to address some of the challenges of examining the influence of culture in a totalitarian age.

For Adorno, there is a definition connection among the commodification of the consumer, mass appeal, and conformity. There is a danger in this, as follows: "As Adorno rightly notes, resignation, avoidance of conflict anti-intellectualism and stereotyping are familiar messages of mass culture that lend themselves all too easily to political propaganda" (Ingram and Simon-Ingram, 1992:xxiii). Adorno's ideas are taken up by Horkheimer, although in a very different style of writing and thinking. For Horkheimer, as for Adorno, the questions raised by a commodification of the consumer were moral ones relating to the very essence of humanity itself. Thus one can easily see the Marxist influence in both their writings, as what troubled Marx in the end was the human suffering created and sustained through capitalism. In *Means and Ends (1941)*, Horkheimer argues that despite the trio of reason, justice, and equality assured us by the writings of the Enlightenment, justice and equality can be tossed aside conveniently on the altar of efficiency and reason. In this essay, Horkheimer vigorously attacks the misuse of reason, the manipulation of its purpose. One can see through his words the dark hours of the Nazi reign:

> Reason has never really directed social reality, but now reason has been so thoroughly purged of any specific trend or preference that it has finally renounced even the task of passing judgement on man's actions and way of life. Reason has turned them over for ultimate sanction to the conflicting interests to which our world actually seems abandoned. (Ingram and Simon Ingram 1992:38)

Although they could easily be seen as an intellectual foil to the policy makers of the day, it did not take long for the work of theorists such as Adorno and Horkheimer to fall prey to political trends they could hardly imagine. Ironically, by the late 1960s the Frankfurt School theorists were victims of an ideology themselves, but not of the Fascist regime they predicted. Rather, it was political conservatives who interpreted their work as somehow synonymous with terrorism (which was one of the political threats of that time) and the School itself was largely dismantled. Its intellectual work, however, lives on in critical traditions of social sciences and philosophers alike.

For our purposes here, then, the Frankfurt School set up some interesting debates: the misuse of reason, the connections between the consumer and mass media, and the critique of the abuse of political power. All of these issues have influenced the study of law in varying forms, for the formation of critical theory in both philosophy and the social sciences disciplines heralded what would later become the critical path in the study of law.

### CRITICAL LEGAL STUDIES (CLS)

Critical Legal Studies (CLS) began with much promise.[6] Originating in 1977 at a conference on Critical Legal Studies, the original group of legal scholars began by examining how law in practice, including teaching in law schools, could be thought of as critical. A second focus was on "law as an instrument of social, economic and political domination, both in the sense of furthering the concrete interest of the dominators and in that of legitimating the existing order" (Kelman, 1987:297). This looked to be exactly what socio-legal scholars were looking for, as that search had taken them to legal realism, legal idealism, and other forms of Marxist interpretation. It was clear that the critical thinkers of this movement, which went on to spawn numerous conferences, publications, and theorizing (especially in the United States for the next decade and a half), revitalized debate on the role of law, encouraged the questioning of the legal status quo, and in some cases incurred the wrath of conservatives. It appeared that law professors associated with CLS recognized the perpetuation of idealized liberalism through the teachings of the law school, and had seen it for what many had already voiced: a reproduction of dominant thinking about the social world. But something went awry on the way to truth and liberation from dogma. The CLS movement, after much highly touted work and discussion, is now seen as little more than a group of white men worrying about their privilege, and that of their students, in such "disprivileged" places as the Harvard or Stanford schools of law. How did this happen? In what ways did the movement lose its footing?

The main contribution of CLS, arguably, is its insistence on a critique of liberalism, especially rights discourses. To the authors of the CLS movement, liberalism's greatest flaws are inherent in its contradictions, and its contradictions are simply penetrated by a dominant class, an idea clearly borrowed from Marxist ideas. However, the war that CLS authors wage is not necessarily against the state, but as a kind of internal wrestling with liberalism itself. Although the ways in which CLS authors have clearly worried about law as a legitimation mechanism, they are a far cry from Habermas. "Crits," as they've come to be known, see legitimation in the form of judicial decision making and become embroiled in arguments about whether law can exist without politics. Specifically they take aim at judges, as Crits see judges as perpetuating a particular kind of elitist politics in their decision making, rationalized by paltry references to precedents. For Crits, this type of "authority" is bogus, politicized, and effectively succeeds in further marginalizing groups that have been traditionally disadvantaged by the system. But Crits go further. In criticizing liberalism's tensions directly, especially its tendency to "fetishize" the individual,[7] Crits demonstrate how prolonged preoccupation with the rights of the individual fail to show how that individual is a very product of both the socio-economic forces and the legal authority that may put them in a position before the law, to begin with. In other words, law may not exactly serve the rights of the individual, since the reasons an individual, or a particular individual, ends up engaging with law are left unexamined. Further, Crits argue, this situation is due to the inability of judges, and therefore the law, to argue for inclusion for groups it neither recognizes nor represents, such as Blacks, women, Hispanics, or in Canada, First Nations.

Although this does seem to be a stride forward in critical thinking, what is more surprising is the CLS attack on rights. Crits recognize, granted without a Canadian Charter to guide them, the failure of the system to guarantee any rights other than individual, and call for their complete elimination. Such calls are criticized quite clearly (Halewood, 1991; Razack, 1993) as elitist and ignorant of the importance of rights discourse in legal guarantees of both sexual and racial equalities. Informality in law is not only dangerously ambiguous, it is ambiguously dangerous; for without the specificities that our Charter offers us in Canada, for example, or in specific legal decisions in the U.S. (*Roe v. Wade, Brown v. Board of Education* come to mind), it is clear that legal rights would still be highly problematic, if not unavailable, for many Americans. In Canada, Charter cases achieve the ends that human rights legislation was simply unable to do, that is, achieve victories in legal cases where the grounds on which decisions were made were written, argued, and found on the basis of women's experiences. But it is how the Crits perform their critique that is of interest to us here. There are, of course, competing narratives within the CLS camp, which includes, as Hutchinson indicates, "the disaffected liberal, the radical feminist, to the utopian anarchist" (1991:182). As a fundamentally American critical movement, this combination of politicos is actually possible. But by doing more than one thing at once, CLS may have actually confused its impetus with its means. For example, although Crits argue that the law and society cannot be separate, they do this in an unusual way. The deconstructionists within the CLS membership (and yes, they do require membership) take apart legal decisions in text, which has come to be known as "trashing," to determine how the arguments themselves reflect the privilege of the arguer. They argue, quite well, that legal arguments are never separate from politics, that judges and laws are not neutral arbitrators, and that rights serve only to perpetuate existing inequalities. But their critique, savage as it is in some quarters, is simply an attempt to radically reform liberalism,[8] rather than radical reform itself. It has been argued that CLS is only a reiteration of the same white male privilege that one finds in other critical theory writings, with little room for women, minorities or any other subalterns.

FEMINISM

Of all the theoretical traditions inherited by the sociology of law, feminism is probably the most eclectic. Feminist theory spans cultural studies, is usually multi-disciplinary (by definition), and has permeated not only the substance of what is to be studied in law, but also the very ways law has been studied in the country.[9] From even a cursory glance at a list of authors, one can see that feminist work in Canada on feminist jurisprudence is extensive and ongoing.[10]

Feminist work in the sociology of law shares one premise: that women are systemically and systematically oppressed in the patriarchal social order, and that this oppression carries over to the formulation of law, the interpretation of law, and the ways in which women come to use (or not use) the legal system. How they go about doing this analysis, and the implications of their varying directions theoretically, however, has had very different impacts on legal order.

Feminists in the aforementioned fields come to the work of feminist legal theorizing from various spaces; many have degrees in law, while others have social science or health backgrounds. Feminist theoretical work is often categorized in various ways.[11] For example, socialist feminism and law are normally found in analyses of family law, daycare, custody and access after divorce or feminist analyses around work. Radical feminist theorizing is to be found predominantly in areas of sexual assault, abortion, or reproductive technology, gay and lesbian couples' rights — their own and that of their children. Liberal feminist theorizing in law tends to focus on equity issues, sexual harassment, and affirmative action. More recent feminist work,[12] such as Rebecca Johnson's chapter in this text tends, to focus on the law as metaphor, a weaving of literary image with the reality of violence against women.

Feminist work in socio-legal matters is wide-ranging, covering much of the traditional canon in law, as well as the areas of usual interest to women legally, including employment equity,[13] reproductive health[14] and social control, family law[15] (custody and access to children), same sex benefits,[16] tax law and its implications for women, pension, interpersonal violence,[17] including sexual assault, harassment, and stalking, and theoretical work on the use of law to ameliorate change.[18] Feminist work has also worked to change the "method" of how law is used and handled[19] and to analyse the contribution of feminism to both the "making" and interpreting of law. Feminist work, of all critical theory, has been the most eclectic — embracing disciplinary boundaries and traditional canons with ease and accuracy. Feminist work has brought together unlikely bedfellows, such as law and psychology,[20] philosophy and social science,[21] and science and law (such as work on reproductive technology). Feminist theory has been with the social sciences since the 1880s, with the early socialist work of Rosa Luxembourg, and not as long as it has been with literature and philosophy (such as the 1750s article by Mary Wollstonecraft on the *Vindication of the Rights of Woman*), but it has spawned much of the exciting critical work today. Not without its detractors, feminist work has embraced its critics often, and emerged more sensitive to difference, more engaging with issues of class, and more accepting of diversity than most of its critical counterparts.

## The Currency of New Critical Theory

This next section will combine some of the findings of chapter one with the new directions presented by critical theory in the opening segment of this chapter.

Both consensus/conflict paradigms are considered to be largely unrepresentative of some of the more critical issues facing people in current legal situations, in today's climate, and are considered largely inadequate to address many fundamental issues. This would include, for instance, the historical nature of the legal oppression of women, revealed in a re-reading of the persecution of witches in the chapter by Noonan. Noonan traces the complicity of law in the persecution of women as witches centuries ago, and more recently as midwives. What is needed is a new paradigm of theoretical/methodological work that is more representative of current struggles in law. The possibilities of such a paradigm exist with a critical standpoint.

The critical paradigm is composed of authors whose work assumes that due to economic, racial, gender, and other factors, current explanations within sociology of law paradigms do not completely capture the everyday experience of people dealing with the law in particular social contexts. The scope of critical theories and methods are far-ranging, but they share a few distinctive features: 1) critical theorists ascribe neither to consensus nor to conflict characterizations of law and legal process, or to micro/macro traditions of method *per se*; 2) critical theorists tend to be characterized by an ability to move easily between micro and macro traditions, and to strengthen theories of conflict by adding new, micro explanations that come from the interpretative tradition, such as feminist theory and social constructionism. This, in fact, is one of the key strengths of critical theory: to move among prior classifications of theory and method with relative ease, blurring the distinctions between these dialectics and opening up the possibility of new research scenarios.

The premise, then, of the critical paradigm is to critique law, legal process, and outcome in terms of the social problems that are created or even exacerbated by the very system designed to root out discord among social groups. Writers within this tradition agree with the two previous paradigms. They assume that the nature of the law itself reflects dominance and submission (as do the writers within the conflict tradition) and reflects status quo values (as does the consensus tradition) but they do not offer set, formulaic ways of viewing these social problems. If anything, critical theorists/methodologists examine situations from the settings of the social groups themselves: the victim of an assault, those denied a benefit, or the historical or legal settings created by ignorance in law of these same social groups — in fact how law perpetuates, by its very nature, the very injustices it seeks to ameliorate. Critical thinkers are wary of large-scale theorizing or methods which ignore the oppressed and serve to reinforce, by default or by design, the legal system. They are also wary of the seemingly self-referential and "fiddle while Rome burns" shortsightedness of wider social contexts that seem to characterize many micro studies.

But the inherent strength in the ability of critical theories to use *macro* theorizing to illustrate the oppressed is found in Machum's chapter on farm wives, which uses political economic theory to illustrate the disentitlement to property many farmwomen face in the death of a spouse or the dissolution of a marriage. Normally, analyses of the plight of women's property is not done from a macro theorizing perspective, but from feminist theory. Machum chooses political economy instead, as she sees the situation of farm women in New Brunswick as inextricably linked to the social organization of work on a farm that agribusiness creates. In a completely different way, Doran does the same thing in his chapter. He takes a traditional area of study — workers' compensation for asbestos miners in Alberta — and applies a non-traditional mode of analyses to explain his findings, that is, Foucauldian analyses of power/knowledge, with Carol Smart's understanding of the "mundane" in law to explain the disenfranchisement of miners in terms of the legal benefits they would normally accrue.

Similarly, Audrey Sprenger analyses the social movements and patterns within what she terms "the industrial forest," not from a macro political economic theme, but from an inductive theorizing standpoint which allows her to easily point out how the social movements she documents are mediated by race, class, and gender. Sprenger's work points out, through inductive theorizing, how we socially construct categories, and yet how easily slippage is possible. In her work, one can identify critical questions; such as how can you "define" a First Nations man with a milltown company jacket on? Through class analysis? Critical race theorizing? How do you separate gender out from a high-school girl's first "Social" (dance event) from her mother who works in a coffee shop down the road, when the girl has more choices and opportunities than her mother? Through an analysis of age? How do you then explain the fact that the milltown in her study hires white and native men, but not women? Through a political economy analysis?

In fact, the varying ways these authors have defied traditional notions of conceptualization have many possibilities for how their work can be categorized. For example, the traditional organization of a book is to put gender, race or class "chapters" together. To do so would be to do a disservice to the creative ways these authors pull their work together. Instead, we might put all of the articles that focus on the worker together (Machum, Sprenger, Doran, and Martin) or the chapters that focus on "women" together (Hughes, Beaman, Noonan, Wachholz, and Machum). Or do we put the chapters that have stories of race politics together (Martin, Sprenger); or, less rigidly, we could categorize the chapters in terms of theory —feminism (Beaman, Noonan, Hughes, and Doran), social constructionism (Doran, Beaman, Wachholz, and Sprenger), socio-legal historical analysis (Noonan, and Martin), and political economy (Machum) . The first thing the reader should note is how some names pop up more than once in this exercise. Yet it is this exercise that reveals my very point, that is, the fluidity and flexibility of critical work. And despite the many and varied ways that these chapters could be organized,[22] there is an underlying pattern that underscores all of the work herein: all authors adhere to one form or another of critical work, theoretically, methodologically or in some cases, the manner by which a "traditional" topic within the discipline was challenged in the choice of analysis mode. It is this type of sociology that this text salutes by presenting these authors' analyses of a variety of problematic areas in the socio-legal context.

CRITICAL RACE THEORY

Critical Race Theory, as we know it here in North America, began as a resistance movement in the United States as both a reaction to, and a supplement for, the Critical Legal Studies (CLS) movement. Another, not unrelated, development was the insistence on the inclusion of black women in white feminist theorizing around the family. Both of these trends were influential in the way we experience the Critical Race Theory movement here in Canada.

In the mid 1980s, at a CLS conference in San Francisco, there was a definite "edge" to the reactions of those attending. According to Carol Aylward (1999), scholars of colour felt alienated from a national conference, the tenth of its kind, that included a mere 30 scholars of colour and six papers on race and law (26). This is not an unexpected occurrence. Despite years of work in the civil-rights movement, the NAACP (National Association of Advancement of Coloured People), and other spaces where the issue of race appeared, it seems that there was "no room at the inn" in the CLS movement for issues of race. Prominent authors such as Mari Matsuda, Richard Delgado, Derrick Bell, Kimberle Crenshaw, and later,

Patricia Williams and Toni Williams, began to frame out some of the cultural critiques that bell hooks and Patricia Hill Collins had made concerning women, social life, and culture. What unites these authors is the primacy of race, racism, and what Canadian author Victor Satezwich would call "racialization" in the shaping of any discourse on social life. What is inescapable in social life, these authors would argue, and what gives immediacy to the contest of how blacks in the U.S. are dealt with in law, is the systemic and systematic racism that people of colour experience.

To exclude race from a discussion of legal progress, for these theorists, would be tantamount to rendering the law "colour-blind," a facet of current practice that critical race theorists find unacceptable. Aylward gives a concise outline of what she feels the Critical Race Theory movement is based on:

1. a need to move beyond existing rights analysis;
2. an acknowledgement and analysis of the centrality of racism, not just as the White supremacy form of racism but also the systemic and subtle forms that have the effect of subordinating people of colour;
3. total rejection of the "colour-blind" approach to law, which ignores the fact that blacks and whites are not similarly situated with regard to legal doctrines, rules, principles, and practices;
4. a contextual analysis which positions the experiences of oppressed peoples at its centre;
5. a deconstruction which asks the question, "How does this legal doctrine, rule, principle, policy or practice subordinate the interests of black people and other people of colour?"; and
6. reconstruction which understands the "duality" of law, recognizing both its contribution to the subordination of blacks and other people of colour and its transformative power. (1999:34)

The basis for critical race theory was an uneasy alliance with the initial promise of CLS, a movement which challenged the basis of the tenets of the "rule of law" as a class-based, imbalanced view of what should be liberal democracy. The CLS movement, at its inception, promised to "deliver," for women and minorities, a challenge to the status quo, a radical claim against form and fantasy which oppressed and gave rise to oppressive laws. It failed to deliver. Its lasting contribution is, arguably, its transformation of the curriculum of law schools, a way of challenging existing canons as irrelevant and transformative, and a space for possibilities yet to be determined. But as a place that welcomed, embraced or even challenged existing legal problems for Blacks and minorities, CLS did not hold up. Black scholars quickly realized the dangers of "abandoning" the formal provisions on equality, anti-discrimination law, and civil rights that had grown for over a century. It is a truism, within most critical movements, that the abandonment of the formal comes as a great peril to women and minorities, for reliance on the informal is something that only white men cementing contracts with handshakes get to do. It is not possible for those whose very lives are sometimes dependent on the legal protections that law offers, even with the knowledge of law's frailty. Indeed, the presence of those protections, weak as they often are, seems much more preferable than their absence, as those who "remember" slavery are quick to note.[23]

For Black women in the feminist movement, the drive toward a critical race theory was moving in a tangential, but similar, direction. Black feminists claimed the term "womanist" as one of their own, one that would truly reflect the lived reality for Black women, a reality that was not only different from that of whites, but unable to be explained by whites. Concepts such as the "double day" became, for Black women, the ultimate insult, as their day consisted of a "triple day" of work, and had for over 150 years. What white women came to discover about their plight in the early 1960s was largely due to the fact that Black women had cleaned their toilets for years. The final insult was the attack on the family unit as a patriarchal, oppressive institution. For many Black women, their family and their church were the few refuges left in a cold, hard, racist world. To attack the one institution that was unfailingly their own, to claim it as part of the oppressive patriarchy, was more than most Black women could take. It proclaimed the ultimate ignorance of white feminists for any theory or experience but their own (Spelman).

And while not exclusively a feminist issue, the trial of O.J. Simpson, a prominent Black football player in the U.S., which created a media circus around the case, reveals some interesting trends around perceptions of race. As illustrated in the following quotation, the race component of this case never went away and was used interchangeably with themes of criminology. This tendency, according to Toni Morrison, did massive damage to already wounded Black sensibilities in the U.S. while simultaneously reinforced white stereotypes.

The narrative of the entertainment media and their "breaking story" confederates was so powerfully insistent on guilt, so uninterested in any other scenario, it began to look like a media pogrom, a lynching with its iconography intact: a chase, a cuffing, a mob, name calling, a white female victim, and most of all the heat, the panting, the flared nostrils of a pack already eager to convict. For many, black and white, the passion they felt in the wake of the media onslaught was real, hinging as it did on violence and treachery. Mr. Simpson became the repository of fear. (Morrison, 1997:xiii)

Such images do little to encourage a critical race theoretical involvement in law; rather, they serve to perpetuate the century-old images of Black criminality.

### POSTMODERNISM

In much of the critical theoretical work since the mid 1970s, the name Michel Foucault has become synonymous with numerous applications of what has been called the theory of the "postmodern." Originally a theory of the aesthetic, postmodernism was taught as a response or reaction to so-called modernists, who, according to the postmodernists, assumed far too certain a subject, far too concrete a reality. Gradually moving into literary criticism, postmodernism became the darling of those interested in the indeterminacy of the subject, questioning the role of identity in explanations of the social. Some of the more interesting and innovative work includes studies on postcolonialism and the subject, which begin and end with fluid rather than fixed notions of identity and state and the interaction between the two.

For the purposes of sociology of law, however, it was postmodernism's foray into the social sciences that held greatest sway for jurisprudential scholars. For many in the sociology of law, it was the work of Michel Foucault, particularly, that garnered most attention. It was interesting to see the shift in sociology when, feminists embraced Foucauldian analyses,[24] whereas most scholars on the left — socialist feminists included — eschewed the theory as too "nonpolitical" and "representational" and therefore at odds with the more staid theories of state discourse.[25] Post-modernist influence, largely from the French philosophers Baudrillard, Lyotard, Derrida, and Lacan, were largely taken up in feminist circles by the likes of Julia Kristeva and Luce Irigaray, both of whom contributed and influenced a wealth of writing focussed on the representation, both in text and in image, of woman, of female sexuality in general, and of mother-hood in particular, for example. Those who read this work were influenced to read law in terms of "signifiers," in terms of the very language used as representational of sexuality.

Still others were influenced by the work of Michel Foucault, particularly his seminal work *Discipline and Punish*. In it, Foucault argued that the work of socialization was largely to reinforce the disciplinary techniques of the state, and the body was largely its canvas. To illustrate this specifically, Foucault chose the "body" of the imprisoned, the condemned, the tortured, in historical context to fully support his thesis that surveillance is a process, a very fluid form of the control over the social actor. Feminists doing jurisprudential work (like Carol Smart) and legal theorists alike were fascinated by the concept of surveillance, and used it as a metaphor to expose the inscribing tendencies of law, the ways in which women's bodies are "written" into text from the viewpoint of those "other" than women.

Postmodernism grew more popular as both a serious theoretical challenge to structural theories of the social but also as a way to "play" with language, with meaning, and with text in ways that theorists rarely do. Postmodernism became the catch-all for many types of theorizing, for the "deconstructionist" language of the 1980s and 1990s to the identity politics of political theory. Many who gravitate to postmodernism are excited by its possibilities as an explanatory tool of social process rather than function, an explanation of power rather than of institutions, and of the myriad ways law can fit into a status quo around "othering" that many on the left would shudder at rather than support. It continues to be an area of socio-legal work that generates many debates.

### SOCIAL CONSTRUCTIONISM AND NARRATIVE: STORIES OF COMMUNITY

One of the lesser-known fields within the discipline of sociology, and arguably the one that has grown the most of late, is the body of work that can be loosely described as "social constructionism." This field of work falls mainly under the rubric of interpretive sociology, which is an older, recognized field within the discipline. Interpretive sociology largely comes from the work of Max Weber, who used both bureaucratic and varying typologies of social life and personality types to illustrate a concept he called "verstehen" or meaningful understanding. Offshoots of interpretive sociology include inherited traditions from philosophy, such as phenomenology, an attempt to understand the social world through phenomenal analyses rather than structural explanations. Of all the theoretical explanations in sociology, interpretive sociology is the most fluid, most concerned with the process of events and with an emphasis on making sense of the social world as a relevant factor in understanding larger social processes. The intimate, the interaction, gestures, the use of words and body language, the nature of our relationships, and how we make sense of our roles with others — these are all part of this tradition.

Social constructionism, loosely defined, refers to that body of work which attempts to de- or re-construct events as they happened, to find explanations for social events that transcend a mere description, to find patterns or trends of explanations within text, ideology, and the rhetoric of the state. Social constructionism seeks to answer the research question, "How do we come to know these phenomena using these words, with particular interpretations, in certain social contexts?" Or, more simply put, "What in the world is real and concrete (such as water or trees) and what is socially constructed (laws and policies about water and trees)?" Social constructionism would then look for meaning within, say, policies and laws around resources to determine how certain policies are designed, for whom, how, and under what circumstances. First Nations work is especially fruitful in this regard, as more often than not, authors in this tradition examine definitions of community and explore ideas of narrative in ways that white authors tend to consider more literary than explanatory. This (mis)understanding leads to a tendency to overlook the contributions of First Nations authors, when in reality their voices tend toward the true narrative often in similar ways to Black theoretical work in the U.S.[26]

When used in areas of law, social constructionism can look to why we call the same event in one context a sexual assault and in another a "normal" sexual activity. How we determine what is normative, and how that normativeness gets either reflected or omitted in text on law, is of great interest to theorists within this tradition. Who is included in the definition and who is by that definition excluded or marginalized by the power of law is also of interest to social constructionists. People working within this tradition are usually de-constructing law or re-analysing its components to determine how and why law has been designed in certain ways and not others, defined to include certain groups and exclude others, and to protect certain interests and ignore others. Social constructionist work can also sometimes be referred to as a method for analysis, a way of looking at data, law, text, and conversation for ideological meaning rather than substance.

Narrative as a form of socio-legal work has become increasingly popular due to certain trends within social life. Life-storying, primary-source interviews, and oral traditions all make up this type of socio-legal work. Life-storying and primary-source interviews are not new at all to disciplines such as anthropology, which has long privileged the words of people from other cultures as part of the attempt to establish the veracity of the pictures of their lives that researchers attempt to draw for explanatory purposes. Gerontology, the new field of studies of aging, also looks at life histories and life-storying as a method of inquiry. Although this may not sound like a very radical way to do research, it is clear from the initial work on aging that the elderly, especially in white North American culture, unlike First Nations or other racial/cultural traditions, have been cast aside by their younger counterparts. Partly because mass media cater to the young, the voices, faces, and concerns of the elderly are not part of common knowledge. Capturing these voices on tape, transcribing their words into text, destroys some of the stereotypes we have of the elderly as helpless, in poor health or of feeble mind. Similarly, primary-source interviews have long been a way to confirm or find fault with dominant structural paradigms. If an institution claims that all needs are met by its services, such as legal aid (as in the Beaman chapter) or in the definition of family (as in the Wachholz chapter), and these claims are refuted with primary-source interviews with participants in that structure, then this constitutes a research finding.[27]

Oral tradition, at least in Canada, is most closely associated with First Nations people. Not to be confused with stories, oral tradition involves a *particular* form of parable, myth or life lesson passed down by word of mouth from one generation to another. Contextualized within First Nations traditions, which revere generations of families, the elderly, and the power of the word in ceremonies of truth, oral tradition is the way by which First Nations peoples have communicated all laws, customs, and health, social, and familial information. It is, for all practical purposes, a tradition of record-keeping that is simply oral, rather than textual, in nature. These traditions have influenced socio-legal work considerably. As Melinda Martin's chapter indicates, it is clear that oral traditions have had a considerable impact on Canadian law, specifically in the recent Supreme Court decision on *Marshall*.

Narratives of other kinds are beginning to crop up as social constructionism and oral tradition are "married" in recent texts that give primacy to the stories of people's experiences with justice, their struggles with and around law, and how law becomes referential to itself, excluding the voice and experience of those with whom it engages (Shreve and Shreve, 1997; Ewick and Silbey, 1998).

In this chapter I have outlined many of the critical theoretical foundations for the readings that follow in this text. I hope that it will give the reader a better sense of the traditions from which the sociology of law springs, and encourage the student to take up the works of one of the many authors cited in this chapter. In so doing, one may discover the rich heritage we are beginning to have in Canada within the sociology of law, an area in which many of us find it exciting to work.

## Notes

1. Audrey Sprenger, "Documenting the social in the Industrial forest," paper presented at the Atlantic Association of Anthropology and Sociology, St. Mary's University, Halifax, Nova Scotia, October 22, 1998.

2. Another historically interesting area is how Marxist thought can be used to analyse the level, frequency, and type of corporate crime. From poaching (McMullen) to Bhopal (Pearce) and all areas in between, sociologists are using frameworks based in Marxism to fully explain social inequalities on the basis of class and law. Analyses of corporate crime, such as those by Colin Goff, France Pearce, and Laureen Snider have also been part of an ongoing tradition in Canadian socio-legal analyses, as has the work of legal scholars such as Judy Fudge. Traditions that have continued on from Marxism include legal realism and left idealism within critical criminology. For an interesting read on this development, see Thomas O'Reilly-Fleming, "Left realism as Theoretical Retreatism or Paradigm Shift: Toward post-critical criminology," in *Post Critical Criminology*, a reader he edits, published by Prentice Hall, 1996.

3. For an interesting collection of readings which go further than this simple classification, see *The Social Basis of Law*, eds. Elizabeth Comack and Stephen Brickey, 2nd ed. (Halifax: Fernwood Books, 1991).

4. Nancy Fraser does an admirable feminist critique of Habermas' lack of gender distinction in his *Theory of communicative action*, and Seyla Benhabib takes on Habermas' "generalized other" (a later version of George Herbert Mead) as an unproblematized category; that is, he does not take into account the emotive-love-care relationships that are mainly left to women to manage in the social realm.

5. Nancy Fraser claims that no improvements have been made over the original definition of critical theory, that of Marx in 1843, as "the self-clarification of the struggles and wishes of the age" (Fraser in Ingram and Simon-Ingram, 1992:357)

6. Authors within this tradition include Roberto Unger, Mark Kelman, Andrew Altman, Duncan Kennedy, Richard Abel, and Lawrence Friedman. Notable Canadian additions to the debates have included those by Richard Devlin, Allan Hutchinson, and Donald Galloway. CLS has also been taken on by feminist critics Dawn Currie, Mari Matsuda, Catharine MacKinnon, and Sherene Razack.

7. This comes from Devlin's statement, "The concern is that this ontological fetishization of the individual (to coin a phrase) fails to appreciate fully the ways in which the individual is the product of the social forces that inscribe her personality" (1994:639).

8. Unger's work fits into this category. It is clear that, for him, a critique of liberalism comes from his very passion with the engagement of the ideas.

9. Notable authors include Susan Boyd, Dorothy Chunn, Elizabeth Comack, Dawn Currie, Lorenne Clark, Mary Morton, Sherene Razack, Laureen Snider, and Mariana Valverde from the fields of sociology and criminology. From the legal field, Constance Backhouse, Bev Baines, Christine Boyle, Mary Eberts, Shelley Gavigan, Judy Fudge, Patricia Hughes, Kathy Lahey, Sheila Noonan, Sheila McIntyre, Patricia Monture-Angus, Mary Jane Mossman, Marie-Claire Belleau, Denise Reaume, and Marlee Kline are names of authors that have shaped the landscape of legal feminism in Canada. More recent authors include Lori Beaman and Rebecca Johnson, both of whom appear in this collection.

10. For a useful and fairly recent summary of trends in feminist legal thinking see *The Canadian Journal of Women and the Law*, "Feminist Reflections on Litigation" (Vol. 10, No. 1, 1998), and "Contexts and Contradictions: Feminism and Social Change" (Vol. 10, No. 2, 1998).

11. The lists I give here are meant to be illustrative rather than exclusive. Many theorists, regardless of orientation, will work on a variety of issues or topics throughout their academic career.

12. See Sylvie Frigon "A Gallery of Portraits: women and the embodiment of difference, deviance, and resistance," *Post-Critical Criminology*, ed. Thomas O'Reilly-Fleming (Toronto: Prentice-Hall, 1996), 78-110.

13. See especially the work of Pat McDermott of Carleton University on legal implications of employment issues for women.

14. The work of Roxanne Mykitiuk of Osgoode Law School is instructive on the intersection of reproduction and new technologies, and the conundrum this creates for women's reproductive rights.

15. See the work of Susan Boyd, chair of feminist legal studies at UBC, for a more complete theoretical understanding of how family law operates in relation to women.

16. Queen's University law professor Martha Bailey organized, with the Law Commission of Canada, a small international conference to look at some of the more pressing issues around same-sex union, titled in the literature as "domestic legal partnerships." This conference, which took place in Kingston in October, 1999, focusses on a variety of issues — same-sex benefits, same-sex marriage, custody/access and birthrights around children, and same-sex partnerships — from jurisdictions as far-flung as New Zealand, the U.K., the Netherlands, various states from the U.S. and, of course, Canada. Discussions around the possible legislative fall-out of *M v. H*, the then-recent Supreme Court same-sex decision of property after separation, were also widely debated, as the counsel for H was present. The legislation on this issue was introduced to Parliament in January of this year.

17. Gillian Walker's work on battering and women is especially instructive here.

18. For contrasting positions on the use of law to effect change for women, compare Carol Smart, *Feminism and the Power of Law*, and Catharine MacKinnon, *Rape Unmodified: Discourses on Life and Law*.

19. Lori Beaman, "Abused Women and Legal Discourse: The Exclusionary Power of Legal Method," *Canadian Journal of Law and Society* 11 (1):1996.

20. The most notable marriage of psychology and law came with family law's embrace of Carol Gilligan's seminal work *In a Different Voice*, which emphasizes the moral decision-making by women compared with men. This has worked its way into law in an "ethic of care," which feminist jurisprudential scholars claim needs to be taken into account in cases of child custody.

21. Ideas that ring philosophical and yet deal with methods of social science can have varying applications in law, including the work of Dorothy Smith. Her recent *Writing the Social: Critique, Theory and Investigations* (Toronto: University of Toronto Press, 1999), in addition to her earlier works that have been so influential, is a prime example of this type of interdisciplinary weaving.

22. My sociology of law students were given two patterns of chapter groupings or the possibility of a third, and asked to title and rationalize their choice of a chapter for each section. They came up with at least five additional ways to group these chapters, in addition to the two patterns given, based on thematic, chronological, theoretical, inductive / deductive / micro / macro traditions or subject. In so doing, they became part of the exercise of the creation of this text, and began to better appreciate the flexibility of critical work within the sociology of law.

23. See any of the numerous books by American author bell hooks for further information on this point.

24. For a comprehensive view of the influence of postmodernism on feminist political thought, see Linda J. Nicholson, ed. *Feminism/Postmodernism* (New York and London: Routledge, 1990).

25. For an interesting discussion on the relationship between varying philosophies behind postmodernism and a rigorous critique of some of the more fleeting uses of the concept, see Christopher Morris, *What's Wrong with Postmodernism?: Critical Theory and the Ends of Philosophy* (Baltimore: Johns Hopkins University Press, 1990).

26. Richard Delgrado, "Legal Storytelling: Storytelling for Oppositionists and Others: A Plea for Narrative," in 87 *Michigan Law Review* 2411, 1989; Naomi Chan, "Inconsistent Stories," *Georgetown Law Journal* 81, 7(1993):2475-2531.

27. This method is not, however, to be confused with journalism, for which three sources or incidents constitute sufficient evidence for a "trend" to be declared.

# References

Adams, David M. (1990). "Skepticism and the Apologetics of Law." *Canadian Journal of Law and Jurisprudence* 3 (1):69-90.

Aylward, Carol A. (1999). *Canadian Critical Race Theory: Racism and the Law.* Halifax: Fernwood Publishing.

Altman, Andrew (1990). *Critical Legal Studies: A Liberal Critique.* Princeton, NJ: Princeton University Press.

Brickey, Stephen, and Elizabeth Comack, eds. (1986). *The Sociology of Law: Critical Readings in the Sociology of Law.* Toronto: Garamond Press.

Chan, Naomi R. (1993). "Inconsistent Stories." *The Georgetown Law Review.* 81:2475-2531.

Devlin, Richard F. (1994). "Mapping Legal Theory." *Alberta Law Review* 32 (3):602-21.

Devlin, Richard F. (1991). "Doubting Donald: A Reply to Professor Donald Galloway's 'critical mistakes'." *The Windsor Yearbook of Access to Justice* 11:178-205.

Ewick, Patricia, and Susan S. Sibley (1998). *The Common Place of Law: Stories From Everyday Life.* Chicago: University of Chicago Press.

Galloway, Donald (1991). "Critical Mistakes." In Richard F. Devlin (ed.), *Canadian Perspectives on Legal Theory*. Toronto: Edmond Montgomery Publishing: 255-68.

Gordon, Colin, ed. (1980). *Power/Knowledge: Selected Interviews and other Writings 1972-1977, by Michel Foucault*. New York: Pantheon Books.

Halewood, Peter (1991). "Trends in American Critical Legal Thought." *UBC Law Review* 25:105-28.

Hutchinson, Allan C. (1991). "Crits and Cricket: A Deconstructive Spin (Or was it a Googly?)" in Richard F. Devlin (ed.), *Canadian Perspectives on Legal Theory*. Toronto: Edmond Montgomery Publishing: 181-205.

Ingram, David, and Julia Simon-Ingram (1992). *Critical Theory: The Essential Readings*. New York: Paragon House.

Kellner, Douglas (1990). "Critical Theory and the Crisis of Social Theory." *Sociological Perspectives* 33 (1):11-23.

Kelman, Mark (1987). *A Guide to Critical Legal Studies*. Cambridge, MA: Harvard University Press.

Kivisto, Peter (1994). "Toward an Antifoundational Yet Relevant Sociology: Can Gottdiener have it both ways?" *Sociological Quarterly* 35 (4):723.

Matoesian, Gregory (1993). *Reproducing Rape: Domination Through Talk in the Courtroom*. Chicago: The University of Chicago Press.

Monahan, John, and Laurens Walker (1991). "Judicial Use of Social Science Research." *Law and Human Behavior* 15 (6):571-84.

Morrison, Toni (1997). "The Official Story: Dean Man Golfing." In Toni Morrison and Claudia Brodsky Lacour, *Birth of a Nation 'hood: Script, Spectacle in the O.J. Simpson Case*. New York: Pantheon Books.

Razack, Sherene (1993). "Using Law for Social Change: Historical Perspectives." *Queen's Law Journal* 17:31-53.

Shreve, Susan Richards, and Porter Shreve, eds. (1997). *Outside the Law: Narratives on Justice in America*. Boston: Beacon Press.

Spelman, E., ed. (1988). *Inessential Women: Problems of Exclusion in Feminist Thought*. Boston: Beacon Press.

Trevino, A. Javier (1996). *The Sociology of Law: Classical and Contemporary Perspectives*. New York: St. Martin's Press.

Unger, Roberto (1986). *The Critical Legal Studies Movement*. Cambridge, MA: Harvard University Press.

Weberman, David (1997). "Liberal Democracy, Autonomy, and Ideology Critique." *Social Theory and Practice* 23 (2):205.

Wiggershaus, Rolf (1994). *The Frankfurt School: Its History, Theories and Political Significance*. Trans. Michael Robertson. Cambridge, MA: Polity Press and the MIT Press. First published in Germany as *Die Frankfurter Schule* (Munich: Carl Hanser Verlag, 1986).

# PART II

*Social Context and the Formation of Law*

# 3

## Legal Treatment of the Body:
## The Example of Sexual Abuse by Doctors

PATRICIA HUGHES

In this chapter, I examine, through a focus on sexual abuse by doctors of their patients, how the law treats women's bodily experience and in particular how different legal *fora* (the civil, the criminal, and the regulatory) mediate what is to the woman the same experience. Although much of what I have to say applies to professionals in different contexts, the application is not automatically transferable from one profession to another. I will limit my examination to the doctor-patient context, since it is in that context that most of the self-examination among professionals has occurred and in which there has been the greatest response.[1]

The doctor-patient relationship relies for its success on the willingness of the patient to trust the doctor and to disclose to the doctor personal information. The relationship between doctor and patient is described by law as a "fiduciary relationship." The doctor, as the fiduciary, has an obligation to act in the interest of the patient, or beneficiary, and not in his or her own interest or with his or her own gratification in mind. In a fiduciary relationship, one party places trust in another: this is "the trust of a person with inferior power that another person who has assumed superior power and responsibility will exercise that power for his or her good and only for his or her good and in his or her best interests" (*Norberg v. Wynrib*, 1992:486 per McLachlin J. [as she then was][2]).[3]

A power imbalance or "power dependency" is almost inherent in a doctor-patient relationship. When the doctor is male and the patient female, the power relations between doctor and patient are reinforced by patriarchal and heterosexual relations between men and women and by racialized sexual assumptions. In this sense, sexual misconduct by professionals

49

is interconnected with other sexualized experiences of women's lives, including rape, sexual harassment, domestic violence, pornography, reproduction, employment (including prostitution), and maintenance.[4] All these experiences involve assumptions about "what women want," "what women need," how women exhibit their sexuality or their desire for sexuality or how women's sexuality is something to trade for other gains. The complexities of the sexualization of women are at play in the professional context: stereotypes about racialized sexuality such as the "easy availability" of black women or the "docile compliance" of Asian women (Austin, 1992; Duclos, 1993) constitute an element in the professional context as in other contexts.

Feminist consideration of these issues must not only come to terms with women's intersecting identities and the different cultural assumptions about diverse women's sexuality held by men, but also with the tension between the individual and the collective. As Kristin Bumiller explores in her analysis of the "symbolic rape trial," we need to recognize women's individual responses to what happens to us at the same time as we need to place what happens to us in a systemic and institutionalized power relation (1991:98, 109). Bumiller's discussion illustrates woman's ambivalent position: "as human she is a free subject who participates in transcendence, but her situation as a woman denies her that subjectivity and transcendence" (Young, 1990:b 144).

Contemporary feminism recognizes that women are not a heterogeneous group; rather, women's experiences vary in conjunction with other sources of oppression or identification (such as those based on race, class or sexual orientation). Feminist claims for the transformation of law are premised on the failure of law to respond to the experiences of diverse women, although it maintains that those experiences are nevertheless different from the experiences of men who might share, for example, racial or class identities. At the same time, each woman is an individual who is not defined solely by her (overlapping, intersecting or sometimes conflicting) membership in these communities; therefore, she will not always conform to expectations or generalizations about the "groups" to which she belongs.

Feminist analysis must therefore grapple with the relationship between the individual and the "group" experience. Sexual abuse in the professional context is based on a collective or systemic definition of women's experience, rather than one delineated as involving individuals existing without linkages through identification with other women, either by choice or, as here, by subordinate status, stereotypes or expectations imposed upon them. This characterization is similar to the changed perceptions of so-called "family" violence or sexual harassment, for example. In these cases, as well as others, activity that was essentially considered private is now considered public; these relations between men and women have moved from outside the boundaries of activities deemed worthy of legal regulation to within the boundaries (from being extra-legal to within the sphere of activity controlled by law), and therefore are considered to be outside *the* law (that is, to be illegal). Rather than being treated as being outside legal (criminal) discourse, abuse (of women) by (male) partners is now seen as a criminal matter, one worthy of public interest. Sexual harassment means that the sexualization of women in the workplace is recognized for what it is and not as a reflection of one man's attraction toward a woman or women.

The doctor-patient relationship, although clearly a commercial relationship and therefore in the public realm, is nevertheless a private relationship in its reliance on trust and confidentiality. As with the family, the "private" professional relationship has been kept from serious public scrutiny. As with family relationships, the client/patient who wants to complain about intimate contact may feel she is betraying the relationship and risking the loss of the professional's approval. As the systemic power relations between doctors and their patients are increasingly recognized, so is their public aspect and the need for public response. But these developments can occur only because we place the individual act within (gendered) patterns and the individual harm within (gendered) patterns of harm; this has been called the difference between "privatized" and "social injuries" (Howe, 1991).

## The Law and Women's Bodies

In mainstream Canadian society, remedies for publicly recognized "wrongs" are enforced through the legal system. To receive validation for one's sense of harm or, in other words, the approbation of law, one is forced to reshape the events leading to, and the harm itself, into legally recognized categories. Thus it is not the experience itself which counts, but the experience as filtered through the legal process. As part of the filtering process, it is necessary to sift through the "facts" of the event, to separate and repackage them so that they become legally relevant and therefore admissible in a legal proceeding. These include "facts" not just about surrounding events (when did this happen? where? who else was there? who said or did what?), but also about the individuals involved. In some cases, it becomes necessary to divide and repackage the individual so that she or he becomes an individual with legal status or meaning within the context of the legal system.

For example, discrimination law establishes specific categories or identities on the basis of which discrimination is prohibited, including race, sex, disability, religion, and marital status, among others.[5] A person who wants to complain about discrimination must choose one of these categories or, at best, separate parts of her identity in order to fit into more than one category. Discrimination law does not easily contemplate a "blended" identity. Thus a black woman who has been discriminated against must decide whether her experience has something to do with her being black or with being a woman: she must divide and ignore part of herself to conform with the law's requirements (Duclos, 1993).[6] A claim by a gay man that his gay partner receive "spousal" benefits (denied because only two people of the opposite sex can be "spouses") is rejected because the claim was made on the basis of "family status"; yet the Court gives strong hints that if brought as a claim of discrimination on the basis of "marital status," a case on much the same facts would succeed (*Canada v. Mossop*, 1993).[7]

Indeed, the law imposes an external definition on most experiences. Anyone who wishes damages for breach of contract must first establish that the "contract" is a form of agreement recognized by law, satisfying certain objective *indicia*. The way in which the female body is made object and separated from the woman as mediated by the legal process may seem simply to be characterization of this kind. But while in some respects reflecting the operation of law generally, the way in which women's bodies are treated in law has ramifications beyond the "breach of contract" situation, in great measure because of the exclusion of female experience from the meaning of law (Smart, 1991).[8] Much of what women are or do has been overlaid by connection with the body to the extent that we become our bodies, not through self-agency, but by externally imposed norms, claims, and expectations, in particular around the value and meaning of female sexuality. Historically, the significance of women's sexuality has derived primarily from external validation: what men want from women sexually becomes, in a heterosexual world, what matters about women sexually in an "objective" sense — and, perhaps even more importantly, it becomes what matters for heterosexual women who strive to satisfy that male (and therefore female) standard.

Women's bodies are specifically characterized as being useful for sexual or reproductive purposes, that is by their use in a society in which women have been subject to obligations, but of which women have not been the designers. In blunt terms, men's sexual activity is for their own pleasure; women's sexual activity is for the use of men. A woman is respectable when she is connected to one man; but she is enjoyable when she is connectable to several men. Because men enjoy her, she is believed to be enjoying men and to be complimented and validated by men's approval. Women's actions are therefore defined not by what women say they mean, but what men have said they mean: screams of terror become screams of pleasure. The law's treatment of women's sexuality has reflected this distortion of women's experience in the protection of men's interests. Thus "legal rules ... encode the female body with meanings" (Frug, 1992:129). While the law claims that these meanings are natural, what is "natural" has been socially constructed by male-dominated thought (Frug, 1992; MacKinnon, 1989). One meaning is the body "in terror": "a body that has learned to scurry, to cringe and to submit"; a second meaning is that the female body is a body " 'for' maternity"; a third meaning is a body " 'for' sex with men" (Frug, 1992:129-30).

Furthermore, because men's concern with women's bodies and, specifically, women's sexuality, is determined mainly by what men want from women, sexuality which men do not want may have no existence. Lesbian sexuality may be seen as subversive or as irrelevant: men either dismiss it (since it does not involve men, it does not exist or it is abnormal) or are threatened by it (because it is evidence of the proposition that women do not need men).[9] Similarly, women's bodies are weapons in men's own battles with each other: white women's bodies have served racism by providing a rationale for lynching black men or as a locus of conquest over white men by black men; black women's bodies are stereotyped to serve as a guilt-free access to sexual adventure (Austin, 1992; Crenshaw, 1992). The "cultural imperialism" by which "a group's ... invisible at the same time that it is marked out and stereotyped" (Young, 1990a:123) applies to women. Women are invisible in the sense that their experience is not recognized, but they are marked out and stereotyped in the sexualized nature attributed to them.

Many of the assumptions about women's (hetero)sexuality and sexual conduct permit the use of women's bodies " 'for' sex with men" in otherwise non-sexual contexts. While generally we are all sexual beings all the time (that is, we all have a capacity for sexual activity at all times), expression of our sexuality is not always relevant or appropriate in all circum-stances. But because women are constituted by our bodies/sexuality, treat-ment of us as "women" necessarily always involves our being seen as available for sexual encounters, of minor or significant degree, *regardless of our own voluntary involvement*. The norm of female-male relations, whether acted on or not, sexualizes women. In the workplace, women have been women before they are workers (MacKinnon, 1979). It has been less than two decades since Canadian law gave a woman the right to refuse her husband's sexual demands: until 1983, a man could not be charged with raping his wife, who was meant to be a ready and able sexualized being at all times.[10] A female patient has also been treated as a woman and available for sexual gratification,[11] something that even recently was not seen by many doctors as cause for significant concern (*Globe and Mail*, 12 Jan. 1994).[12] Nor should we be surprised to learn that one study showed that more than 75 per cent of women doctors were also sexually harassed by their male patients (*Globe and Mail*, 23 Dec. 1993).

For much of our history, the treatment of our bodies has not been seen as worthy of public (i.e., legal) protection, unless men have been injured by that treatment (Smart, 1991; Pateman, 1988). Women's own injuries were less likely to be recognized; how could women be injured when they did not "own" the locus of the injury? The concepts of mind/body, thought/feeling, rationality/instinct, civilization/nature, public/private have posited hierarchical dualities in which men have defined themselves on one side and have defined women as on the other — and then defined "their" side as superior (Smart, 1991; Scott, 1990). Only those who are able to separate ("disembody") their mind and its processes from their body and its processes are worthy of public recognition and protection; only they can be injured.

Therefore, women who have sought the protection of the legal system *vis-à-vis* their bodies have for the most part had to redefine their bodily experiences to conform not only to the way an abstract body of knowledge or set of processes requires, but to the way in which those who have the most interest in controlling women's bodies have defined them. This is because the "abstract body of knowledge" is merely a reflection of (certain) men's perception of the world. In considering the place of women in law, therefore, feminists must consider "the ways in which legal reasoning transforms the embodied imaginings from male lives into the 'objective' form of doctrine which passes for the 'normative.'" (Grbich, 1991:69).

In "real life," the apparently shared experience of men and women — they are physically in the same place at the same time — have often been quite different experiences. For example, "for the man, the office pass was sex (and pleasurable), for the women [sic], it was harassment (and painful); for the man the evening was a date—perhaps not pleasant, but certainly not frightening—for the woman, it was a rape and very scary indeed" (West, 1991:115). But these different characterizations have not been given the same credence. The male interpretations of these experiences have been superimposed on women's experience to render the latter invisible.

As women we have been reclaiming our bodies as part of our integrated selves. We have been making ourselves visible and defining the way in which we are visible. The pro-choice slogan of the right to control our bodies has been criticized as over-emphasizing the choice of middle-class, mainly white women *not* to be compulsory child-bearers, while ignoring the choice of many poor, racial or cultural minority and physically or mentally disadvantaged women to *be* voluntary mothers; regardless of its particular focus for a particular purpose, however, that slogan underlies our assertion of a more general right to bodily integrity. During the second wave of feminism, "[o]n a wide range of fronts women have struggled to assert or regain control over our bodies, seeking to wrest control away from the state, the medical establishment, institutionalized religion, pharmaceutical companies, advertisers, pornographers, institutionalized censorship, the violence of men" (Pierson, 1993:98). Thus incest, sexual assault, spousal abuse, professional sexual abuse, and similar manifestations of male violence against women have received widespread public attention.

Feminist praxis has forced the treatment of women's bodies onto the public agenda. For example, previously "normal" sexual relations between men and women have new names: "sexual harassment" and "date-rape." Similarly, the husband's "right" to chastise his wife through corporal punishment is now "wife battering." The medical profession itself has acknowledged society's growing intolerance of sexual abuse, even in cases of "consensual sexual intercourse" (*Macdonald v. Council of the College of Physicians and Surgeons* [N.B.], 1992).[13]

Remembering Carol Smart's admonition that "law has entry into minute aspects of the life of the body and has the potential to regulate women's activities whilst appearing most liberal and benevolent" (Smart, 1991:97), we need to understand how law defines, reconceptualizes, and recategorizes women's experiences even as it purports to validate them. In a sense, the norms of one culture (that is, a private sphere in many respects significantly outside the realm of law) are being transmitted onto the circumstances of another (the imposing of legal sanctions on behaviour considered in large measure to be "normal"); even if we want to do so, we must recognize that there is not always an easy fit and accommodation must be made. In short, all aspects of a particular situation do not change at the same rate, and even the most well-intentioned attempts at reform must recognize that.[4]

This transition occurs in ourselves. Having been defined by our bodies, and rewarded or punished for daring to use our bodies without permission, women are in a complex relationship with our bodily/sexual selves. Claiming bodily autonomy, on the one hand, we may also strive to please through the way we display ourselves; or we may deny that we lack autonomy. The "ever-present possibility that one will be gazed upon as a mere body, as shape and flesh that presents itself as the potential object of another subject's intentions and manipulations," has the consequence that "the woman herself often actively takes up her body as a mere thing" (Young, 1990b:155). After all, "[w]oman lives her body as seen by another, by an anonymous patriarchal Other" (Bartky, 1993:459).

She may also treat herself as an object to be taken, the pain of being treated as object, as sexualized being, as disembodied body as "punishment, or flattery, or transcendence, or unconscious pleasure" (West, 1991:118). The threat of male violence against women is so pervasive (it is there for all women, even if the violence does not actually happen to all women) that women "*reconstitut[e]* themselves in a way that controls the danger, suppresses the fear. Thus: women define themselves as 'giving selves' so as to obviate the threat, the danger, the pain, and the fear of being self-regarding selves from whom their sexuality is taken" (West, 1991:122; emphasis in original). Women's capacity to move autonomously, to set out parameters, to exclude is constrained: "Woman's space is not a field in which her bodily intentionality can be freely realized but an enclosure in which she feels herself positioned and by which she is confined" (Bartky, 1993:456).

An ostensibly positive (male) response to the (female) body is thus responded to positively by the heterosexual woman; and when a male doctor engages sexually with a female patient, he is invading and becoming part of the space in which she is enclosed. His act attracts all the ambivalence connected to the woman who is perceived mythically, while she seeks autonomy, is defined collectively while she seeks to be an individual, whose parts are considered to be sum, forced to dance the dance of gendered relations masquerading as individual attraction.

## One Real Experience: Many Legal Meanings

The treatment of the body by the law in the context of sexual misconduct by a doctor may be best illustrated through a story, one which, although fictional, reflects real experiences of women with their doctors.

About 18 months ago, Jane Colter moved to a town somewhat smaller than the city in which she had spent the last decade. She became a patient of Dr. Alan Hodges, a general practitioner. They are both white, straight and able-bodied; they are both in their early forties; she owns her own business. Dr. Hodges has seen Ms Colter for regular examinations and the odd minor ailment, including a vaginal infection. For most of the time, she has been suffering a mild depression; Dr. Hodges referred her to a psychologist for treatment, but he and Ms Colter have discussed it from time to time, as well. On one visit, as he performed an internal examination in connection with the vaginal infection, Dr. Hodges smiled and said "have I told you how much I enjoy my work?". The exam did not seem like most internal exams Jane Colter had been given, but since this one was to check for an actual infection, she thought it might have to be different. As the doctor removed his gloved finger from her vagina, Jane was sure that he stroked her clitoris. She did not say anything and later she wondered if she had imagined it. On another occasion, he came into the examination room before she finished undressing, apologized and said he would simply prepare some paper work while she finished and put on the gown. He then did a lengthy breast examination, mentioning how firm her breasts were. As time went on, she became quite reliant on him; she looked forward to discussing some of her problems with him, as well as their shared interests in cooking and films. As she requested when she first called the office, her appointments were usually scheduled at the end of the day to avoid interrupting her work. The doctor got into the habit of telling the nurse that she could leave if he was running a bit late. One day, Alan suggested to Jane Colter that if she liked, they could talk about her situation more informally, over a drink. Eventually they became more intimate and had sexual relations. He did not use force and she did not resist his overtures. On the contrary, she enjoyed it. She mentioned this new relationship to a friend. As a result of this conversation, she started to question the events of the previous few months. She thought about the sequence of events, the small touches or comments, the way in which she was drawn into the relationship by his displays of caring and affection and his references to her depression. She began to feel that the trust she had placed in him had been a mistake.

If Jane Colter decides she wants to complain about Dr. Hodges' conduct, there are three ways she can do so: report him to his professional body, the provincial college of physicians and surgeons ("the regulatory context"); bring a civil suit against him for damages for the tort of battery,[15] breach of fiduciary duty or breach of professional duty ("the civil context"); or file a complaint with the police that he has sexually assaulted her ("the criminal context"). The three forms of legal regulation, control, or prohibition of sexual misconduct have different purposes and methods or procedures.[16] Professional regulation combines features of both criminal prosecution and civil actions but, from the doctor's point of view, does not contain the procedural safeguards of either criminal nor to a lesser extent, of civil suits (Campbell and Lisus, 1993). Although Jane Colter's experience remains constant, the law would redefine her experience to conform to its requirements. Thus the same events might well have different (and inverse) consequences for both the doctor and the patient: her experience may in effect change from one that is considered worthy of compensation or legal recognition to one that is not so considered. Her description of the events may be "truth" in one proceeding and not in another. She may be believed in all the proceedings, but denied redress in one forum because of how she is found to have behaved, while being granted a remedy in another.

It will quickly become clear that her ability to tell her own story is affected by the forum she chooses. While she will always find that she must describe her experiences in ways that conform to legal categories, if she decides to file a criminal complaint or a complaint with the regulatory body, the case is taken from her: it is the state (the Crown prosecutor) or the regulatory body itself which decides how the case is to proceed. While this process reduces her financial cost, it also reduces her participation to that of a "bystander" (Smart, 1991:34). The extent to which her views matter will depend on the individual Crown or the lawyer for the college.

If she decides to bring a civil action against Dr. Hodges, she will have to bear the financial cost, but she will have the greatest involvement in the case (to the extent that any client is able to influence the course of a lawsuit). In the criminal and regulatory processes, on the other hand, the "victim" becomes a witness to her experience; she is disembodied from it and it becomes shaped by what matters to those prosecuting the case. She has no way of framing the discourse; she simply answers questions about what happened as if she had observed it rather than experienced it. She is expected to be a rational, objective witness to the events which had her at their centre. She is supposed to treat what happened to her body as if she is observing it from the outside.

The end of the process reflects the beginning. Dr. Hodges may be jailed if convicted of criminal sexual assault or lose his licence to practice for a specified period permanently and fined if the College is successful in its disciplinary proceeding. Jane Colter herself will not be granted a remedy in either case. In the civil proceeding, however, she could be awarded damages, including damages for the distress she has suffered.

Jane Colter's role and the remedy in each case reflect the purpose of each form of proceeding. Criminal law, as codified in Canada in the *Criminal Code* and other statutes, is intended to reflect "societal" interest in encouraging (mostly by implication, but sometimes explicitly) certain types of behaviour and, usually explicitly, preventing others, including sexual assault. The legal fiction is that the harm is done to "society," as represented by "the state." The individual who is *actually* harmed is an actor with a part to play, along with other witnesses, if there are any. The person is almost incidental, the vehicle by which the drama between the state and the accused comes to be staged.[7] The purpose of a professional body's code of conduct is to ensure that the public can rely on a professional to practise in accordance with the standards established by the profession. Disciplinary proceedings serve to control the profession's members. It is the regulatory body's interest that is protected more than the complainant's. In legal appearance, then, it is not really Jane Colter, but the state or the College of Physicians and Surgeons which has been "sinned against."

Private law, on the other hand, is designed to attain redress for the person actually harmed. It is less to punish or to regulate, than to try to make the victim "whole." In this case, the law cannot undo what Dr. Hodges did, but it can force him to compensate Jane Colter for any harm he did to her. In broad terms, the issue is between them and societal values come into play mainly as background noise.[18] The different ways in which the cases would be named reflect the "ownership" of the case, and thus of the events: *R. v. Hodges* (the criminal proceeding, "R" being The Queen, represented by the Crown); *The College of Physicians and Surgeons v. Hodges* (the disciplinary proceeding); and *Colter v. Hodges* (the civil suit).

Two other important questions concern how the "facts" are perceived or how they are translated into legal constructs and which version of the story is to triumph in case of conflict. What "facts" matter here? Whose "facts" are they? I place "facts" in quotation marks because what is or is not "fact" in real life may be quite different from what is legally recognized and therefore relevant "fact." The judge's treatment of the facts in the case of *L.T. v. McGillivray*, referred to earlier, illustrates this point. The judge found as fact that L.T. had suffered sexual abuse when she was seven or eight years old (he also found as a fact that the doctor was counselling her for emotional problems resulting from the early abuse); he found, as well, that before they began to have sexual intercourse, they discussed contraception and Dr. McGillivray gave L.T. birth control pills from his samples. The judge treated L.T.'s use of birth control as relevant to whether she had consented to the sexual intercourse (so relevant that he concluded that she had consented on that basis and dismissed the tort action in sexual assault or battery); he did not consider the early sexual abuse and the doctor's knowledge of it as relevant to whether she had voluntarily consented, however, nor did he seem to think that Dr. McGillivray's promises of marriage at a later time (which he stated at a session with a third party) might have had some impact on her apparent "consent." In short, some facts mattered and some did not as far as "the law" (in the person of the judge) was concerned even though in "real life," it is impossible to separate L.T.'s early experience from her response to the doctor ten years later.

In our scenario, Dr. Hodges may deny the events occurred at all (that is, he may deny the *existence* of the "facts" as presented by Jane Colter); he may characterize them in ways which show him at best to be a caring doctor and person and, at worst, to be someone who made an error in judgement (he will dispute Jane Colter's *version* or characterization of the "facts"). He may simply deny that he stroked her clitoris at all, or turn her uncertainty at the time into evidence that she must have had no objection to his action: his testimony will be firm, hers will be tentative. He will use her confusion, ambivalence, and depression, her need for approval or caring, her "giving self" against her. He will say that he used no force, nor even any untoward persuasion. He will say that she enjoyed the relationship and that her second thoughts now are merely a reflection of her unstable state or need for attention (he will introduce new "facts"). He will point out that she had no complaints about his medical treatment of her. He will stress their relative equality in age, education, sophistication, and other characteristics. These "facts," it is obvious, are amenable to slipping and sliding across the boundaries between Dr. Hodges' pleasure and Jane Colter's sense of violation; what to him is gratification is to her a sense of betrayal; his relationship of "equality" is a manifestation of her life's training to be a body "'for' sex with men."

For example, Dr. Hodges' comments about his work and Ms Colter's breasts may be seen as ascribing sexualization to a professional examination; or they may be seen as efforts to make his patient more comfortable and increase her self-esteem. She becomes a woman like other women: she needs praise about her body. In a case in which a doctor made derogatory remarks to his patient (calling her a "slut," for example) as well as making inappropriate suggestions about having an affair or showing him her breasts "to make [her] day," the disciplinary committee of the Ontario College of Physicians and Surgeons and the Ontario Divisional Court characterized the comments as attempts at humour, albeit misguided ones, intended to make the patient more comfortable (*Re College of Physicians and Surgeons of Ontario and Lambert*, 1992). In that case, according to the patient, the doctor had also apparently fondled her clitoris, but this was lost in the translation into law. The comments were unprofessional conduct (circumspection in language is essential for a doctor to maintain a satisfactory relationship with a patient), but words alone did not constitute sexual impropriety without sexual touching.

Faced with a criminal charge of sexual assault or with a civil claim in the tort of battery, Dr. Hodges will defend himself by claiming that Jane Colter consented to the activity. Section 273.1 of the *Criminal Code* now defines "consent" in the context of "sexual assault" as "the voluntary agreement of the complainant to engage in the sexual activity in question" (prior to 1992, the Code did not define "consent"). But the *Criminal Code* also provides that there can be no consent under certain circumstances. In other words, even if as a matter of "fact," one would conclude that the person had consented, if these circumstances exist, the question of consent is foreclosed. In the context of the doctor-patient relationship, consent is foreclosed when "the accused adduces the complainant to engage in the activity by abusing a position of trust, power or authority." The doctor-patient relationship is one of trust. Whether Dr. Hodges "adduced" Jane

Colter to have sex "by abusing" his position as her doctor will be determined by whose version of "truth" is accepted. A doctor does not need to use physical force or a weapon to induce a patient to engage in sex, when he has the "weapon" of trust available to him (College of Physicians and Surgeons of Ontario, 1991:79). But sexual conduct by a doctor with his patient is not automatically a criminal offence.

In the Supreme Court of Canada case *Norberg v. Wynrib* (1992), in which a doctor provided drugs to a young female patient in exchange for sex, the majority of the judges held that Ms Norberg had not *voluntarily* consented to the sexual activity because of the power imbalance in the particular relationship (the differences in age and education and the drug dependency all contributed to the imbalance; Ms Norberg is an Aboriginal woman and Dr. Wynrib is white, but this "fact" played no part in the case for the judges) and because of the doctor's exploitation of the patient's drug addiction, in the relationship of doctor-patient. Dr. Wynrib was therefore liable for the tort of battery. While the mere fact of the relationship will not vitiate consent, it will be a major factor. Furthermore, while both parties might have responsibility in the relationship, the doctor had special obligations; the doctor is also in a position of advantage in knowing the patient and what he thinks he can "get away with" (*W.[B.] v. Mellor*, 1989, cited in *Norberg v. Wynrib*, 1992).

Other civil claims treat consent differently. The two female judges in *Norberg v. Wynrib*, who based their finding of Dr. Wynrib's culpability directly on his breach of the fiduciary relationship, held that Ms Norberg had consented to the sexual activity, but that does not save him. One judge held that the doctor had breached his professional duty by not treating Ms Norberg's addiction, and again, on this ground, consent plays no part; the sexual activity was of little import in his decision.

In the regulatory context, professional bodies are increasingly recognizing that any kind of sexual conduct by the doctor should receive sanction. Consent may be more significant to penalty than to liability, therefore, but it will still be important for the doctor to present the patient's behaviour as consent. Thus where the patient is a "sophisticated" woman, as Jane Colter may be seen to be, this will be taken into account, even though the doctor's conduct may be "disgraceful, dishonourable and unprofessional" (*College of Physicians and Surgeons v. Boodoosingh*, 1990).

The judge, the jury or the disciplinary committee will hear different stories or different characterizations of the same event. Torn between these versions, how will they determine the single "truth" which law permits to define Jane Colter's experience?

In a criminal proceeding, the Crown bears the burden of proving beyond a reasonable doubt that the person charged with an offence is guilty. The burden and other protections afforded the accused in a criminal proceeding are justified on the basis that the accused is an individual against whom is arrayed the full panoply of the state. Thus if the trier of fact (who may be a judge or a jury) has some (reasonable) doubt about whether Dr. Hodges did assault Jane Colter, he will be acquitted. In her civil suit, on the other hand, Jane Colter has the onus of showing on the basis of the preponderance of evidence (or balance of probabilities) that the other person did commit the action complained of and that it resulted in the harm alleged. This is the same standard before a regulatory body (*Re Bernstein and College of Physicians and Surgeons of Ontario*, 1977). It is not difficult to see, therefore, how the same events can result in culpability in civil proceedings or the regulatory context, while in the criminal proceeding, the doctor may be acquitted.

In this scenario, Dr. Hodges will likely be held culpable only because he has abused the doctor-patient relationship; the power imbalance is *structural*, rather than a *personal* imbalance of power between him and Jane Colter. The acknowledgement of women's different power position involves some risks; among them is that women will be treated as "victims," as vulnerable and weak, and as less than independent, autonomous beings who are capable of making decisions about our lives. For example, it might be argued against a total ban on sexual activity by doctors with their patients in the regulatory context, that the capacity of women to make a choice to engage in a sexual relationship is being impaired, and that it is assumed *for all women* that they are not competent to make that decision.[19] From this point of view, the absolute ban is another version of protecting a class of persons who are considered incapable of acting in their own interests. Furthermore, patients may be seen as escaping responsibility for their own actions when they initiate the activity (not the case in our scenario). Yet in today's world of gender hierarchy, "women" in the collective sense *are* more vulnerable to sexual abuse, and "where such a power imbalance exists it matters not what the patient may have done, how seductively she may have dressed, how compliant she may have appeared, or how self-interested her conduct may have been—the doctor will be at fault if sexual exploitation occurs" (*Norberg v. Wynrib*, 1992:498 per McLachlin J.).

## Conclusion

A few years ago, the Supreme Court of Canada had occasion to review the decision of a motions judge in British Columbia to sever and divide a number of counts of sexual assault which had been filed against a doctor (*R. v. Litchfield*, 1993). The judge ordered three trials, depending on whether the allegations related to the genitals, to the breasts or to other areas of the body; this pre-trial order was upheld by the trial judge and the Court of Appeal. The initial order reflects the disembodied woman with whom we are familiar, the woman carved into pieces, whose identity is externally imposed, determined in part by how she is perceived by a man, here the doctor, for whom she is a discrete set of body parts apparently assembled for his pleasure, as well as by the judge, for whom the female patients apparently had no existence outside the paper descriptions of their body parts.

In part because of the technical vagaries of legal process (vagaries which the Supreme Court denounced in its decision), it was necessary to take this amazing decision (amazing only in its blatancy) to the Supreme Court of Canada to have it overturned. In doing so, Iacobucci J. wrote for all members of the Court that

> The order [to sever the counts] denies the reality of how the complainants experienced the conduct which they have alleged constitutes sexual assaults. Each aspect of one complainant's contact with the respondent [doctor] interlocks with all the other aspects to form the larger context within which the complainant felt the respondent's actions were inappropriate. Further, the message that a divided and severed order in a sexual assault case based on the complainant's body parts sends to women is that the complainant's physical attributes are more important than her experience as a whole person. The order severed the complainants as well as the counts. (*R. v. Litchfield*, 1993:19 per Iacobucci J.)

For the Jane Colters of this world, the *Litchfield* decision at least tells them that they might begin the hearing with their individual parts intact. The requirements of the legal process will nevertheless almost guarantee that they will have to traverse the remainder of the process by trying to maintain a firm grip on their own "truth." Jane Colter's experience is insidious in its "normalcy." It is therefore all the more difficult for the law, concerned as it is with pathology, to identify it as "wrong." In order to be successful, Jane Colter must deconstruct her experience and reconstruct it so that it conforms to structural imperatives. While this process has been increasingly challenged by feminist legal theorists, and while there have been significant changes, we need always to remember the systemic (gendered/multi-identity) nature of these experiences. Otherwise, we will find ourselves again the prey of "benevolent" law.

## Notes

1. Colleges of Physicians and Surgeons in most Canadian provinces have established task forces or committees to examine sexual misconduct by doctors, with resultant reports (see the *Final Report*, "Beyond the Silence," and "First, Do No Harm" as examples). As of January 1994, Ontario established an extensive regime to respond to sexual abuse of patients; for example, doctors (and other health professionals) could lose their licence to practise for up to five years and be fined up to $35,000 for having sex with a patient: *Regulated Health Professions Amendment Act*, 1993, S.O. 1993, c.37.

2. McLachlin C.J.C. was elevated to Chief Justice of the Supreme Court of Canada in January 2000, the first woman to be so appointed.

3. As an example of how the law fails to treat women's bodies as their own, take note of a case in which a man was awarded damages for breach of the fiduciary duty owed to him by his lawyer when his lawyer engaged in sex with the client's wife (*Szarfer v. Chodos*, 1986).

4. For example, "[w]omen seek maintenance awards from judges who decide that little maintenance is required as an attractive body will soon find another spouse to assist in maintaining a home" (Grbich, 1991:75).

5. Human rights acts or codes list grounds upon which discrimination in the specified contexts is prohibited; for instance, it is common to prohibit discrimination in employment or in the renting of accommodation. For examples, see *Human Rights Code*, R.S.O. 1990, c.H-19 (Ontario); *Human Rights Code*, R.S.N.B. 1973, c.H-11 (New Brunswick); *Canadian Human Rights Act*, R.S.C. 1985, H-6.

6. The Supreme Court of Canada has said that an "intersection of grounds" could constitute an analogous ground under the equality guarantee of the *Canadian Charter of Rights and Freedoms*: *Law v. Canada (Minister of Employment and Immigration)*. Section 15 of the Charter guarantees equality without discrimination on the basis of an open-ended list of grounds which were common to human rights legislation in 1982 when the Charter was enacted; the Court has held that any added grounds should be "analogous" to these enumerated grounds. There has not yet been a case in which a synthesis or intersection of grounds has actually been considered.

7. In 1995, the Supreme Court of Canada considered an application alleging discrimination on the basis of sexual orientation by a gay man in a same-sex couple claiming spousal benefits when his partner received the old-age pension: *Egan v. Canada*. Although all members of the Court held that sexual orientation was an analogous ground under section 15 of the Charter, four judges held that the limitation of benefits to different-sex couples was not discrimination; of the five judges who considered it discrimination, one decided it was justified under section 1 of the Charter and therefore the couple were unsuccessful.

8. It would be inaccurate to leave the statement about contract law as it is; while the statement is in essence correct, the law does address itself to whether the process leading to the contract was "fair" by permitting consideration of whether there was unequal bargaining power. The assumption that a contract is reached between two equal individuals, that is, the liberal individualism underpinning contract law, may be upset in a number of ways, including the respective status of the parties to the agreement. Nevertheless, this is really only "tinkering" with contract principles (Pateman, 1988; Frug, 1985).

9. In this regard, the Supreme Court of Canada has held that the support provision of the Ontario *Family Law Act* which excluded same-sex couples is a contravention of section 15: *M. v. H.* (1999). M. and H. were a lesbian couple. This and other related cases and legislative changes are a recognition of lesbian (and gay men's) sexuality.

10. Section 278 of the *Criminal Code*, R.S.C. 1985, c.C-46, states that a spouse may be charged with sexual assault of his or her spouse, whether they were living together at the time of the events constituting the sexual assault or not. Until amendments to the *Criminal Code* in 1982, conduct that is now considered "sexual assault" was called by a variety of different names, the most important of which was "rape," a crime which could be committed only by a man against a woman "who is not his wife."

11. There are instances of male patients being subject to sexual misconduct, but usually by male doctors (*Brand* v. *College of Physicians and Surgeons (Saskatchewan)*, 1990; X v. *College of Physicians and Surgeons of British Columbia*, 1991).

12. There was a gendered distinction among doctors who believed that physicians who had sexually violated a patient should permanently lose their licences: 40 per cent of female respondents and 22 per cent of male respondents thought that they should.

13. In this case, the College of Physicians and Surgeons suspended the doctor for a year; however, the New Brunswick Court of Appeal reduced the penalty because it said that there had been no evidence presented of society's views. The same doctor was convicted of eight sex-related charges in criminal proceedings. The Ontario College's lifetime suspension of the licence of a psychiatrist who had had one instance of (consensual) sex with an ex-patient was reduced by the courts and the Supreme Court of Canada refused leave to appeal those decisions (*College of Physicians and Surgeons* v. *Boodoosingh*, 1993).

14. In the context of spousal violence, for example, the commitment to charging spousal abusers has not always been accompanied by an appreciation of the complexity of the situation for the abused wife who is subpoenaed to testify (Hughes, 1994).

15. A "tort" is a legally recognized harm done by one person against another for which the harmed person can be awarded damages. "Battery" is a particular kind of tort involving the unlawful touching of another person (that is, touching without the person's consent); the tort of "assault" merely requires a threat to touch without a person's consent. Because the definition of the wrong requires that it be carried out without the person's consent, it is a defence to being sued for the tort of battery to show that the person consented to the touching.

16. These processes are not mutually exclusive. A doctor may be subject to two or all three proceedings in connection with the same set of events. A doctor convicted of sexual assault is likely to face a disciplinary proceeding initiated by the professional body itself, for example. But there may also be consequences for a patient who attempts to use all three proceedings (*L.T.* v. *McGillivray*, 1993). L.T. sued Dr. McGillivray in a civil action for the tort of sexual assault and breach of fiduciary duty after her complaint to the College of Physicians and Surgeons resulted in a fine and a postponed two year suspension of the doctor's licence (if he did not engage in sexual impropriety for five years, the suspension would be revoked) and after she had been unsuccessful in having him charged for criminal sexual assault. The judge hearing the case concluded that one of her motives for bringing the civil action was "vindictiveness," apparently on the sole basis that she was dissatisfied with the results in the other

forums. As a result, although he held that the doctor was liable for breach of fiduciary duty, he took the "vindictiveness" into account in assessing the damages he awarded.

17. Section 722 of the *Criminal Code* provides that a victim may make a victim impact statement at time of sentencing about the effect that the accused's behaviour had on her or him.

18. These three forms of legal proceeding do, of course, share some characteristics. All types of legal process have a social aspect at the same time as they respond to harms suffered by individuals. There may well be similarities in issues approached through civil and criminal processes (*Norberg* v. *Wynrib*, 1992; *R.* v. *Litchfield*, 1993). And modifications such as victim statements on sentencing in criminal proceedings may at least give the victim a sense of involvement. What I have described, however, in the most general terms, is the essence of each type of process.

19. A zero tolerance attitude is gender-neutral on its face (it would apply to men and male doctors, women and female doctors, men and female doctors, and women and male doctors), but underlying it is a recognition that occurrences of sexual abuse occur far more often in the male doctor-female patient combination than in any of the others.

## Cases Cited

*Brand v. College of Physicians and Surgeons* (Saskatchewan) (1990), 86 Sask. R. 18 (C.A.).
*Canada v. Mossop*, [1993] 1 S.C.R. 554.
*College of Physicians and Surgeons v. Boodoosingh* (1990), 73 O.R. (2d) 478 (Div. Ct.); aff'd (1993) 12 O.R.(3d) 707; lv. to appeal to SCC denied (9 December 1993).
*Egan v. Canada*, [1995] 2 S.C.R. 513.
*L.T. v. McGillivray* (December 10, 1993 (N.B.T.D.)).
*M. v. H.*, [1999] 2 S.C.R. 3.
*Macdonald v. Council of the College of Physicians and Surgeons* (N.B.) (1992), 126 N.B.R.(2d) 118 (C.A.).
*Norberg v. Wynrib*, [1992] 2 S.C.R. 226.
*R. v. Litchfield*, [1993] 4 S.C.R. 333, rev'g (1992), 120 A.R. 391 (C.A.).
*Re Bernstein and College of Physicians and Surgeons of Ontario* (1977), 15 O.R.(2d) 447 (Div. Ct.).
*Re College of Physicians and Surgeons of Ontario and Lambert* (1992), 11 O.R.(3d) 545 (Div. Ct.).
*Szarfer v. Chodos* (1986), 54 O.R.(2d) 663 (H.C.J.).
*W.(B.) v. Mellor* (1989), 16 A.C.W.S.(3d) 260 (B.C.S.C.).
*X. v. College of Physicians and Surgeons of British Columbia* (1991), 2 B.C.A.C. 112 (C.A.).

## References

Austin, Regina (1992). "Black Women, Sisterhood, and the Difference/Deviance Divide." *New England Law Review* 26:877-87.
Bartky, Sandra Lee (1993). "The Feminine Body." In Alison M. Jagger and Paula S. Rothenberg (eds.), *Feminist Frameworks*. 3rd ed. Toronto: McGraw Hill. 454-61.
Bumiller, Kristin (1991). "Fallen Angels: the Representation of Violence against Women in Legal Culture." In Martha Albertson Fineman and Nancy Sweet Thomadsen (eds.), *At the Boundaries of Law: Feminism and Legal Theory*. New York: Routledge. 95-111.

Campbell, Colin L., and Jonathan Lisus (1993). "Procedural Fairness in the Defence of Professionals Charged with Sexual Abuse." *Advocates' Quarterly* 15:308.

College of Physicians and Surgeons of Alberta (1992, June). *Beyond the Silence Toward a Solution ..., the Final Report of the Committee on Sexual Exploitation in Professional Relationships.*

College of Physicians and Surgeons of New Brunswick (October, 1993). *"First, Do No Harm:" The Report of the Special Committee on Sexual Exploitation of Patients by Physicians.*

College of Physicians and Surgeons of Ontario (1991, November). *Independent Task Force on Sexual Abuse of Patients: The Final Report.*

Crenshaw, Kimberlé (1992). "Whose Story Is It, Anyway? Feminist and Antiracist Appropriations of Anita Hill." In Toni Morrison (ed.), *Race-ing Justice, En-gendering Power: Essays on Anita Hill, Clarence Thomas, and the Construction of Social Reality.* Toronto: Random House of Canada. 402-40.

Duclos, Nitya (1993). "Disappearing Woman: Racial Minority Women in Human Rights Cases." *Canadian Journal of Women and the Law* 6:25-51.

Frug, Mary Joe (1992). *Postmodern Legal Feminism.* New York: Routledge.

Frug, Mary Joe (1985). "Re-Reading Contracts: A Feminist Analysis of a Contracts Casebook." *American University Law Review* 34:1065-1140.

*The Globe and Mail.* "Sex with patient not seen as abuse by 40% in survey" (12 Jan. 1994) A1.

*The Globe and Mail.* "Female MDs often harassed, study finds" (23 Dec. 1993) A4.

Grbich, Judith E. (1991). "The Body in Legal Theory." In Martha Albertson Fineman and Nancy Sweet Thomadsen (eds.), *At the Boundaries of Law: Feminism and Legal Theory.* New York: Routledge. 61-76.

Howe, Adrian (1991). "The Problem of Privatized Injuries: Feminist Strategies for Litigation." In Martha Albertson Fineman and Nancy Sweet Thomadsen (eds.), *At the Boundaries of Law: Feminism and Legal Theory.* New York: Routledge. 148-67.

Hughes, Patricia (1994). "Twice a Victim." *Canadian Journal of Women and Law* 6:502-12.

MacKinnon, Catharine (1989). *Toward a Feminist Theory of the State.* Cambridge, MA: Harvard University Press.

MacKinnon, Catharine (1979). *Sexual Harassment of Working Women: A Case of Sex Discrimination.* New Haven: Yale University Press.

Pateman, Carol (1998). *The Sexual Contract.* Stanford: Stanford University Press.

Pierson, Ruth Roach (1993). "The Politics of the Body." In Pierson, Marjorie Griffin Cohen, Paula Bourne, and Philinda Masters (eds.), *Canadian Women's Issues: Strong Voices.* Toronto: James Lorimer. 98-122.

Scott, Joan W. (1990). "Deconstructing Equality-versus-Difference: Or, the Uses of Poststructuralist Theory for Feminism." In Marianne Hirsch and Evelyn Fox Keller (eds.), *Conflicts in Feminism.* New York: Routledge. 134-48.

Smart, Carol (1991). *Feminism and the Power of Law.* Toronto: Routledge.

West, Robin L. (1991). "The Difference in Women's Hedonic Lives: A Phenomenological Critique of Feminist Legal Theory." In Martha Albertson Fineman and Nancy Sweet Thomadsen (eds.), *At the Boundaries of Law: Feminism and Legal Theory.* New York: Routledge. 115-34.

Young, Iris Marion (1990a). *Justice and the Politics of Difference.* Princeton: Princeton University Press.

Young, Iris Marion (1990b). *Throwing Like a Girl and Other Essays in Feminist Philosophy and Social Theory.* Bloomington: Indiana University Press.

# 4

## Legal Discourse and Domestic Legal Aid: The Problem of Fitting In

### Lori Beaman

Oh my gosh when I tell people they tell me that I should have went to a shelter. It got to the point when the police would tell me to leave my home and I took my kids and left my home. And I wasn't allowed back in my home. I got really angry because I want to know what they consider abusive. I wasn't allowed back into my home because all these police departments and doctors were scared for me. I had to hide out for 2 months with my kids. I lived in a car with the kids going from relative to relative without him knowing where I was. I had to do that. They recommended that. It wasn't an abusive case for a legal aid lawyer but it was too abusive for mediation. Now you make sense of that one in a clear head. (28-year-old mother of two children)

The Canadian Charter of Rights and Freedoms guarantees women equality and security of the person in theory, yet in practice it is often quite different. While an abused woman might seem to be an obvious case for legal protection under the Charter's security of the person provisions,[1] the woman's experience described above is an example of the power of legal discourse to shape women's stories so as to minimize or exclude them. How does legal discourse serve to discount women's experiences and ignore their voices? One way is through limiting women's access to justice through a variety of practices.

This chapter will focus on the ways in which women's experiences of the legal system speak to the power of legal discourse to control their access to justice. The first section explores what exactly is meant by access to justice and the variety of ways in which access can be denied. The reasons that this issue is important to examine specifically in the context of women's experiences will also be discussed. The second section of the chapter explores how legal discourse works through legal method to preserve its own authority, particularly as it relates to "boundary setting." The last sections of the chapter explore two particular aspects of access to justice: the first is an exploration of women's experiences in one domestic legal aid program; the second is a consideration of the ways in which legal discourse is able to define constitutional challenges to provincial domestic legal aid programs.

Law has been described by a number of feminist theorists as a discourse, the most central feature of which is its ability to exclude accounts of women's lives. Legal discourse extends beyond traditional understandings of discourse that include language, texts, and interactions which define and confine (O'Donovan, 1989). It also includes a body of knowledge that is often accepted as the truth and processes that are presented as somehow facilitating the determination of the truth, such as the trial. It is this latter aspect of legal discourse — the process dimension — that is the focus of this chapter. The disqualification of women's voices is achieved at a local level through legal method, or the way in which law processes claims. Legal method exemplifies law's ability to define its own boundaries.

While much feminist work has been done at both the practical and theoretical levels in relation to substantive legal problems, it is only recently that women have begun to challenge issues relating to process and access to law. One such process-related issue is the inadequate provision of what is known as domestic or civil legal aid, which has begun to attract attention as being rooted in inequities based on gender (see, for example, Mossman, 1993; Hughes, 1995). Here access to justice needs to be conceptualized broadly, moving beyond the simplistic notion that having a lawyer translates into a guarantee of justice.

## Access to Justice

Access to justice (or lack of it) is shaped and framed at a variety of stages in the legal process. It takes place at the *statutory* level through the inclusion or exclusion of certain groups of people. For example, if a woman is living in a "common law" relationship, and she is not "legally married," she may be excluded from provincial marital property legislation which gives her, at least in theory, the right to claim half of the marital assets if the marriage/relationship breaks down. While there may be other legal solutions[2] available to the woman, those remedies are frequently more time-consuming and costly to prove than is a claim under marital property legislation. Women[3] in this case are thus excluded from justice at the statutory level.

While some people might argue that this understanding of access broadens the concept of access to justice too much, it is important to realize the debilitating impact of exclusionary legislation on those who are left out; most women do not have the time, energy or money to enter into the legal arena to challenge their exclusion. Thus for some people, access to justice is precluded simply on the basis of statutory exclusion.

Linked to statutory exclusion is *statutory interpretation*; access to justice also includes the possibility of using legal arguments to advance one's position before the courts. The example I will explore later in this chapter is that of the possible Charter challenge to domestic legal aid programs on the basis of equality and security of the person arguments. Statutory interpretation works at two levels: first, what actually takes place when a judge interprets a statute to exclude or limit a particular case; second, the way in which these decisions impact on shaping the stories of those who have not actually appeared before a judge. In other words, lawyers and their clients are guided in their applications by decisions in other cases. It is particularly difficult to document this effect, yet lawyers are guided both by Supreme Court decisions, but probably more so in their everyday practices by decisions made in their local judicial districts. After all, one of the rudimentary rules of practice learned by law students is to "know your court." Inherent in this maxim is the understanding that judges and court practices differ from jurisdiction to jurisdiction. While law presents itself as neutral and objective, lawyers negotiate which judge they will appear before with court staff so as to best advantage themselves and their clients. The practices of shaping the case and determining who "has" a case and who does not are linked to what Carol Smart calls the "mundane" level of law (1990).

Drawing from the work of Michel Foucault, Carol Smart views law as a discourse from which women's voices are excluded or reshaped (1987). The mundane level of law involves the process by which women's experiences are sorted, shaped, and framed to fit into legal discourse as a "case." This process takes place long before the "facts" ever reach the courtroom. Some cases are excluded altogether as being irrelevant, hopeless or simply bad. Impoverished women are especially vulnerable to the sorting processes that take place at the mundane level of law. It is these processes within legal discourse, more than any other, that have been largely exempt from scrutiny. Smart explicates the importance of examining routine practices:

> Primarily the job of the solicitor is to translate everyday affairs into legal issues. On hearing the client's story, the solicitor sifts it through a sieve of legal knowledge and formulations. Most of the story will be chaff as far as the lawyer is concerned, no matter how significant the rejected elements are to the client. Having extracted what law defines as relevant, it is translated into a foreign language. (1990:197)

Access to justice includes mundane, or practical, everyday aspects of being able to present one's arguments using all of the advantages available to "ordinary" litigants, primarily through representation by a lawyer in court, or through the use of a lawyer's skills to achieve one's purpose through negotiation and settlement. This aspect of access to justice includes the process of finding and obtaining the services of a lawyer.[4] While lawyers are not technically necessary for the presentation of one's case, the disciplinary practices within legal discourse often render them a practical necessity.

Concomitant with the interplay of power and knowledge in the production of "truth" in legal discourse is the notion of disciplinary practices, which are at work in law through protocols such as court-room dress, the manner in which judges are to be addressed, and even requirements about the size of paper on which applications are to be submitted. These disciplinary practices work to preserve imbalances in access to justice by rendering it unknowable to those who do not have special knowledge (i.e., legal training). Since many women are financially disadvantaged, they cannot hire the services of private counsel, and therefore must turn to legal aid programs for help. It is this mundane aspect of access to justice with which we are concerned in the following section.

The information and analysis in the following sections are based on a study of domestic legal aid. State workers (social workers and lawyers) and private legal practitioners were interviewed, but I will focus on the voices of the women who told their stories. This research was conducted by LEAF N.B. (The Legal Education and Action Fund for Women, New Brunswick) in an attempt to understand whether the domestic legal aid program meets the needs of women. The sample size in this component of the research was small (25 women) but included participants who had received legal-aid services, and those who had been denied legal aid.[5]

## Legal Aid in New Brunswick

In May 1993 a new legal-aid program came into effect in New Brunswick. While, previously, domestic legal-aid services had been offered by the private bar in the province (judicare model), these services were now to be offered by Department of Justice staff (staff model). Under the judicare model, private practitioners are issued with certificates for individual legal-aid cases. Under this model, at least in theory, clients have a choice of legal counsel. Under the staff model, lawyers are employed by the state to represent clients in domestic legal-aid matters. Domestic legal aid refers to those services that deal with the breakdown of marital relationships — custody, access, support, division of marital property. It is important to remember that while New Brunswick is the focus of this discussion, it is somewhat representative of the inadequate state of legal aid in most Canadian provinces. While the program — delivery protocols may differ from province to province, the impact on women is the same.

The New Brunswick domestic legal-aid program is integrated with services already offered through the Department of Justice, including mediation and representation on support applications and enforcement hearings. Each of the eight judicial districts has one full-time or part-time family solicitor. Legal representation is offered only to women who are living in, or who have recently left, abusive relationships. The determination of who qualifies as a victim of abuse is made by a court social worker, who, at least in theory, acts as the intake worker. I say "in theory" because some screening may be conducted over the telephone by receptionists. If a woman is deemed to be eligible, the majority of her legal representation will actually be provided by the court social worker, who drafts affidavits, applications, and other documents necessary for proceeding to court. The legal-aid lawyer may only see the client once, often just prior to the court appearance. Clients are represented in divorce "only when necessary," necessity being narrowly defined to include only those cases in which a client becomes the respondent in a divorce action. In addition, marital property will only be dealt with if the marital assets do not exceed $20,000. The harshness of such an artificial barrier is illustrated by the experiences of this woman, who, like many of the women who had contact with the domestic legal-aid system, was included on one basis only to be excluded on another:

> I said look I have been seeing an abuse counsellor for the last 2 months for emotional abuse. So I went back to the court counsellor and I told her that I found out that one of the criteria for Domestic Legal Aid was abuse. She never mentioned it during any of the previous meetings or during the mediation sessions and she saw the bruises on my arms and she asked me where I got my bruises and I told her I got them in a fight, trying to break up a fight between my husband and my daughter. I was always ending up getting hurt. She asked me about emotional abuse. I said yes and she handed me this pamphlet to fill out. Six pages of questions and it took me four hours to fill out because it upset me. I was to fill it out and bring it out to her. It was difficult. I called her as soon as I had it done and she said that's fine and she told me that I was still not going to get legal aid because of the $20,000.00 limit. So I didn't bother to send it in. (Forty-two-year-old mother of two children who had applied for child support and marital property division)

Under court services, mediation is offered for all issues, including division of "simple" marital property. However, "simple" marital property division has been so narrowly construed that even the presence of a pension amongst the marital assets is reason to deny mediation on that issue. Once the issues have been mediated, the couple is given a separation agreement, prepared by the social worker and reviewed by the court solicitor, and advised to seek independent legal advice. If the parties do not want to seek or cannot afford independent legal advice, they are asked to sign a waiver giving up their right to such advice. Presumably the reason many people go to legal aid in the first place is because they cannot afford private lawyers. Mediation is the *only* access impoverished women have to justice, unless they have been abused.

In summary, access to justice for women in New Brunswick is extremely limited, to say the least. Women who aren't abused or are not willing to admit their abuse[6] are forced to turn to mediation. For many women, this option is not realistic, either because their partners are unwilling to cooperate or because an agreement simply cannot be reached. In this respect they are deprived of access to the adversarial system simply because they are poor. In this sense, the state appears to have created a two-tiered system of justice: one for those with economic resources and one for those without. Women are also denied access to justice on problems that are concomitant with their poverty, such as appeals of income assistance rulings, landlord/tenant problems, and custody and supervisory proceedings by the state. Proceeding through the adversarial system without legal representation is beyond the contemplation of many impoverished women.

In 1995, the National Council of Welfare released a report entitled *Legal Aid and the Poor*, which cites research that found a strong relation between having a low socio-economic status and inaction in relation to legal problems. In addition, women who are victims of family violence are probably the least likely of any group to seek legal assistance. While men experience poverty too, as Mary Jane Mossman points out in her article "Gender Equality and Legal Aid Services" (1993), women may experience poverty for different reasons and in different circumstances than men, and therefore legal aid services must be defined according to women's experiences.

The limited nature of New Brunswick's domestic legal-aid system, and the legal-aid systems of most provinces in Canada, exacerbates the disadvantages already faced by women by further discouraging women from pursuing their legal options. The exhaustion that results from pursuing access to justice only to have the door slammed in their faces precludes the possibility of further legal action for many women. This 46-year-old woman who had applied to have access to her children legally documented describes her frustration:

> I don't want nothing from the system. I'm exhausted from the system. It didn't do much for me. Nothing whatsoever. My question is why do they have this service, 'cause it is full of loop holes? Everything has loopholes. Where is the service to help these people who need it? This was a year ago and it frustrated me so much that I don t even like to talk about it, really. I just want to forget that that part of my life ever existed

> and pray to God that I never have to walk down that road
> again. No, mine was not a positive experience at all.

Encouraging mediation in a case based on the fact that there is no evidence of abuse fails to recognize the power differential that often exists between men and women. It also ignores the shame, embarrassment, and fear many women feel which prevents them from disclosing abuse. The legal aid system magnifies an abused woman's feelings of hopelessness and reinforces her belief that she has made her bed and must now lie in it.

It is important to examine the "mundane" practices through which access to justice is controlled. In some measure these practices link to broader policies based in the notion that the state knows best. The rhetoric guiding the justification for limited domestic legal aid is that the state has limited financial resources and that the problem of access to justice is not a serious one. Further, access to justice through legal aid in New Brunswick operates on the premise that it is only battered women who need state assistance to meet their legal needs. While it is true that battered women are uniquely vulnerable, this assumption has the effect of pitting those who argue against the legal-aid system as it presently exists against abused women and their legal needs. Since most of the activists in relation to this issue are women, it plays women off against other women. Another "truth" is that family law is private law, and that interests relating to public law are not as important as those relating to public law (criminal law) and therefore are not as worthy of state support. These truths work to set the boundaries within which women have access to justice. In relation to access to justice, legal method plays an important role in the preservation of law's image as a producer of truth.

## Legal Discourse: Boundary Setting and Access to Legal Aid

Traditional legal method continues to be one of the most unexplored aspects of the gendered nature of legal discourse. Although some feminists have contributed to the articulation of feminist legal methods,[7] an invaluable project in and of itself, the explication of the ways in which traditional legal method works to replicate legal discourse as exclusive of women's experiences remains relatively immune from feminist theorizing and action. One notable exception to this void is the work of Mary Jane

Mossman, in particular her article "Feminism and Legal Method: The Difference it Makes."

Mossman raises the question of whether feminism has the ability to transform legal method. She ultimately concludes that legal method, "law's process of determining facts, choosing and applying principles, and reaching reasoned decisions" (1986:31), may well be impervious to feminism. In the process of reaching this conclusion, Mossman analyses two cases of significance to women's legal history in Canada,[8] centring her discussion around three aspects or principles of legal method: "1) the characterization of the issues; 2) the choice of legal precedent to decide the validity of the women's claims; and 3) the process of statutory interpretation, especially in determining the effect of statutes to alter common law principles" (1986:38). In her conclusions, Mossman highlights three points that are relevant to our consideration of legal aid: first, law has a unique ability to define its own boundaries; second, while law presents itself as being neutral and objective, it is in fact value-laden and full of opportunities for choice or discretion; and finally, legal method defines what is relevant, and is thus able to exclude ideas which challenge the status quo (1986:332-33).

Legal method has often been understood as something that relates predominantly to courtroom procedures, and yet much of the important work of processing cases takes place in the behind-the-scenes work of lawyers and their interactions with their clients. It is therefore especially critical that, as suggested by Carol Smart, we continue to explore legal method, particularly at the mundane level. Expanding the conceptualization of legal method as a process that includes not only those elements or principles outlined by Mossman, but also the more mundane and insidious aspects in the daily practice of law discussed by Smart, enables us to reveal the depths of the exclusionary practices of legal method and the harm suffered by women as a result. The experiences of the women described in this chapter are unique in that they allow us insight into aspects of legal method that normally remain obscured from scrutiny.

## Discounting Women's Claims: the Legal-Aid Process

In this section, I will attempt to make sense of the experiences of a group of women who have used or tried to use the legal-aid system in New Brunswick in the past few years. As we will see, Mossman's discussion of boundaries, neutrality, and relevance is helpful in explaining the themes that emerge from the women's experiences. However, these are not discrete categories, but interrelated and overlapping. They are used as an analytical tool only, and should not be read as replacing or superseding the women's discussion of their own experiences.

These women's experiences exemplify the power of law in relation to the mundane aspects of access to justice, the disciplinary practices of legal discourse that serve to demean and discount women's stories, and the ability of legal discourse to remain an unknowable authoritative voice that is removed and somehow "superior" to the knowledge gleaned from everyday experiences. It is important to note that both women who received legal aid and those who did not had experiences which they described as negative.

### BOUNDARY SETTING

Part of the characterization of the issue or the boundary-setting process of legal discourse is the coding of stories to exclude the legal "junk" and include the relevant "facts." However, for a woman who applies for legal aid and who is rejected, her story never reaches this sorting phase. When her story does not meet the narrow criteria for qualification for legal services, she may assume that the law has nothing to offer, and in fact that she is excluded from legal processes, which, in essence, she is. (Two of the women interviewed did not apply for legal-aid assistance simply because they believed that they were ineligible. Most economically disadvantaged women do not have the resources to pursue other alternatives.) While we might say that her story never reaches the characterization stage, I would argue that this pre-sorting practice administered by the legal-aid program is one of those mundane practices which often escapes notice, but which is an important adjunct to the process of characterizing the issues and the boundary-setting abilities of law. By barring access to the adversarial system to the poor, the legal-aid program acts as a filtering system, smoothing the way for those who can pay, freeing up court time and other legal resources. Boundaries are set on the basis of "truths," like the availability of family resources to women. The treatment of women as adjuncts to their husbands reminds us of an age we may have thought had passed. This woman describes the basis on which the decision to reject her for legal-aid services was made:

> What she said was that my husband did his (financial statement) and brought it in and she decided by his that I was not eligible for legal aid. Because what she could tell from his was that our assets were above the $20,000 limit. (Woman — she had wanted child support and division of marital property)

Boundary setting operates not only in relation to who is eligible for legal aid, but also in relation to the services offered to those who are admitted through the gates. The nature and range of services are dependent not on need, but on seemingly elusive criteria that are unknown both to the women who enter and to those who are rejected.

> I thought it was like when you get arrested that if you can't afford a lawyer that they would appoint you one. Therefore, if you can't afford a lawyer Family Court will give you a lawyer. It's not criminal. It's family law. That's what I went in there thinking what it was. When I came out they gave me this pamphlet and yet rejected me. So I don't have a clue what legal aid is? Because I haven't been that close to find out, whether it is a court-appointed lawyer, if you can't afford one, or if you find your own lawyer whether the court will pay for your lawyer ... I haven't got a clue what I was denied of. (Woman — had wanted advice on whether or not to take legal action)

The impact of boundary setting in many cases cannot be assessed. Some women never apply for legal aid, believing themselves to be ineligible. Others, after applying and being rejected, resign themselves to the limited options they have for access to justice, as is illustrated by this woman's statement:

> Sometimes you can't afford it and you have to wait and then if the house is not sold then you have to wait and you are stuck. Because now he doesn't want to give me my half and he says that if I apply for my half that he will kill me. So I have to do something about it but I can't afford to right now ... I wish that I could get my legal separation or divorce, whatever. But that's another thing that I can't afford right now. It has to wait. (Woman — had wanted a marital property division)

The determination of "what counts," or the characterization of the issues as Mossman would call it, is made long before the story reaches a courtroom in the form of a case. We rarely focus on these processes as part of legal method, yet they are often the most damaging in terms of women's access to the law. Excluding women who are economically disadvantaged from access to the legal system predetermines the type of cases that enter the legal arena. If you are poor, and many women are, your story is far less likely even to be framed for entry into the process. Thus the needs of impoverished women as issues to be characterized remain almost invisible within legal discourse. How can economically disadvantaged women enter legal discourse? Indeed, Carol Smart might ask whether they even want to.

### THE OBJECTIVITY OF THE LAW
### AND THE POSSIBILITY OF CHOICE

Integral to law's ability to retain its authority is its claim to be neutral and objective; the law applies equally to everyone. While we most often think of the myth of legal neutrality and objectivity in relation to courtroom decision making and judicial interpretations of the law, it also permeates mundane legal processes outside of the courtroom, like the process of applying for legal aid. Underlying the authority of the process are assumptions about fairness, neutral rules, and their objective application. However, discretionary practices in the legal-aid application process were described not only by the women we interviewed, but also in our interviews with those who work in the system, like court lawyers and social workers. Clearly, there exists not only the possibility of choice about whether and how a case should be supported by legal aid, but the probability of human biases entering into the process. The following woman was on sick leave when she applied to legal aid. She had suffered a nervous breakdown precipitated by failed mediation with her husband, insufficient support to maintain herself and her primary school-aged child, the death of her father for whom she had been the primary caregiver every day after work, and, finally, the suicide of her 16-year-old son. She describes the response of the court mediator to her request for legal assistance:

> I spoke to [the court mediator] and he said get your shit together and get back to work. There is nothing we can do here.... You had a lawyer. You went to court. Like, be satisfied and get off your ass and go back to work.

Part of the myth of objectivity and neutrality is the authority of legal actors like lawyers and judges, that somehow, they have knowledge which means that they "know best." This intersection of knowledge and power means that many women accept what they are told or directed to do, even when they object to it or do not understand its consequences. The following woman, who received legal-aid assistance on issues of access, child support, and division of marital property, but was denied assistance for a divorce, describes her experience in settling her case before it went to court:

> He [legal aid lawyer] told me it was in my best interest to sign it at the time and I did. He submitted it and it was signed and that was the end of it. No court appearance. Then I was faxed a copy of the consent order-I didn't even understand my consent order, I had to pay [private lawyer] $55.00 to explain it to me. After I got my order I had to go pay a private lawyer $55.00 to explain it to me because my lawyer [legal aid lawyer] never did.

Obviously women do exercise agency in managing their experiences in the legal system, but they expect that the lawyers who have been appointed to represent them will provide a certain level of service. The following woman, who received assistance with child support, recognizes the advantage her own education gave her in dealing with the legal system. She is also cognizant of the disadvantages other women might face:

> All I was told by my lawyer was that I would have just to confirm that I have custody. That's all I was told that I would have to do on that stand. I didn't know that I would have to be put on trial. I was in no way prepared and thank God everything worked out and I know how to use my head. I have a degree for God sakes, what happens to the women that don't. I was up on that stand for a good two hours defending myself. I was not told that would happen. I was hurt, it hurt my ideal of the court system. If I can't get good legal representation, if I can't be allowed to know these things prior, what defence do I have or somebody else. At least I'm smart enough and able to talk, but what happens to somebody that doesn't have that education or doesn't have time to think about the double barreled

> questions that are coming at them. That man [the legal aid
> lawyer] is in there every day, he could have prepared me a
> hell of a lot better.

Again, the idea that the lawyer knows best[9] is reflected here, even though
this woman felt stranded and abandoned by the lawyer who was appointed
to represent her.

Despite the promise of access, neutrality, and objectivity, some women
felt that they received a different level of service than that which they
would have received from a private practitioner. This woman received
assistance from legal aid on the issue of access to her children. She was
worried about the possibility that they were being exposed to "hard core"
pornographic materials that her husband was importing from the United
States. On expressing her concern, her legal-aid lawyer asked her whether
she was a "born-again Christian."

> I feel the legal aid lawyers looked at me like I can't afford to
> pay a real lawyer sort of thing and they didn't show any con-
> cern at all for what I was telling them, they made me feel like
> I was over reacting, that I was prudish, that I made a big deal
> over pornography, I was just made to feel like I did something
> wrong and I was just trying to turn it around and he was in
> the wrong and I was only trying to be vindictive and nasty and
> just trying to make his life miserable. That's basically what
> they made me feel like. They don't care, you're just another
> welfare mother coming in who can't afford to pay for a
> lawyer, as far as I'm concerned they don't care. If I hadn't
> been on Income Assistance I bet that I would have been
> treated with more respect, I would have been treated differ-
> ently. I don't believe the staff lawyers are doing anything but
> lining the people up and saying "next."

By instilling in women a sense that they somehow deserve less because
they are receiving state-assisted legal services, women are encouraged to
expect that they are entitled to less access to justice than someone who can
pay for it. Therefore, although the law presents itself as neutral and objective, justice is not equally accessible to everyone, nor does everyone have
the same legal choices.

## DEFINING RELEVANCE

The ability of law to sort through experiences and evidence and determine what will be considered and what will be discarded as legal junk involves the process of determining relevance. While we usually think about legal relevance in relation to admissible facts and pertinent case law in the courtroom, the assessment of relevance also operates at the mundane level in law, in this case through the acceptance criteria (set out in state policies) of the legal-aid program. While it is useful to talk about boundary setting, neutrality/choices, and relevance as analytic categories, they are interrelated. Determining relevance involves both choices and the boundary-setting process.

Women who apply for legal-aid assistance often present their stories with no prior knowledge of the criteria on which their applications will be based. Issues that they feel are relevant frequently will be discarded and a new story created by the state worker based on the invisible framework of state policy. The mystery of this process is part of law's power to control women and their access to justice. The theme that emerges most often from the interviews is that of disjuncture between women's experiences and the relevance criteria for legal aid. Women's stories are ignored in the process of assessing their eligibility, as is illustrated by this woman's experience:

> She [the court social worker] said go and get your own lawyer. I said that I have no money, none, and he has sold the house for less than what the mortgage was. She said any money left-over from the house, any lawyer would gladly take your case because they know they are going to be getting money. I said there isn't any, he sold it for $2,000 less than what the mortgage is left owing on it, plus he had to pay the real estate cost on top of that, which he did to just get out of the house, to sell it and make sure that the kids and I were out on our own and gone and that way he would not have any responsibility for us. Well she said, you will have to go to your family to get money and go get your own lawyer. End of conversation.

The social worker imposes one set of facts on this woman: "you will have money left from the sale of your house." When the woman is able to introduce information to counter this, the worker creates a new option "your family has money." The relevant "facts" are those worked up by the social worker, not those that reflect the woman's situation as told by her.

Not only is the legal-aid applicant's story regularly dismissed as irrelevant to the process, but often her husband's circumstances are deemed to be the relevant "facts." The following woman identifies not only the disjuncture between her circumstances and the assessment process, but also between social and legal expectations to leave an abusive relationship and the realities imposed by economic circumstances:

> They fail to realize that just because your husband makes big money and you're in a big money bracket, that does not mean that the wife has any hands or any way of getting any means of money to do a legal fight. And that's where they tell you to leave abuse, but if you don't have any money, where are you? He's the one who holds all the purse strings.

This woman's story is a stark reminder of the power of law and of the limited options available to women whose stories are deemed not to be "relevant."

> And they told me that unless I was physically abused that they could not help me. And I said well (what about) mental abuse. Actually I would have preferred to be physically abused than mentally abused. And they said that didn't matter and that unless it is physical abuse that there was nothing that they could do ... they told me that it didn't count.

The power of legal discourse extends beyond the mere denial of access to the legal system, it also impacts on how women view their own experiences; mental abuse doesn't count.

Despite the claims that abuse is the only relevant criterion in assessing whether or not a woman is eligible for legal aid and that abuse is broadly defined to include more than physical abuse, of the 14 women we interviewed who were rejected by domestic legal aid, only three did not describe their relationships with their partners as abusive. The following are descriptions by women who were rejected by legal aid; apparently they were not abused "enough":

> Can you imagine sitting in a court room to tell a judge that my husband when he didn't get sex would kick me out of bed

or he would stick his rear end in my face and fart and tell me that "Pete's" upset. If that's not abuse what is?

As I say I was not physically abused, but I was never able to go out of the house, I was never able to speak back to him, I was never able to have any bank account or chequing account, nothing, he controlled everything, I had nothing. So this is why I thought ... I mean I was destitute, but I didn't have bruises on me, so I didn't think that made me any less destitute than the person standing beside me with bruises.

Discarding the abuse suffered by these women as irrelevant, the legal-aid process is able to control not only women's access to justice, but it delegitimizes their experiences in the process.

Finally, one of the major concerns to arise out of women's descriptions of their experiences in the legal-aid system is the extent to which determinations of relevance could endanger them. One woman described how her lawyer insisted on requesting an amount of support that she knew was unreasonable given her husband's circumstances. Though she explained that an exorbitant request had the potential to anger her ex-husband, the lawyer ignored this information and filed the application despite her protests. Her ex-husband did in fact react angrily, not, this time, against her directly, but by taking their children from the school and the babysitter. The babysitter called the police. When the woman called the legal-aid lawyer for help she says that he replied in the following manner:

> "Calm down. He has to bring them back.... Look I can't have you phoning me every 10 minutes hysterical." The police contacted [the legal aid lawyer] because they wanted some sort of action taken, some sort of interim consent and he [the legal aid lawyer] called me up and yelled at me for it, "Don't you ever have the police contact me again."

Although the lawyer had created the crisis through his determinations of what was best and what was relevant, he recreated the "facts" so that the woman, and not he himself, appears to be the cause of the crisis.

## Validating Women's Claims:
## The Charter Challenge to Legal Aid

In her paper "Domestic Legal Aid: A Claim to Equality," Patricia Hughes argues that the domestic legal-aid program may be able to be challenged under sections 7 and 15 of the Canadian Charter of Rights and Freedoms.[10] Hughes challenges the disparate resources made available to criminal and domestic legal aid, and argues that women and men need the legal system for different reasons. Therefore, simply to say that women have equal access to the system begs the issue. She states,

> the reasons women require access to the legal system are imbedded less often in their own actions than in their status as a subordinate class economically, socially, and, in the broad sense, politically; this subordination has been reinforced by the legal system and the state itself and it is therefore incumbent upon the state to ensure that economically-disadvantaged women have the means to use the legal system to remedy their subordinate status at least to the extent that economically-disadvantaged men have the means to protect themselves. (1995:12)

The difficulty lies, however, in persuading the courts that women's rights are being violated, and it is here that we see the power of legal method (and more generally legal discourse) to define the issues; the choice of precedent and the interpretation of the Charter can work to exclude women's claims to equality in relation to access to the justice system. For example, while Hughes argues that access to legal aid is not an economic issue, but one which goes to the heart of the integrity of the legal system and its ability to protect all members of society, it cannot be denied that in part women need access to the justice system because they are economically disadvantaged. However, since there is no precedent that would support an economic argument, and the Supreme Court of Canada has been reluctant to extend protection (at least overtly) to those who are economically disadvantaged, the arguments must be framed to fit within existing legal boundaries.

The power of legal discourse to exclude women's interests is also illustrated by section 10 (b) of the Charter, which explicitly guarantees in the criminal context the "right to retain and instruct counsel without delay and to be informed of that right." The idea that a person should not be deprived of liberty without strict attention to procedural fairness extends only to persons — mostly men — in the criminal context.[11] But what of the woman who is trapped in a marital relationship with no access to legal protections, whether that means division of marital property and debts, custody of children, or support payments? Why has the law minimized her interests, her liberty?

## Conclusion

In this chapter I have sought to make two points. First, it is important to pay particular attention to the mundane aspects of legal method. By mundane I mean those things that happen outside of the courtroom, behind the lawyer's or mediator's door, those sifting and shaping processes that are rarely brought to light as important determinants of how an issue comes to be characterized or even silenced.

As we have seen through the stories of the women who have had contact with legal aid, legal "choices" are made within narrowly prescribed boundaries. Those boundaries work to eliminate information deemed to be legal junk within legal discourse, but which is central to the lived experiences of women.[12] Determinations of relevance are based on a framework that remains largely hidden from women who seek access to the justice system. Thus, while some women experience a disjuncture between their experiences and the state-imposed criteria (but I was abused!), others come to delegitimize their own interpretations of events in their lives (I guess I wasn't really abused). The myth of the objectivity and neutrality of the law infiltrates the mundane processes involved in decisions related to access to justice. While using discretionary practices in decision-making, the process of applying for legal aid is protected under law's umbrella of neutrality. The authority of the state and its workers to make decisions "for the good of" women remains relatively unchallenged, even when it endangers their lives or the safety of their children.

The second point I have made in this chapter is that even when women seek to challenge law and extend the boundaries of legal discourse, they must shape their experiences so that they fit within the confines of established precedent and patterns of statutory interpretation. In this way, law has the power to organize and define women's lives. Mary Jane Mossman argues that, ultimately, legal method may be impervious to feminism; the stories of the women who participated in this research would seem to support that claim.

## Notes

1. Section 7 of the Charter states, "Everyone has the right to life, liberty, and security of the person and the right not to be deprived thereof except in accordance with the principles of fundamental justice."

2. Known as the common-law solutions of constructing and resulting trusts, these remedies have been developed by the courts to address situations when women who are living in conjugal relationships make contributions to property and other material assets, but have no "legal" title to them. See *Pettkus v. Becker*, [1980] 2 S.C.R. 834; and *Peter v. Beblow*, 1993 3 W.W.R. 337.

3. It is not only women who are excluded from legal solutions. Gays and lesbians have suffered similar, and in many cases more pronounced, discrimination.

4. People can present cases without legal representation, but often they are disadvantaged by doing so, for a variety of reasons, including the fact that they do not know the court rules and protocols. In addition, as will be discussed later in this chapter, people who are economically disadvantaged are less likely to represent themselves than are other groups. Since women are economically disadvantaged in comparison to men, women are also less likely to represent themselves in legal proceedings.

5. See *Access to Justice in New Brunswick: The Adverse Impact of Domestic Legal Aid on Women* (LEAF)-NB, September 1996). See also Hughes (1997).

6. I personally know of one such case; the woman lived in an abusive relationship for approximately 20 years. She had been beaten and raped by her husband. She was unwilling to disclose her abuse and went through a number of mediation sessions. The abuse was never detected by the court social worker.

7. See, for example, Bartlett (1990), MacKinnon (1987; 1989; 1991).

8. Those cases are *In re French* [1912] 1 D.L.R. 80 and the *Persons Case* (Reference re Meaning of the Word "Persons" in s. 24 of the B.N.A. Act, [1928] SCR 276; *Edwards v. A.G. for Canada*, [1930] AC 124.

9. For an excellent analysis of lawyers as mediating voices, see Worrall (1990).

10. Every individual is equal before and under the law and has the right to the equal protection and equal benefit of the law without discrimination and, in particular, without discrimination based on race, national or ethnic origin, colour, religion, age, or mental or physical disability.

11. Even women who commit crimes do not have equal access to legal aid; legal aid programs often limit the provision of services to indictable offences. Most of the crimes committed by women are summary conviction property offences.

12. For a more detailed discussion of this idea, see Beaman (1996).

## References

Bartlett, Katharine T. (1990). "Feminist Legal Methods." *Harvard Law Review* 103:829.

Beaman, Lori G. (1996). "Legal Ethnography: Exploring the Gendered Nature of Legal Method." *Critical Criminology: An International Journal* 7(1):53-74.

Hughes, Patricia (1997). New Brunswick's Domestic Legal Aid System: New Brunswick (Minister
Health and Community Services v. J.G.). *Windsor Yearbook of Access to Justice* 16:240-51.

Hughes, Patricia (1995). "Domestic Legal Aid: A Claim to Equality." *Review of Constitutional Studies* 2(2):203.

LEAF-NB (1996). Access to Justice in New Brunswick: The Adverse Impact of Domestic Legal Aid on Women

MacKinnon, Catharine A. (1991). "From Practice to Theory, or What is a White Woman Anyway?" *Yale Journal of Law and Feminism* 4 (1):13.

MacKinnon, Catharine A. (1989). *Toward a Feminist Theory of the State.* Cambridge, MA: Harvard University Press.

MacKinnon, Catharine A. (1987). "Feminism, Marxism, Method, and the State: Toward a Feminist Jurisprudence." In Sandra Harding (ed.), *Feminism and Methodology.* Bloomington: Indiana University Press.

Mossman, Mary Jane (1993). "Gender Equality and Legal Aid Services: A Research Agenda for Institutional Change." *Sydney Law Review* 15:30.

Mossman, Mary Jane (1986). "Feminism and Legal Method: The Difference it Makes." *Australian Journal of Law and Society,* 3:30-52.

National Council of Welfare (1995). *Legal Aid and the Poor.* Ottawa: Minister of Supply and Services.

O'Donovan, Katherine (1989). "Engendering Justice: Women's Perspectives and the Rule of Law." *University of Toronto Law Journal* 39:127.

Smart, Carol (1990). "Law's Power, the Sexed Body, and Feminist Discourse." *Journal of Law and Society* 17:197.

Smart, Carol (1987). *Feminism and the Power of Law.* London: Routledge.

Worrall, Anne (1990). *Offending Women: Female Lawbreakers and the Criminal Justice System.* London and New York: Routledge.

# 5

# Of Death, Desire, and Knowledge: Law and Social Control of Witches in Renaissance Europe[1]

### SHEILA NOONAN

Historically, women have long been associated with the body and its processes. Our association with reproduction and our consignment to the private sphere of home and family established the body as a subject of central concern to feminist scholars. The bulk of feminist legal writing on the body has tended to centre on the contemporary relation between the female body, and institutions of social control, including the criminal justice system.[2] It is the body as a site of inscription of various strategies of legal control which is the topic of this chapter. The lens through which this issue will be addressed is an exploration of the European witch-hunts, since some of the discourses pertaining to law and the female body seem to resonate with those from a distant past. During the witch-hunts the female body became inscribed in law in ways that display a haunting familiarity. It is thus the female body, situated within a framework that emphasizes the significance of law, that receives particular attention in this account.

My interest in the witch-hunts stems in part from the high number of females who were prosecuted[3] and executed. From a criminological perspective, this period is fascinating because it represents the first instance in the modern legal period in which women were criminalized in large numbers. It was particularly during the sixteenth and seventeenth centuries that hundreds of thousands of women were killed across Europe.[4] The peak of the trials and executions in most countries occurred between 1560 and 1670.[5] While the extent of accusation and prosecution was subject to considerable geographic disparity, women were almost consistently the vast majority of those accused.[6]

Various theories have been advanced as to the combination of circumstances that produced the mass-scale executions. In the English context, Thomas places emphasis on increased tensions in village life which produced hostility toward elderly and dependent neighbours.[7] The witch-hunts in his work function to reinforce notions of charity during times in which it was under attack from social and economic forces. Prior to the Reformation, the Catholic Church encouraged acts of charity toward the destitute. The collapse of this mechanism for social welfare, the duty to care for the poor and infirm, was transferred to the State. With the rise of capitalism, the primary social unit became the individual, not the community. Macfarlane's analysis of English witchcraft is quite similar; he sees the accusations as assisting in the transition from a neighbourly village society to an individualistic one.[8] Moral panic created by the absence of machinery for law and order and the gradual consolidation of the state are among several factors identified by Larner in her work on Scottish witch trials of 1620,[9] and this social dimension also figures in the analysis by Midelfort of South West German trials. Others have stressed the significance of religious conflict[10] and the influence of both ruling-class and peasant beliefs in the construction of the mythical imagery of witches.[11]

However, within this context, it is staggering that so little academic attention has been devoted to the gendered nature of the killings.[12] Some work appearing in the 1970s acknowledged the role of misogyny in the executions.[13] Similarly, some marvellous feminist work began to appear around the same period which brought a gendered analysis to this issue. Recently, rich documentary detail has been provided by feminist historians, criminologists, and others who are re-examining the witch-hunts in light of the intervening sociological and historical literature.[14]

Unquestionably, the collusion among juridical, ecclesiastical, and medical authorities around the detection, surveillance, and punishment of witchcraft was an extremely important feature of this history of gynocide.[15] Though there is considerable academic disagreement on the number of women killed, and the social roles of the victims, there appears to be widespread consensus that poor and single women were overwhelmingly the target[16] of the so called "witch-craze."[17] It is still the case that in the academic literature (with the exception of the literature noted above), if they are addressed at all, women enter the analysis indirectly. Additionally, there are very few accounts that systematically address the significance of the legal system.[18]

## Part I: The Insatiable Body

### FEMALE SEXUALITY

Female sexuality outside or beyond male control must be located as a prominent feature of the witch prosecutions. Women have long been associated with and subject to the body and its demands. Unable to transcend its demands or to regulate its excesses through piety, prayer, or reason, woman has become the negativity attached to the body. It is men alone who are able to contain its effects.[19] In Bordo's analysis the consequence of the projection of desire onto the female body is that women come to symbolize "distraction from knowledge, seduction away from God, capitulation to sexual desire, violence or aggression, failure of will, even death."[20] The construct which situates women as the body luring men to evil also simultaneously permits men to disavow male ownership of the body and its desires.[21]

Clearly, the genesis of woman as evil derives from Eve's seduction of Adam, culminating in banishment from the Garden of Eden and man's fall from grace with God. The philosophical mapping of bodily appetites and desires onto the female body can be traced at least to Greco-Roman times, but its gradual incorporation into official Catholic theology derived in significant measure from the work of Augustine, who stressed that asceticism was a precondition of moral virtue.

Although strands of the ascetic ideal are to be found in the work of St. Paul, it was Augustine who formulated a theology, extant today, that equated sex and sin. Since it was man's body that was created in the image of God, it was woman's body that represented the temptation that seduced man away from God.[22] To approach God was to renounce the body and its passions. Asceticism in Church doctrine had profound implications for women, who could only achieve moral virtue by effacing or renouncing their femaleness:

> The equation of woman with sexuality and body ... and the exclusion of sexuality and passion from the divine opened up a chasm between woman and God. Only by repudiating her sexual identity and renouncing femaleness could this chasm be bridged. The equation of woman with sexuality meant that she was both subordinated to man and alienated from God.[23]

Representations of female saints during the Middle Ages were of extremely thin figures whose female form could no longer be readily discerned.[24]

Furthermore, the papal struggle to enforce celibacy of male clerics was assisted by a theory of demonized sexuality which drew heavily upon Augustinian precepts of sexual drives as morally evil. The Church deployed emissaries to preach the danger of female sexuality, and the drive to control the pernicious lure of the female body assumed a demonic cast. As Torjesen notes, "It was a short step from the idea that female sexuality was dangerous and an instrument of the devil to the idea that female sexuality itself could be a demonic power."[25]

Historically, witch prosecutions must be located against the backdrop of the Inquisition. Preceded by the Crusades against Islamics that started in 1095, and sanctioned by Pope Urban II, the killing of infidels was undertaken. While the Crusades were underway in the Holy Land Pope Innocent III permitted military action against a more local Christian target — heretics, known as Cathari or Alberigensians. Officially in 1233, Pope Gregory IX issued a Bull allowing Dominican Inquisitors to eradicate heresy. The Inquisition began with legal authority to convict heretics without appeal and provided authority for the Inquisitors to pronounce death sentences, though torture and lesser forms of punishment were initially counselled to permit the accused an opportunity to repent. The possibility of mass extermination was given the imprimatur of Papal seal. While evidence of prior torture and execution of heretics dates back to the fourth century, it had not occurred at the behest of Papal edict.[26] Indeed, the battle against paganism to this point had been largely an unofficial one. While some Pagan cities such as Pan and Diana were demonized, pagan rituals and festivals persisted, and the "broody, sinister, malevolent energies" residing in the surrounding forests began. The Inquisition saw participation in such activities as witchcraft or sorcery and classified such behaviour as heresy.

Prior to the mid-fifteenth century, the Church denied the reality of witchcraft: belief in witchcraft was a delusion created by the devil. The gradual acceptance of diabolical beliefs was particularly noteworthy given that in 1215 the Catholic Church had expressly stipulated that "belief in witchcraft was an illusion."[27] Currie cites the *Capitulum Episcopi*:

> Some wicked women ... seduced by the illusions and phan-
> tasms of demons, believe and profess that they ride at night
> with Diana on certain beasts with an innumerable company

of women, passing over immense distances ... priests every-
where should preach that they know this to be false, and that
such phantasms are sent by the Evil Spirit, who deludes them
in dreams....

While the loss of faith accompanying such belief was heresy, beginning in
1458 Church policy underwent a transformation that acknowledged the
reality of witchcraft. This step was officially taken by the Church in 1484
in the papal bull of Innocent VIII, which extended the powers of the
Inquisitors to prosecute witches. Suddenly healers, sorcerers, infidels, and
those believed to create chaos or disasters were subject to the jurisdiction
of the Inquisition.

The evil associated with the female body is most clearly expounded in
the *Malleus Maleficarum*, which was officially commissioned by the
Church, and which broaches the question of why women are more likely
to become witches than men. Women are more credulous, and hence,
more easily corrupted. Feebler both in body and intellect, women are
more impressionable and therefore make easy targets for the Devil.
Ultimately, however, it is their inordinate passions and the insatiable
nature of their carnal lust which lay women open to wickedness:

> To conclude. All witchcraft comes from carnal lust, which is
> in women insatiable.... There are three things that are never
> satisfied, yea, a fourth thing which says not, It is enough; that
> is the mouth of the womb. Wherefore for the sake of fulfill-
> ing their lusts they consort even with devils.[28]

As Brauner notes, women's libidinal drives threatened to disrupt realization of the ascetic spiritual ideal.[29]

That woman was reputed to be more carnal than men was especially
relevant to her propensity to engage in sex with the Devil. Women accused
of witchcraft, particularly on the Continent, were subject to excruciatingly
detailed interrogations of their sexual interaction with the Devil. The
Inquisitors were salaciously eager to discover information relating to sex
with the Devil. Kramer and Sprenger analyse in great detail the type of
body the Devil assumed when he had sex with women, the circumstances
under which the Devil would inject semen from another, why the carnal
act was often invisible to one who was not a witch, and the degree of pleasure imparted by the Devil in contrast to regular heterosexual relations.

The depictions of wild and frenzied sexual orgies at the sabbath featured women as both the initiators and the primary participants.

Women were seen to be responsible both for desire and its failures. For example, witches were believed to be capable of preventing erections in men. In a classic illustration of the profound depth of men's castration anxiety, Kramer and Sprenger discuss the ability of a witch to create the illusion that a man has lost his penis:

> And what, then, is be thought of those witches who in this way sometimes collect male organs in great numbers, as many as twenty or thirty members together, and put them in a bird's nest or shut them up in a box, where they move themselves like living members, and eat oats and corn, as has been seen by many and is a matter of common report? It is to be said that it is all done by the devil's work and illusion, for the sense of those who see them are deluded.... For a certain man tells that, when he lost his member, he approached a known witch and asked her to restore it to him. She told the afflicted man to climb a certain tree, and that he might take which he liked out of a nest in which there were several members. And when he tried to take a big one, the witch said: You must not take that one; adding, because it belonged to a parish priest.[30]

The impact of the *Malleus Maleficarum* was muted in England in part because the Inquisition had not extended there, but also due to the Protestant reworking of theology pertaining to sexuality. Nevertheless, it must be stressed that both Catholics and Protestants tried and executed women for witchcraft. However, there were fundamental differences. Luther believed that because sexual desire was so powerful, the best ideal was not ascetic celibacy but marriage. Because sex was integral to marriage, Luther advocated divorce on the basis of adultery, impotence, sexual incompatibility, abandonment, or refusal to engage in sex.[31] Sex was good due to its ability to promote marital harmony, not simply because of its procreative power.[32] The clearly defined gender roles morally sanctioned the deployment of an extant household ideal. Clerics were permitted to marry. However, symbolically sexual difference becomes instantiated as natural fact.[33]

Protestant Reformers established marriage courts whose jurisdiction expanded to include gambling, blasphemy, failure to attend Church, as well as sexual complaints. The Protestant ideal of the nurturing wife and mother led to a reconceptualization of her negation—the witch. Thus, the seducing carnal woman is replaced by the inverse of wife and mother in Protestant projections:

> [T]he witch is the inverse of Luther's obedient and restrained housewife — a nagging shrew who refuses to obey her husband, a mother who loves her children so obsessively that she resorts to magic on their behalf, or an unmarried old woman who casts spells on children and disrupts marriages.[34]

Renunciation of the body gave way to acceptance of its desires as holy, provided those urges found expression within the institution of marriage. Women were required to sublimate their sexuality in service of the moral imperative of wife and mother. They were to use their sex in part as an incentive to educate their new husband and children in "proper deportment" in the familial and social realms.[35] For Luther, marriage was a "direct route to the rewards of heaven"; however, the affirmation of sexuality was a limited one.[36] Calvin, like Luther, rejected marriage as a sacrament: he was adamantly opposed to extra-marital or adulterous sexual activity. Even within marriage he was markedly more circumspect and stressed "measure and modesty so as not to wallow in extreme luridness."[37]

Literature during the period of the witch-hunts stressed women's sexual unruliness.[38] The Essex trial pamphlets examined by Hester found that accusations of sexual deviance, particularly in trials occurring prior to 1645, accounted for almost half the witch prosecutions.[39] Disproportionately, the women who were the targets of the witch-hunts were those beyond, or at the margins, of the social control of men. In most countries, widows and spinsters were over-represented proportionately; poor and elderly women were more likely to be targets of the accusations.[40]

The fifteenth and sixteenth centuries witnessed a pattern of late marriage and a high rate of people remaining single. In a patriarchal order, the seditious potential of women unconstrained by marriage raised profound ramifications for the social fabric:

> Women belonged under the protection and legal power of their father until they married. When they married, their husbands took over this power intact. Maids and servants too were part of the household in which they lived and were sub-

ject to the discipline of the family. The structure of society was so completely geared to the family that persons without families were automatically peculiar, unprotected, and suspect. Widows in particular were defenceless until they remarried. So were spinsters. For this reason, husbands urged their wives to remarry if death should separate them.[41]

Social isolation from men left women at risk of suspicion of witchcraft, as did women's failure to sublimate desire to the marriage contract.

Thus women (and some men) who failed to adhere to the norms of monogamous, heterosexual existence were also subject to prosecution: women who bore illegitimate children, women who were known to be "lewd" or adulterous, women who were lesbians, and men who were gay.[42] "Sexual deviance" of these types increased the risk of successful prosecution as a witch. In the words of Wiesner-Hanks, "[a] godly society that could not include fornicators, adulterers, or sodomites could certainly not include witches."[43]

THE BODY ACTED UPON: WOMEN AS HEALERS

The processes through which men have consolidated juridical and medical control over women's reproductive lives are complex and varied. Unquestionably, juridical, religious, and medical authorities exercised significant power in the detection, surveillance, and punishment of witchcraft. The assiduous efforts to consolidate power over reproduction started with the purgings of the witch trials and extended to encompass formal regulation of healing practised by women. The principal target was the village wise woman or man who was consulted about general matters of health, hygiene, fertility, and childbirth.

There remains a strong link between healing and faith. Though faith is largely discounted in medical circles, some patients who believe or engage in spiritual practice may fare better than others who do not when faced with the same illness. Larner tells us that the word "salvation" means healing:

> Healing is salvation from disease and, even if temporarily, from death. The churches have, with varying degrees of intensity and conviction, offered direct healing to the sick and dying. The exorcist will cure madness caused by the pres-

ence of an evil spirit. The sacrament of last unction has sometimes been thought to have healing qualities, though it is
properly only given to the moribund. The laying on of hands
as a healing art is practised in a number of churches today.
Pilgrims visit shrines in the hope of a cure. Those sceptical of
the efficacy or propriety of such rituals may, nevertheless,
attribute cures directly to the power of prayer — the personal
intervention of God in an individual case in response to
prayer when He might otherwise have let nature take its
course.[44]

Many believe spiritual practice to be of assistance in attaining healing.
Historically, the close relationship between religious piety and physical
well-being developed from the understanding of the etymology of disease
in the medieval period: disease was the manifestation of a vengeful God.

Indeed, the Church played a crucial function in the professionalization
of medical practice. In part, the Church's interest in medical matters must
be placed alongside its efforts to curb pagan practices and beliefs. Pagan
conceptions attributed illness to the workings of demons which could be
battled by amulets, prayers, or incantations. Christianity, however, construed sickness as a sign of the vengeance of a just God who alone had the
power to promote healing through forgiveness. At least officially, healing
was associated with sorcery and priests were prohibited under pain of punishment from engaging in healing practises. Yet the Church commanded
that in every community there must be at least one woman appointed to
assist women who were ill. She was directly accountable to the village
priest who required her to submit to the authority of God. Incantations
were henceforth converted into prayers. Once schools of medicine were
opened in Europe, the Church relaxed its stance against healing, but
asserted control over the curriculum: medical training consisted largely in
the study of theology.[45]

Women in the Middle Ages were engaged in a variety of healing
practices. In some European countries they were physicians, surgeons,
barber-surgeons, apothecaries, healers, and midwives. However, most of
the healing performed by women was unofficial. In a study of registered
health practitioners in the British Isles from Anglo-Saxon times to the
beginning of the sixteenth century, Talbot and Hammond were able to
find records relating only to eight female practitioners. A later study
discovered three additional names. In reviewing the later medieval period,

Gottfried claims to have discovered 28 women — 8 leeches, 16 barbers, and 4 apothecaries.[46] However, research that shifted the emphasis away from licensed practitioners discovered that in the city of London around 1560 there were approximately sixty female practitioners, and in Norwich between 1570 and 1590 there were ten female practitioners known by name.[47] Introduced with the intention to drive women out of medical practice, legislation was placed before Parliament in England in 1421 to ensure "that no Woman use the practyse of Fiysk [medicine] under ... payne of long imprisonment."[48]

Nor was there much distinction in practice between the methodologies of lay healers and physicians. When William Cullen took up a medical faculty appointment at the University of Glasgow in 1751, the pharmacopia he found consisted of "spider's web, ants, eggs, snakes, skin, extract of wood lice, extract of foxglove, beetles blood, and ... an elixir with seventy-nine ingredients."[49] In reality, the only distinguishing feature between lay and official healers was their proportional representation on the basis of gender. Official healers had been trained within the emergent professions and taught in universities.[50] Official medicine even in the sixteenth century consisted of such treatments as purging, cauterization, and blood-letting. These treatments were not only painful but left in their wake a flood of iatrogenic disease.[51] The majority of the population received treatment from wise women and some men who, through "treatments" such as the use of charms, herbs, or rituals performed on urine, enjoyed considerable popular faith in their practices. Although male physicians relied on the humours to diagnose, there is evidence that they too employed techniques used by wise women.[52] Given that there remain people whose faith in Western medicine is less than absolute, it is unsurprising that the physicians and the Church, acting jointly, were unable to wholly eradicate belief in lay healing:

> If this is true today, when medical techniques have made such striking advances, we can hardly wonder at the attitude of 17th century villagers, when medical therapy still proceeded along its traditional paths of purging and bloodletting. There is little more reason for asking why the wizards were able to retain their prestige than for enquiring how it was that the pretensions of Galenic physicians remained so long unchallenged.[53]

In relation to women's health, there is perhaps reason to believe that women healers might have possessed greater knowledge and skill than their licensed male counterparts.

England first introduced state regulation over medical practice in 1512 when Henry VIII acceded to pressure from surgeons, physicians, and apothecaries and forbade the practice of medicine, save by graduates of Oxbridge or those who passed an examination with either the Bishop of London or the Dean of St. Paul's Cathedral in conjunction with "four doctors of Physik."[54] University-trained physicians were necessarily men since women were excluded from admission. Physicians were permitted to practise only on advice from the local priest; the Church lent assistance in curbing unlicensed practitioners through excommunication.

In fact, there were few licensed practitioners, and lay healers continued to dispense care in the face of both ecclesiastical sanction and the prospect of potential prosecution for witchcraft. Though the provisions of the 1512 legislation were loosened in 1542, it was in that same year that the first legislation on witchcraft was introduced. The 1563 act against witchcraft was strengthened in 1604 to permit attempts to cure by unauthorized means to be evidence of witchcraft, and inexplicable injury or illness to be construed as an act of witchcraft.[55]

MIDWIFERY

While Catholicism stressed an expression of sexuality in spite of procreation, the theology of the Protestant Reformation also preached that child-rearing was an act of service to God.[56] Ensuring control of female sexuality, purity of a patrilineal blood-line, and the administration of proper baptismal rites was thus of interest to both Catholics and Protestants. Integral to the healing role performed by women were the care of infants and the assistance conferred in childbirth. The arcane knowledge of midwives in relation to conception, pregnancy, and parturition were of special significance to the Church in its efforts to ensure adherence to its moral precepts. Church authorities viewed midwives as implacable opponents largely due to their knowledge pertaining to fecundity. Midwives were known not only to assist in childbirth but were able to assist in procuring abortions and to provide counsel to women on how to prevent conception. In short, they dispensed requisite information to assist women in controlling the reproductive process.

Nonetheless, it is the association between childbirth and the supernatural which is revealing. The Church regarded the arsenal of techniques deployed by midwives as problematic. To the Church, the pain of labour was God's punishment for Eve's sin; midwives were able to lessen the pain of labour by using various herbs, incantations, girdles, and stones. A midwife who possessed "virgin-nuts" (a stone with a cross) were in demand, or the woman could be scattered with urine, or served "groaning-malts" by the midwife.[57] Furthermore, the caul, umbilical cord, and after-birth have long been credited with magical forces.

In countries where Catholic and Protestant forces struggled for ascendancy the battle for the newborn's soul was particularly important. However, under either religious paradigm, failure to baptize a child resulted in eternal damnation of the child's soul. Therefore, where the newborn was in danger of death, midwives were charged with the obligation of baptising the child. This duty was so weighty that midwives were instructed that where a woman died in childbirth, the midwife was to perform a caesarian section in order to christen the offspring. And still-born infants, once thought to possess healing properties, were regarded as a source of evil under Christianity. Having not been released from original sin by baptism, they were regarded as children of the Devil.[58]

By virtue of their association with unbaptised children, midwives were subject to regulation either by municipal or ecclesiastical authorities from the mid-fifteenth century. This regulation was designed not to govern medical competence but rather to safeguard the midwife's moral character.[59] In England, midwives were required under legislation passed in 1512 to obtain a licence upon application to the Bishop's Court. The oath administered by the Bishop declared that midwives were not to employ "any witchcraft, charms, relics or invocation to any saint in the time of travail." Other promises extracted included administering the Protestant form of baptism, ensuring safe disposal of the corpses of still-born children, abjuring use of abortifacient, preventing false naming of fathers, ensuring children were neither substituted nor destroyed, and not permitting a woman to deliver in secret.[60] Midwives were required to produce character witnesses who could attest to their moral rectitude and the competency of their skills. Practising without a license or operating in defiance of the oaths could lead to punishment by the ecclesiastical court.

Beyond the sphere of quasi-legal regulation lay the risk of prosecution as a witch. The authors of the *Malleus Maleficarum* declared, "No one does more harm to the Catholic Faith than midwives":

The Canonists treat more fully than the Theologians of the obstructions due to witchcraft and they say that it is witchcraft, not only when anyone is unable to perform the carnal act, of which we have spoken above; but also when a woman is prevented from conceiving, or is made to miscarry after she has conceived. A third and fourth method of witchcraft is when they have failed to procure an abortion, and then either devour the child or offer it to a devil.[61]

In demonological accounts, witches were eager to devour children, sacrifice unbaptized babies to the devil, or use their remains in magical potions.[62] The *Malleus Malleficarum* details a confession of child-murder/cannibalism extracted from a Swiss witch

We set our snares chiefly for unbaptized children, and even for those that have been baptized, especially when they have not been protected by the sign of the Cross and prayers ... and with our spells we kill them in their cradles or when they are sleeping by their parents' side, in such a way that they afterwards are thought to have been overlain or to have died some natural death. Then we secretly take them from their graves and cook them in a cauldron, until the whole flesh comes away from the bones to make a soup which may easily be drunk. Of the more solid matter we make an unguent which is of virtue to help us in our arts and pleasures and our transportation.[63]

At least theoretically, midwives were able to supply infants to witches for these purposes. Boguet, another prominent French demonologist, was particularly suspicious of the link between midwifery and child murder:

[T]hose midwives and wise women who are witches are in the habit of offering to Satan the little children which they deliver, and then of killing them, before they have been baptized, by thrusting a large pin into their brains. There have been those who have confessed to having killed more than forty children in this way. They do worse; for they kill them while they are in their mother's wombs.[64]

Midwifery was a perilous profession given that any mishap surrounding the birthing process, including sickness, death and disease, was frequently attributed to witchcraft. Many women were charged with the practice of witchcraft on account of hapless deaths in an era when the infant mortality rate was high. But it should also be noted that midwives were known to assist in witch prosecutions by deciphering whether bodily protrusions were created naturally by the childbearing process, and so women played a significant role in accusing other women of witchcraft. However, the charge of witchcraft served much more directly to shore up the integrity of the emerging medical profession. Illness which could not be cured by a physician was believed to be caused by witches.

Concomitantly, illness spread by unnatural means was by definition incurable. Interestingly, the *Malleus Maleficarum* vested authority for establishing the distinction between natural and unnatural disease with physicians. Inexplicable injury, death, or illness were extremely important features of witch-prosecutions, particularly in England. Evidence in English witchcraft trials frequently consisted of one neighbour testifying as to a prior unpleasant encounter with another neighbour believed to be a witch. Where it was followed by illness or death, the case had in many instances been established. In other words, it was sufficient for a bodily manifestation of illness, coupled with previous disharmony, to suggest that the body had been acted upon by witchcraft.

As Macfarlane has noted, the particular illnesses or diseases linked to witchcraft did not possess any uniquely defining quality.[65] Temporally, the lag between offending a witch and falling victim to an ailment caused by her could be as long as a decade. It is the lack of any discernible pattern to these accusations which led Macfarlane to conclude that at issue was the social relationship between witch and accuser. The work of Macfarlane and Thomas on witchcraft in England has found that the accusations of witchcraft often followed refusal of charity to the witch. Witchcraft accusations, they suggest, were thus not linked to illness or death unless the accuser had reason to fear retaliation by a witch.

Recent academic work has questioned the overall significance of the role of female midwives and lay healers and the consolidation of the male monopoly over medical practice in understanding the witch-prosecutions. This is an appropriate criticism of some accounts, particularly those which centrally locate the prosecution of healers and midwives as witches. However, while in some countries the social role of healers and midwives did not feature prominently among those accused of witchcraft, belief by the local populace in the ability of women to act upon bodies is a feature of the prosecutions that should not be overlooked.[66] Moreover, the salience of the body acted upon must be assessed in light of the authority of Church and state to distinguish between the practice of medicine and that of witchcraft. In this respect, the power brought to bear in the regulation of women was both legal and extra-legal.

Professionalism, like religion, remains intimately connected, in the words of Dostoyevsky, to "miracle, mystery, and authority."[67] Much of women's healing has been periodically driven underground; therefore, knowledge of the ancient arts of healing have remained subject to medical delegitimation. While legislation regarding alternative healing has begun to surface recently, physicians have a long history of seeking to ensure that alternative models of healing lack professional status and scientific credibility.

## Part II: Legal Regimes

It is crucial to underscore that the numbers of women killed in the European witch hunts could never have reached epic proportions without shifts in legal process to accommodate and facilitate these events. The witch-hunts were, as Levack has argued, essentially a judicial operation.[68] It is worth emphasizing that the entire process of discovering, prosecuting, and executing witches was a lucrative business. The accused were required to pay for trial expenses, including costs associated with the application of torture. Judges, priests, executioners, guards, and torturers profited from the witch-hunts. Additionally, the court retained the power to confiscate the property of those accused.[69]

One of the chief impediments to a detailed examination of these legal shifts is the sheer number and variety of legal regimes existing in the numerous countries where witch prosecutions and executions arose. For ease of simplicity, in this paper I will follow the customary practice of bifurcating these regimes into the continental procedure adopted in countries such as Germany, Italy, and France, and the common-law procedure followed in England.[70] A cursory overview of the various systems of accusation, prosecution, and punishment is thus in order. Levack has argued that a series of legal developments facilitated the witch-hunts.[71] Of these, two matters are uniquely germane to the unfolding of events on the continent and warrant closer attention here: changes in legal procedure and the use of torture. These will be discussed in greater depth below.

Under medieval European criminal justice, the accusatory system of procedure prevailed. The system contemplated that an individual accuser was responsible for providing evidence to substantiate a charge. Talion dictated that should the accuser fail to satisfy the Court, he/she would be subject to the same penalty as that specified for the crime unsuccessfully prosecuted. Guilt or innocence was often determined by processes whose outcome was potentially auspicious for the accused, e.g., an acquittal was possible where the accused successfully performed an ordeal.[72] Innocence could also be established by victory in a duel, or in a trial by compurgation in which "oath-helpers" attested to the honesty of the accused. In effect, innocence was established by evidence of divine intervention, and human judgement played a limited role. However, from the thirteenth to the fifteenth century human agency assumed greater salience. The Church initiated the lead by adopting its own techniques and by formally prohibiting clerics from engaging in ordeals.[73]

It warrants mention that the jurisdiction over witchcraft was a "mixed" one; that is, both ecclesiastical and secular authorities had an interest in it. Prior to the fifteenth century, secular courts assumed jurisdiction over sorcery where it caused physical harm to people or property, or where it displayed a political dimension.[74] Expanding the definition of heresy to include diabolic activities permitted Papal Inquisitors to deal with magic as a spiritual transgression. It should be emphasized (though such a claim is not universally true and subject to some considerable geographic and temporal disparity) that in general the sentences dispensed by ecclesiastical authorities were significantly more lenient than their secular counterparts. Therefore, it would be both empirically incorrect and distorted to suggest that the Inquisition (rather than secular and, especially, local authorities) was responsible for the scale of mass witch-hunting across Europe.

Many witches were dealt with as heretics in episcopal courts or by the Inquisitors; however, the ecclesiastical authorities rarely worked at arm's length from their secular counterparts. Secular authorities, even where they did not themselves claim initial jurisdiction, facilitated the exercise by locating suspects, bringing them to trial, furnishing names of accomplices, and ultimately executing the punishment pronounced upon conviction. It is accurate that in southern France in the fifteenth century the hunts were driven by the Inquisitors in their search for Waldesian heretics; however, the trials in other parts of Europe manifested extensive co-operation between religious and secular courts.[75]

Secular authority increased over the course of the sixteenth and seventeenth centuries as witchcraft underwent redefinition as a crime. Correspondingly, ecclesiastical courts waned in the face of the Protestant Reformation and growing reluctance on the part of its officials to adhere to procedure. Italy and Spain were countries in which primary responsibility was retained by religious authorities; elsewhere, local courts fulfilled this function.

### CONTINENTAL PROCEDURE

Changes in criminal procedure initiated by the Church were gradually adopted in secular proceedings and secured by the sixteenth century. While accusations could still be laid by an individual, communities or Court officials were able to commence proceedings, often on the basis of rumour. The office of official prosecutor replaced the interpersonal accusatory model. Court officials assumed the responsibility for investigating the crime by secretly questioning witnesses. Judges were also permitted to interrogate the accused to elicit information. *Lex talion*, whereby the accused stood at risk of prosecution, was abandoned.

These alterations to legal process were justified on the basis that witchcraft was an exceptional crime. However, further modification to rules governing proof were vital in facilitating the large-scale prosecutions. Conviction generally required a confession, or the proof of two eye-witnesses. Given that the latter were difficult to find, at least in the absence of a confession which named accomplices,[76] a confession was often crucial to successful prosecution. The legal system became a tool of the moral order and its rules were adapted to meet the needs of Christendom.[77] Among the most salient modifications in procedure was a revival in the use of torture deployed to extract confessions.

Though the mode of torture and the rules governing its application were not uniform, generally there were limits imposed on its use. Judges could not torture without some proof that the crime had been committed. There were restrictions on the duration (torture was not to be repeated if unsuccessful in generating a confession) and severity of the procedures implemented (pregnant women and children were not to be tortured); subsequent endorsement or ratification of the confession was necessary after torture had ceased. However, many of these rules were significantly altered or abridged in pursuit of witches. Levack suggests that although complete statistical data are not available, where torture was used the rate of conviction could be as high as 95 per cent.[78] More significantly, the use of torture provided authorities with the names of hundreds of accomplices, which dramatically fuelled the scope of the hunts. The confessions produced under torture also legitimated the witch prosecutions in that the evil deeds confessed to were publicly read at the execution and often distributed in written form.

While torture was practised more in continental regimes than in common-law procedures, another key difference between the Continent and England is in the substantive content of "witchcraft." Under Roman civil law a distinction was drawn between "black magic" or *maleficium*, generally causing deliberate harm, and white magic, which arguably fulfilled a socially desirable function such as healing or finding lost objects. Under the *Corpus Juris*, engaging in the former activity carried the death penalty, while engaging in the latter did not.[79] It must be stressed that popular culture emerging from pagan beliefs firmly accepted the notion that women, and some men, possessed the power through sorcery, charming, divination or healing to bring about particular ends, either good or harmful. The traditional secular jurisdiction over harmful magic dates to Roman times and formed the mainstay of subsequent statutory prohibitions.[80] In this respect, the concept of *maleficium* more closely adhered to widespread beliefs among the populace concerning the harm that could befall the hexed.

However, Canon Law stressed a different conception, namely that witchcraft was either a private pact with the Devil or a conspiracy among persons who were in his service.[81] In this way, the role of *maleficium* was diminished in that any supernatural power outside the control of the Church was viewed as emanating from demonic sources. The emphasis shifted from proof that supernatural powers had actually been used, but centred rather on the renunciation of the Church as implicit in the formation of such a pact.[82] The significance of the distinction between *maleficium* and the ecclesiastical views generated by the Church is vital; it was the conception of evil, widely disseminated through the publication of texts on demonology, which formed the basis of mass executions.

Though the populace feared *maleficium*, the abstract diabolical accounts of evil were generated by ecclesiastical and lay elites:

> ... [T]he sabbath ... is simply and solely a figment created by theologians, whose ideas governed the imagination of the

elite classes of Europe in the Middle Ages. Drawing on the composite tradition of persecution of the Jews, the early Christians, and various heretical sects ... the theologians revived stereotypes that had no popular basis, in order to demonstrate the existence and progress of a huge satanic plot designed to make the powers of evil triumph upon earth.... Persecutors and heirs of the Inquisition, the new fraternity of demonologists imagined that they were themselves persecuted, that the world was given up to diabolism, and that secret devil-worshippers were plotting to frustrate their purposes.[83]

Muchembled goes on to say that the key distinction between these two conceptions was that under folk beliefs such extra-ordinary power was innate and unrelated to the Devil. Yet it is doubtful if the demonological conception could have taken hold without the belief in *maleficium*. The virulence of the witch-hunts must in large measure be understood in relation to peasant beliefs. During the fifteenth-century search for heretics, the Inquisitors encountered peasants who under torture confessed to folk magic, night-flying spirits, devil's pacts, and secret meetings which were attributed to diabolic activity.[84]

Although charges of sorcery (traditionally conceived of as a practice that might cause *maleficium*) persisted alongside or in combination with charges of diabolism, the latter became the primary focus of the charges. In such cases, emphasis was placed on the significance of the witch's sabbat, sexual orgies, night-flying, and the cannibalization of children.[85] Bishop Bisfield, a notorious demonologist, listed as among the most serious indications of witchcraft denunciation by an accomplice, pact with the Devil, association with known witches, common report, acts of evil following threats, and the possession of magical equipment, especially flying ointment.[86]

COMMON LAW PROCEDURE

In contrast, statutory regulation of witchcraft in England more closely adhered to traditional notions of *maleficium*, or harm. In particular, far fewer English trials centred around events or activities in which the sabbath or pacts with the Devil featured prominently. The laws generally provided for lesser punishments than were adopted on the Continent.

The first English statute precluding the practice of witchcraft was passed in 1542, but it was repealed in 1547. It was replaced by a 1563 "Act against Conjuracions Inchantments and Witchecraftes." While most convictions carried the punishment of imprisonment for one year for a first offence, and life for a second, two offences were deemed capital in nature. These two offences — i.e., causing death of a human being by witchcraft, and conjuring spirits — are closely related to *maleficium*. Similarly, injuring people or property by witchcraft was well within the conventional harm feared by the populace. A second conviction for this offence also carried the death penalty.[87] Where death was decreed, it was by hanging. Burning at the stake, the more common form of witch execution practised in Scotland and on the Continent, was reserved in England for cases of treason. It should be noted, however, that petty treason by a woman encompassed using witchcraft to murder her husband or employer; accordingly, it seems at least some women might have been put to death in this manner in England.[88]

The 1563 legislation was replaced by a significantly more severe act in 1604 that remained in force until 1736. In addition to the two capital offences noted above, the death penalty was applied to taking bodies out of graves, and for a first offence of injuring people or property by witchcraft which now included the use of evil spirits to perform these deeds. In the event of a second conviction, the death penalty also applied to using witchcraft to search for treasure or lost property, intending to injure persons, intending to cause death or injure property, or provoking a person to unlawful love by witchcraft. Again, these offences adhere more closely to traditional understandings of sorcery, divination, and *maleficium*.

The attenuated influence of demonological accounts served directly to limit the scope of the English witch-hunts:

> English witches did not fly. They did not go to the sabbath. They did not copulate or make pacts with the devil, or make powders and ointments with the bones of murdered children. They kept "familiars" — homely, though diabolical, pets. They were accused, not of being heretics, but of harming their neighbours' cows. They were not tortured or burned.[89]

The focus on *maleficium*, emerging from below through accusations between neighbours, coupled with the greater adherence to the restraints imposed upon common-law procedure, certainly appears to have played a role in curbing the extent of prosecutions and executions in England.

Apart from the Star Chamber, English courts operated on an accusatory model. Public trials were initiated by a private complainant, and were held before a judge who had no role in investigating or prosecuting the case. Far more significantly, English trials were held before juries and a unanimous verdict was required to support a conviction. Although the presumption of innocence provided some protection for the accused, the English courts in principle relied upon less strict methods of proof. "Just and sufficient proofs" of witchcraft consisted in the testimony of two witnesses (who could be children) as to the accused having made a pact with the devil, or having used devices for divination or engaging in the practice of witchcraft, including having entertained a familiar spirit; the other certain proof was a voluntary confession.[90] Torture was not legally permitted, although there are accounts of enforced wakefulness, continuous questioning, withholding food or immersion in water yielding confessions.[91] Generally, however, confessions were rare.[92] In the absence of this evidence, discovering witches by other means assumed significance.

It is here that the female body, bearing witness to its own excesses, was used to justify prosecution. Although some of the forms of evidence to be discussed below were also of significance in continental trials, a number were distinctively British.

## Part III: Discovering Witches: The Body As Evidence

### CONCERNING THE DETECTION OF WITCHES

In some jurisdictions, the detection of witches primarily fell to the local populace, who supplied accounts of *maleficium* directed against them, their loved ones, or their property. However, in the wake of the enterprise of witch-prosecution, expert knowledge was generated to assist in the detection, surveillance, and prosecution of witches. Particularly salient in formulations respecting the discovery of witches was the publication of the *Malleus Maleficarum*[93] and other texts on demonology. These publications provided detailed guidance to assist in hunting witches. The surface of the body often played a crucial role in the establishment of guilt or innocence. One of the key pieces of evidence that could be introduced against a suspected witch was the presence of the "Devil's mark."[94] The witch's body was therefore stripped of clothing and thoroughly searched.

The Devil's mark was alleged to be imparted by the Devil during carnal relations consummating the pact. In the accounts of demonologists, the Devil could engage in sexual relations by appearing either as a human or as an animal. If the Devil took the form of a woman this bodily transformation was termed succubus, or if it appeared in the shape of a man, incubus. In the Swedish witch trials of 1668-76, the Devil often took the form of a black dog. Witches were said to engage in arguments over who should be first to go under a table to copulate with him.[95] The mythical theme of intermingling between animals and humans was also present in the functional purpose ascribed to the Devil's mark. It was allegedly used by the witch to nurse her familiar or imp. A familiar spirit could take the form of another human, but more frequently its shape was that of an animal such as a dog, cat, foal, fowl, hare, rat or toad. The familiar was personal to the witch, and believed to be assigned to her by the Devil.[96] The witch employed the familiar in executing her magic, and familiars were often sent on missions to harm or destroy the persons or property of enemies of the witch. By way of reward, the witch either gave the familiar drops of her blood or suckled the animal at some supernumerary nipple on the body. Witches were closely "watched" to establish whether or not they were visited by familiars.

Many bodily markings of an accused could be read as indications of guilt.[97] Cysts, scars, warts, supernumerary teats or other excrescences particularly where swelling was present suggested evidence of nurturing a familiar. The Devil's mark was believed to be insensitive to pain. Accused were subject to diligent bodily searches for suspicious marks, and then suspicious marks were tested by the insertion of a pin or other sharp device, known as "pricking." In particular, genitals and breasts were subject to rigorous searching. If a mark was found which failed to bleed, or was insensitive to the application of the pin, guilt was often assumed. Witch-hunters also engaged in the practice of "swimming" the accused, similar to a trial by ordeal. It was believed that those who were agents of the Devil were incapable of sinking in water.[98] The practice has been described as follows:

> The victim was stripped naked and bound with her right thumb to her left toe, and her left thumb to her right toe, and was then cast into the pond or river. If she sank, she was frequently drowned; if she swam she was declared guilty without any further evidence being required.[99]

Professional witch-hunters were compensated lucratively for their role in subjecting women to these tests. Perhaps the most notorious in England was Matthew Hopkins, the self-styled "Witch-Finder General" who, with his assistant John Stearne, carried out a brief but devastating campaign of witch-hunting. The witch-hunter was believed to be trained in the art of discovering witches. For a fee these men amassed proof and testified at prosecutions. During the space of only a few years, Hopkins and company were directly involved in finding around two hundred witches who were subsequently executed.[100]

However, the female body, even where it failed with expert assistance to inculpate itself, ultimately yielded the secrets of its own excesses. The female form, not created in the image of God, was open and receptive to the temptations of the Devil.

### ESTABLISHING BOUNDARIES:
### ABJECTION OF BODILY FLUIDS

Subjectivity which seeks acceptance within the domain of the social relies upon the violent expulsion and destruction of those aspects of "self" submerged in fear and horror. Kristeva's concept of abjection defines the socially configured boundaries of the clean and proper body.[101] As Young points out, "rule-breaking is necessarily *expelled* from the community.... The outlaw can never belong to the community, in that the community's very existence is founded upon her prior and symbolic expulsion from it."[102] The expulsion thereby constitutes demarcation of corporeal links and assists in the maintenance of orderly boundaries.

The effort to eradicate evil is often symbolically assisted by redefinitions of crime and criminality. However, it also relies upon constructing certain individuals as hazardous to the body politic such that solutions that would normally be unpalatable become acceptable:

> The method is a simple one, and consists less in fresh descriptions for crimes for which people may be punished than in fresh descriptions of human beings themselves. What is redefined is the nature of those who are to be regarded as legitimate members of human societies ...[103]

Thus, my argument is that the social contract relies upon the expulsion of individuals who threaten the maintenance and containment of proper social boundaries.

Much recent French feminist work has stressed the fluid nature of women's embodiment — our menstrual flows, lactation, viscosity, and inter-penetrability. In this sense, boundaries are "masculine products that seek to 'contain' women's corporeal 'flows' and the amorphous nature of feminine desire."[104]

Moreover, what is expelled from the body, that is from the configuration of the proper "self," is renounced as waste. Waste products — fecal, menstrual or nasal (to provide a few examples) — are involved with the "power of horror."[105] These rejected aspects of self are typically viewed with revulsion, loathing or disgust:

> The social organization of disgust as it related to bodily substances was mostly subsumed into the moral and social economy of shame and honor, but we can begin to discern it taking on a life of its own.... In the world of the high Middle Ages disgust, in some contexts, grew so large as to break away from the shame that organized it in more routine settings. Intense disgust in this period is not focused on vile substances like excrement but on people who inspire horror, fear, and loathing: the leper, the Jew, the heretic, and for monks and priests and hence much of official discourse, women.[106]

To return to the notion of abjection, or the boundaries around which the body is expelled, the law-abiding social body emerges as a consequence of the culture seeking to assert its limits or boundaries in order to maintain its fundamental integrity. If women are unruly by virtue of their uncontainable bodies and desires, those at greatest risk of expulsion are those located on the periphery. Those who are unruly, disruptive, resistant, or outlaws in Young's terms, are most likely to find themselves forcibly eradicated from the social contract.

Witchcraft fantasies mapped fear, horror, and revulsion onto the female body whereby nurturance and sustenance were transmuted to represent hazardous fluids, the risk of contamination, and the chaos implicit in merger. Roper expresses these fears as follows:

> Sexual fantasies to which witches give voice often display a similar vision of the disorganized body: in English witch fantasies, teats appear not confined to the breast, but all over the body as the Devil's mark; they are often to be found near the

anus or vagina, as if the bodily orifices had become inter-
changeable. Sexual activity, when it takes place at the
witches' sabbath, is an orgy in which "sodomy" ... becomes an
imprecise term for every kind of unorthodox coupling ...
Rather what we encounter is a disordered imagination ... fantasies to do with sex and death, with non-reproductive intercourse, sexual union as an engulfment which destroys the
identity, and behind this, the horror of sex with the mother
herself, the return to the death of the womb.[107]

Kristeva identifies the abject with bodily fluids which are likely to
arouse loathing, such as urine, excrement, nasal discharges, blood and
menstrual discharges. These fluids represent impurities which are generated by the body to which the "self" no longer wishes to lay claim.
Similarly the corpse, or body in which the self no longer resides, can figure as the ultimate horror. Her work relies upon that of Mary Douglas,
who stressed the permeable and leaky quality of female bodies.[108] During
pregnancy a woman's boundaries are breached and distended. Lactation
again furnishes a connection in which self and other are no longer clearly
demarcated. These functions fulfilled by the female body attest to its inde-
terminate nature and chaotic structure. The consequences for women in
the social construction of the symbolic order are profound.

## Part IV: Power, Law, and the Female Body

The emphasis on legal and religious institutions in this paper may be trou-
bling, both because it distorts the many other factors that produced the
witch-hunt, but also because of recent work that dislocates the importance
of law in historical analysis. Within some circles, this new scholarship is
perceived as eclipsing "older," less sophisticated, and currently unfashion-
able feminist work that concentrates on the analysis of male dominance
and female submission or on male oppressors and female oppressed. In
this sense, there is something of an attitude of exoneration within the new
scholarship. Men, it seems, should not be held solely accountable for their
acts of violence, on the basis that they too are embedded in cultural institutions and practices that they neither define nor control. But, as Bordo
contends, such an analysis often fails to attach significance to the fact that
men have a stake in the development and maintenance of these same cul-

tural institutions and practices. The degree to which women have inter-
nalized and reproduced the cultural norms and practices of a profoundly
racist and sexist culture and participate in reproducing the effects of the
particular orders that inscribe it quickly becomes transmuted into women's
responsibly for, and complicity in, the abuse they suffer at the hands of
men.[109]

Much post-structuralist scholarship has centred on Foucauldian conceptions of power, which emphasize the self-regulating subject and the
varied and minute ways in which the process of normalization unfolds.
This work has been illuminating especially in its application by feminist
scholars to the micropractices that school the female body in keeping with
cultural demands.[110]

Foucault sought to develop a new "analytics"[111] of power which would
remove itself from what he termed the older "juridico-discursive model"[112]
such as the characterization of power deployed by the monarch (or state).
Modern power must be understood, he suggests, by freeing it from its older
juridico-discursive representation.[113] His position on modern power
(though difficult to summarize) includes the view that power should be
characterized neither as primarily repressive, nor as emanating from a unitary source above, but rather as emerging from below, as the product or
effect of a "multiplicity of force relations."[114] Modern power under this conception rests less with the law than with the multiple, minute, and varied
strategies and practices through which normalization is achieved. Power,
in short, has become pre-eminently extra-legal.

Part of the difficulty associated with eschewing previous categories of
analysis is that the degree to which power also comes "from above" tends
to be obscured. In particular, the coercive power of law and of law-enforce-
ment practices becomes relegated to relatively obsolete expressions of
power; modern power has moved beyond the reign of law.[115] One might
argue that the witchcraft prosecutions are paradigmatic of the older representation of power assuming legal form, pre-dating what Foucault terms
the modern period. In this sense, the significance of the legal form in
which power manifested itself during the witch-prosecutions is unsurprising. This argument, however, is somewhat problematic.

Although I have concentrated in this chapter on the role of the legal
apparatus within witchcraft prosecutions, the scholarship to date has
placed much greater emphasis on a dispersed and heterogenous constella-
tion of force relations affecting the scope of the executions. In fact, the law
has received comparatively scant attention. This could be taken to suggest

either that power's self-representation, as juridico-discursive, has not masked the workings of other networks of authority, or that the break between older and newer representations of power is not as clean as Foucault posits. It is the latter claim that I find more tantalizing.

Without wishing to deny the historical specificities of the marking of authority on the bodies of women during the witch-hunts, there are certainly shades of familiarity. One need only examine the deployment of current textual representations of female sexuality (I include here both legal and other cultural forms) to discover hauntingly familiar qualities. Variations upon the theme of woman as temptress have been among the most powerful and pervasive in legal discourse. It finds expression particularly in rape and child-abuse cases. The evil of woman threatening to consume or otherwise destroy children is deployed in debates around abortion, infanticide, and in child-welfare statutes that problematize women's failure to protect children or provide adequate nurturance in the face of male violence.

The hegemonic force, to say nothing of the resilience, of particular juridico-discursive attitudes toward the female body could also be taken to suggest that law, as a form of power, is less unstable and more unitary than many would care to admit. I do not wish to be taken to suggest here that historical accounts afford the kind of richness, texture, and depth of understanding that analysing shifting sexual and other cultural representations can provide. Rather, I wish to question whether the entrenchment of certain discourses pertaining to women might suggest that as a site of resistance, law is not altogether malleable.

In relation to post-structuralist conceptions of power, Carol Smart has forcefully argued that there is little evidence to support the view that modern law is withering.[116] In fact, she suggests that law has become refracted, that it has simply merged with other systems of regulation, expanding and consolidating the degree of regulation of everyday activity.

Female bodies are still subject to significant legal, medical, and moral regulation in terms of sexuality. Criminologists continue to search for the cause of female criminality, and are willing to locate either women's madness or badness in the excesses of the female body, as evidenced recently through the legal incorporation of the medical pathology of Pre-Menstrual Syndrome (PMS) and Battered Woman Syndrome (BWS). Medical delegitimation and legal regulation over the practice of midwifery and other alternative forms of healing have been consolidated in a way that centrally maintains the power of the medical profession. And Christian theological doctrine and practice still conceptualize God in male form.

### READING WITCHES: THE GENDERED
### CONSTRUCTION OF THE WITCH

I have not analyzed or alluded here to the rich narratives to be found of the witch: trials, including Assize records; confession pamphlets; and the transcriptions of ecclesiastical proceedings. Such work is increasingly emerging and has begun to be infused by complex strategies of "reading" such records. These representations were designed for specialist audiences, but co-existed alongside popular representations of witches in novels, plays, poems,[117] and more localized knowledge. This, however, perhaps begs the central question of interpretation and the light that present readings can shed on past events.

Brauner argues that the "modern" notion of witch became gendered in the latter part of the sixteenth century, but that earlier Medieval notions of witches as purveyors of sorcery and supernatural powers were not gender-specific.[118] One of the fundamental problems here is that the vast majority of historians dismiss notions of magic and witchcraft as patently untrue, in this sense both counter-intuitive and counter-factual. Margaret Murray was the first notable exception; she viewed the witches as participating in a pagan fertility cult in active resistance to the imposition of Christian authority.[119] For her efforts, she was regarded as a heretic of historical method.

What is overlooked in most historical analysis is the degree to which the constructed nature of religion relies upon rituals which, to an innocent outside observer, might appear scandalously implausible. Roper draws parallels between the construction of the possessed in Catholic rites of exorcism and the demonic cast of corporeality in the witch prosecutions.[120] In my view, the parallels between magic and religion run much deeper than this. My claim is that they cannot be clearly demarcated without reference to the very authorities which seek to produce and enforce them. For example, many religions, including Catholicism, Judaism, Hinduism, and Buddhism, rely upon incantations, ritual observances, and prescriptive formulas in pursuit of what may be regarded by some as ultimate truth, and by others as ludicrous superstition (if not outright madness). The distinction between the mystic and the heretic has thus always relied upon traces of authorized discursive conceptions and repressed, subjugated knowledge. In short, the distinction is a construct and by-product of the exercised effects of power.

The potential of ritual, meditation, and prayer to radically alter consciousness, both of the self and of the external world, might be regarded as entirely a matter of faith. Some schools of Buddhism reflect deeply magical precepts and beliefs. As many post-structuralists have only recently observed, the dualisms (including self and other) upon which ordinary understanding rests are themselves mere illusions that we imbue with meaning and equate with an externally identifiable reality.

Historical accounts that rely upon the renunciation of the uncivilized past in favour of the romanticization of the rational present, miss what the witch-craze might have meant to the populace and to those accused of witch-craft. Magical abilities may have presented a vocation by and through which women came to lay claim to social power. Only Carlo Ginzburg has been able to credibly navigate this terrain. In *Ecstasies*, Ginzburg examines ecclesiastical tracts, folklore, legal records, and iconography to trace and map the meaning of ritual practice. Rather than stressing an imposition of demonology from above, Ginzburg weaves often inchoate local beliefs together with the disciplines that sought to eradicate them. However illuminating his work may be, like most of his male colleagues he does not focus on gender analysis to any extent. In this respect, the work of Purkiss, Roper and Gibson are truly ground-breaking. The narratives of the witches are read with a view to both psychic and popular understanding. Infused with rich psychoanalytic and nuanced reading strategies, they raise fundamental questions about how one should approach the project of interpretation. As I rhetorically (albeit indirectly) raised at the outset of this paper: why witches?

There is no doubt that while I wish to raise the complicity of centralized and localized deployment of the moral, professional, and juridical domains, the sub-text suggests a valorization of resistance and unruly feminine disorder. Women may have genuinely possessed or believed that they exercised extraordinary abilities, or that other women did. In this sense victimization, in the sense of false allegation, can be misleading as a heuristic tool. However, its rejection in a broader sense can result in the obscuration of the forest for the proverbial trees.

## Conclusion — the Significance of Gynocide

The prosecution of witches emerged from the spiritual crimes of apostasy and heresy. What began in some regions as co-operation with ecclesiastical authorities in the punishment of spiritual offences soon gave rise to gradual acquisition of secular authority over the various crimes of witchcraft. Despite the persistence of the belief that it was the clergy and ecclesiastical courts that prosecuted and executed witches, in fact it was predominantly local authorities and secular courts that fulfilled this role.[121] Without the assistance of the state, and the array of punishments deployed by secular courts, the scale of gynocide in Renaissance Europe would never have reached the proportions it did.

Unquestionably, the Church played an active role both in the formulation of the concept of witchcraft, and also in the prosecution of heresy, magic, and witchcraft.[122] In particular, the preference for traditional secular jurisdiction over *maleficium*, which came from Roman law, was extended with the adoption of specific laws prohibiting witchcraft during the sixteenth century. The influence of ecclesiastical concerns about diabolism were often manifested in the law. Exceeding traditional notions of *maleficium*, some states allowed prosecution on the basis of having formed a pact with the Devil, or for entertaining evil spirits.

As authorities sought to "discover" witches, the bodies of women were fragmented, scrutinized, and subjected to routinized tests and tortures to reveal the secret crimes believed to have been perpetrated. Ultimately, though, failure to discover corporeal evidence of guilt did not preclude the female body from collapsing under the weight of its excesses. The witch-hunts represent a concerted effort to contain female sexuality, both spurned and feared, and to re-assert male dominion over "un-manned"[123] female bodies. A corollary of ensuring regulation of female sexuality was the control over midwives and healers to prevent their skills from undermining the fabric of the patriarchal family. The suppression of women's healing practices stemmed in part from the seditious potential of women scorned or abused to seek malevolent revenge.

Women were clearly the primary victims of the European witch-hunts. The fact that they were not its only victims,[124] or that women may have participated in accusing each other, does not detract from how the witch prosecutions should be largely viewed: as an effort by men to punish and contain women. While the witch-hunts cannot be reduced merely to this, desire or arcane bodily knowledge unleashed could, and did, lead to the fiery deaths of countless women.

While legal apparatuses should not be viewed as the only or perhaps even primary instruments that fuelled the gynocide we remember as the European witch-hunts, neither should the participation of legal officials, legislators, and judges in this event be trivialized or overlooked. In the words of Monter, the legal systems of Europe "carried out misogynistic campaigns of unique savagery."[125] Insufficient attention has been devoted to the complicity and centrality of law in this history of gynocide. The witch-hunts represent perhaps the graphic and violent example of the practices of containment and legal control enacted upon the female body. While the strappado, the rack, and other instruments of torture are no longer among the sanctioned arsenal of the legal order, vestiges of the attitude toward the female body made manifest by the witch-hunts have been refined and exist within legal discourse today.

## Notes

1. I would like to thank Jane Koster, Andrea Timoll, and Emily Grabham for their invaluable research assistance. I would like to thank Peggy Tugwood and Kathleen Lahey for their support and encouragement in this project. Finally, and most importantly, I am forever indebted to eight years of successive students in Feminist Jurisprudence, whose interest in the witches and belief in their power provided the alchemical impulse behind this paper.

2. See, for example Carol Smart, *Feminism and the Power of Law* (London: Routledge, 1989).

3. For example, Marianne Hester suggests that of those formally charged with witchcraft in England, more than 90 per cent were women. Marianne Hester, *Lewd Women and Wicked Witches* (London: Routledge, 1992), p. 108.

4. While precise knowledge of the number of deaths is lacking, estimates range from several hundred thousand to nine million. See Karlene Faith, *Unruly Women* (Vancouver: Press Gang Publishers, 1993), p. 17 and sources cited therein.

5. William Monter, "Protestant Wives, Catholic Saints, and the Devil's Handmaid: Women in the Age of Reformations," in R. Bridenthal, C. Koonz, and S. Stuard (eds.), *Becoming Visible: Women in European History* (Boston: Houghton Mifflin, 1987), p. 214.

6. Monter, "Protestant Wives," p. 214.

7. Keith Thomas, *Religion and the Decline of Magic* (London: Weidenfeld and Nicolson, 1971).

8. Alan Macfarlane, *Witchcraft in Tudor and Stuart England: A Regional and Comparative Study* (London: Routledge and Kegan Paul, 1970).

9. Christina Larner, *Enemies of God: The Witch-hunt in Scotland* (London: Chatto and Windus, 1981).

10. Such as Hugh Trevor-Roper, *The European Witch-Craze of the Sixteenth and Seventeenth Centuries and Other Essays* (New York: Harper and Row, 1969).

11. Many of the images that found expression in demonological accounts of witchcraft generated by the Church and ruling elites also relied upon some popular conceptions of witchcraft has been explored in some considerable detail. The most notable is Carlo Ginzburg, *Ecstasies: Deciphering the Witches' Sabbath* (New York: Pantheon, 1991).

12. However, there have been some wonderful efforts by women scholars to address the gendered dimension of the killings. Beginning in the 1970s Barbara Ehrenreich and Deirdre English wrote the pamphlet *Witches, Midwives, and Nurses: A History of Woman Healers* (Old Westbury, NY: Feminist Press, 1973), which stresses male efforts to monopolize the heal-

ing professions. Similarly Andrea Dworkin, *Woman-Hating* (New York: Dutton, 1974) wrote eloquently of the misogynistic character of the witch-hunts and Mary Daly, *Gyn/Ecology* (Boston: Beacon Press, 1978) explored the role of the Church in controlling women's sexuality. More recently, Larner, *Enemies of God*, for example, acknowledged that to some degree witch-hunting is synonymous with woman-hunting. Marianne Hester, *Lewd Women*, provides a sustained and detailed analysis of male domination in her account of English witch trials. See also the literature detailed in n. 14 below.

13. See for example, H.C. Midelfort, *Witch-Hunting in Southwestern Germany 1562-1684* (Stanford: Stanford University Press, 1972) and Robert Muchembled, "The Witches of the Cambresis: The Acculturation of the World in the Sixteenth and Seventeenth Centuries" in J. Obelkevich (ed.), *Religion and the People 800-1700* (Chapel Hill: University of North Carolina Press, 1979), pp. 221-76.

14. A number of important feminist interpretations highlight the roles of misogyny and patriarchy in the witchhunts (for example Marianne Hester, *Lewd Women*, and "Patriarchal reconstruction and witch hunting," in Barry, Hester and Roberts [eds.], *Witchcraft in Early Modern Europe* [New York: Cambridge University Press, 1996]); Anne Llewellyn Barstow *Witchcraze* (San Francisco: Pandora, 1994) and Sigrid Brauner, *Fearless Wives & Frightened Shrews: The Construction of the Witch in Early Modern Germany* (Amherst: University of Massachusetts Press, 1995). This approach has been contested, *inter alia*, by James Sharpe, *Instruments of Darkness: Witchcraft in England, 1550-1750* (London: Hamish Hamilton, 1996), pp.169-89. For criticism of his view see Garthine Waler, "Witchcraft and History," *Women's History Review* 7.3(1998): 423-32. A careful re-examination of this period from a criminological perspective is contained in Karlene Faith's *Unruly Women*. There have been explanations for the persecution of women as witches involving psychoanalytic approaches (Diane Purkiss, *The Witch in History* [London: Routledge, 1996]; Lyndal Roper, *Oedipus and the Devil: Witchcraft, Sexuality and Religion in Early Modern Europe* [London: Routledge, 1994]) and anthropological approaches using conflict theory (Andrew Sanders, *A Deed Without a Name: The Witch in Society and History* [Washington, DC: Berg Publishers, 1995]). Some approaches place prime importance on the development of ideas. In this vein, Sigrid Brauner in *Fearless Wives and Frightened Shrews* examined samples of learned texts, as well as texts produced by the learned classes for the uneducated majority, in order to root out the gender-specific imagery which, she hypothesized, provided the link between women and witches. The most recent contribution to the debate is Stuart Clark's *Thinking with Demons: The Idea of Witchcraft in Early Modern Europe* (Oxford: Oxford University Press, 1997), which focuses on binary oppositions in the characterization of witches as women.

15. Dworkin, *Woman-Hating* was one of the first to identify the witch-hunts as gynocide. See also Daly, *Gyn/Ecology*.

16. See Larner, *Enemies of God*; Hester, *Lewd Women*; Richard Horsley, "Who Were the Witches? The Social Roles of the Accused in the European Witch Trials," *Journal of Interdisciplinary History* 18 (Spring 1979): 689-715.

17. This expression was coined by Hugh Trevor-Roper, *The European Witch-Craze*.

18. Among the work that deals substantially with legal issues are Brian Levack, *The Witch-Hunt in Early Modern Europe* (London: Longman, 1987); Elliott Currie, "Crimes Without Criminals: Witchcraft and its Control in Renaissance Europe," *Law & Society Review* 3(1968): 7-31; Norman Cohn, *Europe's Inner Demons: An Inquiry Inspired by the Great Witch Hunt* (New York: Basic Books, 1975).

19. Dorothy Dinnerstein in *The Mermaid and the Minotaur: Sexual Arrangements and Human Malaise* (New York: Harper and Row, 1976), p. 133 comments, "'I'ness wholly free of the chaotic, carnal atmosphere of infancy, uncontaminated humaneness, is reserved for man."

20. Susan Bordo, *Unbearable Weight: Feminism, Western Culture and the Body* (Berkeley: University of California Press, 1993), p. 5.

21. Bordo, *Unbearable Weight*, p. 6.

22. K. Torjesen, *When Women were Priests: Women Leadership in the Early Church Scandal of their Subordination in the Rise of Christianity* (San Francisco: Harper, 1993), p. 211.

23. Torjesen, *When Women were Priests*, p. 222.

24. See Caroline Walker Bynam, *Fragmentation and Redemption* (New York: Zone Books, 1991).

25. Torjesen, *When Women were Priests*, p. 228.

26. Michael Baigent and Richard Leigh, *The Inquisition* (London: Viking, 1999), pp. 1-4, 20-21.

27. Currie, "Crimes Without Criminals," p. 346.

28. Montague Summers (ed. and trans.), *The Malleus Maleficarum of Heinrich Kramer and James Sprenger* (London: Arrow Books, 1971), hereinafter cited as *Malleus Maleficarum*.

29. Brauner, *Fearless Wives & Frightened Shews*, p. 114.

30. *Malleus Maleficarum*, p. 121.

31. See generally Merry Wiesner-Hanks, *Christianity and Sexuality in the Early Modern World: Regulating Desire, Reforming Practice* (London: Routledge, 2000), p. 26.

32. Wiesner-Hanks, *Christianity and Sexuality*, especially pp. 60-100.

33. Roper, *Oedipus and the Devil*, pp. 18-19.

34. Brauner, *Fearless Wives and Frightened Shrews*, p. 66.

35. Brauner, *Fearless Wives and Frightened Shrews*, p. 66.

36. Torjesen, *When Women were Priests*, p. 236-38.

37. Calvin, *Institutes* 2.844 (Louisville, KY: Westminster, 1989), p. 408. See also Wiesner-Hanks, *Christianity and Sexuality*.

38. Carol Merchant, *The Death of Nature: Women, Ecology and the Scientific Revolution* (London: Harper and Row, 1980).

39. Hester, *Lewd Women*, pp. 196-97.

40. Macfarlane, in his research on English witchcraft trials in Essex, found that almost 40 per cent of those accused were widows. See Macfarlane, *Witchcraft in Tudor and Stuart England*, and Hester, *Lewd Women*.

41. Midelfort, *Witch-Hunting in Southwestern Germany*, pp. 184-85.

42. Hester, *Lewd Women*; Carolyn Dinshaw, *Getting Medieval: Sexualities and Communities, Pre- and Postmodern* (Durham, NC: Duke University Press, 1999), p. 63.

43. Wiesner-Hanks, *Christianity and Sexuality*, p. 92.

44. Christina Larner, *Witchcraft and Religion: The Politics of Popular Belief* (Oxford: Basil Blackwell, 1984), p. 141.

45. See M. Chamberlain, *Old Wives Tales; Their History, Remedies and Spells* (London: Virago Press, 1981), pp. 35 ff.

46. Monica Green, "Women's Medical Practice and Health Care in Medieval Europe," *Signs* 14.2(1989): 440.

47. Green, "Women's Medical Practice," p. 445.

48. Green, "Women's Medical Practice," p. 449.

49. Larner, *Witchcraft and Religion*, p. 142.

50. Larner, *Witchcraft and Religion*, p. 142.

51. Larner, *Witchcraft and Religion*, p. 145.

52. See Chamberlain, *Old Wives Tales*, p. 65.

53. A. Clark, *The Working Life of Women in the Seventeenth Century* (London: Routledge, 1992), p. 245, cited in Chamberlain, *Old Wives Tales*, pp. 64-65.

54. See, generally, Chamberlain, *Old Wives Tales*, pp. 57-62.

55. Chamberlain, *Old Wives Tales*, p. 60.

56. Torjesen, *When Women were Priests*, p. 240.

57. M. Chamberlain, *Old Wives Tales*, p. 56.

58. J. Donnison, *Midwives and Medical Men: A History of the Struggle for the Control of Childbirth* (London: Historical Publications, 1988), pp. 14-16.

59. M. Green, "Women's Medical Practice," p. 450.

60. Donnison, *Midwives and Medical Men*, p.20; J. Fowler and J. Bromall, *Midwives in History and Society* (London: Croom Helm, 1986).

61. *Malleus Maleficarum*, p. 66.

62. Levack, *The Witch-Hunt in Early Modern Europe*, p. 128.

63. *Malleus Maleficarum*, pp. 100f.

64. H. Boguet, *An Examen of Witches* (New York: Barnes and Noble, 1971), p. 137.

65. Macfarlane, *Witchcraft in Tudor and Stuart England*, pp. 178-82.

66. Hester, *Lewd Women*, p. 194.

67. Fyodor Dostoyevsky, *The Brothers Karamazov* (London: Penguin, 1982), p. 301.

68. Levack, *The Witch-Hunt in Early Modern Europe*, p. 63.

69. See Currie, "Crimes Without Criminals," p. 356.

70. Obviously, Scotland's legal regime doesn't properly fit within either category. However, it would add little to the analysis which follows to treat it separately. Also, while there may appear to be differences on a macro-level in terms of process, substantive prohibitions, rules of evidence, and so forth, there are compelling reasons to believe that such generalizations might not withstand closer scrutiny. This method of classifying legal regimes is an admittedly crude one, and is adopted here only in Part II to elaborate on the procedural and substantive disparities between the two systems where it appears appropriate.

71. Levack, *The Witch-Hunt in Early Modern Europe*, pp.63-64. Namely: the adoption of inquisitorial procedure; the sanctioned use of torture to extract confessions and names of accomplices; the gradual acquisition of secular jurisdiction over witchcraft, supplementing or supplanting ecclesiastical authority; and the relative autonomy of local and regional courts.

72. Examples of ordeals provided by Levack include carrying a hot iron, or immersing a limb in hot water, and subsequently revealing a healed limb after bandaging; sinking when thrown into a body of cold water; or swallowing food whole without choking. Levack, *The Witch-Hunt in Early Modern Europe*, p. 65.

73. Levack, *The Witch-Hunt in Early Modern Europe*, p. 66.

74. Levack, *The Witch-Hunt in Early Modern Europe*, p. 78.

75. Levack, *The Witch-Hunt in Early Modern Europe*, p. 79.

76. Since witches were known by reputation, accusations could be laid on the basis of another's claim that someone was a witch. See generally Jeanne Achterberg, *Woman as Healer* (Boston: Shambhala Publications, 1990).

77. Elliott Currie, "The Control of Witchcraft in Renaissance Europe," in D. Black, and M. Mileski (eds.), *The Social Organization of Law* (New York: Seminar Press, 1973), p. 348.

78. Levack, *The Witch-Hunt in Early Modern Europe*, p. 77.

79. *Corpus Juris Civilis*, Codex 9, Tit. 18. For a discussion of these distinctions see Christina Larner, "Crimen Exceptum? The Crime of Witchcraft in Europe," in V.A.C. Gartell, B. Lenman, and G. Parker (eds.), *Crime and the Law: The Social History of Crime in Western Europe since 1500* (London: Europe Publications, 1980).

80. Levack, *The Witch-Hunt in Early Modern Europe*, p. 78.

81. Larner, *Enemies of God*, p. 51.

82. Currie, "Crimes Without Criminals."

83. Robert Muchembled, "Satanic Myths and Cultural Reality," in B. Ankarloo and G. Henningsen (eds.), *Early Modern European Witchcraft* (Oxford: Clarendon Press, 1990), p. 140.

84. Brauner, *Fearless Wives and Frightened Shrews*, p. 8.

85. Horsley, "Who Were the Witches?", p.690, explains diabolism in the following manner: "In a Christian society, since witchcraft could only be apostasy from the true religion, witches had therefore been seduced by Satanic forces and had made a formal contract with the Devil. Hence, also, all magic done by (non-christian) supernatural powers, beneficent as well as maleficent, was viewed as diabolism." See also Cohn, *Europe's Inner Demons*. For a fuller analysis of the sabbat see Ginzburg, *Ecstasies*.

86. *Commentarius*, 1608, cited in R. Robbins, *The Encyclopedia of Witchcraft and Demonology* (London: Spring Books, 1959), p. 178.

87. Macfarlane, *Witchcraft in Tudor and Stuart England*, pp. 14-15.

88. Christina Hole, *Witchcraft in England: Some Episodes in the History of English Witchcraft* (Totowa, NJ: Rowman and Littlefield, 1977), p. 19, cites the example of Mary Lakeland who suffered death by burning in 1645 at Ipswich for having murdered her husband. Hole suggests that where witches were burnt, in all cases heresy, poisoning or treason were also present.

89. Robert Rowland, "Fantastical and Devilishe Persons: European Witch-Beliefs in Comparative Perspective," in B. Ankarloo and G. Henningsen (eds.), *Early Modern European Witchcraft* (Oxford: Clarendon Press, 1990), p. 173.

90. Robbins, *The Encyclopedia of Witchcraft and Demonology*.

91. See generally Macfarlane, *Witchcraft in Tudor and Stuart England*, p. 20.

92. Currie, "Crimes Without Criminals," p. 354.

93. *Malleus Maleficarum*, p. 47.

94. Under the category of "uncertain or less sufficient proofs" of witchcraft, Perkins included "ordeal by the red-hot iron, scratching a witch to draw blood, and ducking a witch to see if she would float." Perkins listed the Devil's mark among his category of "presumptions of guilt." Familiars and the Devil's mark remained primary sources of evidence in English trials. See Robbins, *The Encyclopedia of Witchcraft and Demonology*, pp. 174-75.

95. Jonas Liliequist, "Peasants against Nature: Crossing the Boundaries between Man and Animal in Seventeenth-and Eighteenth-Century Sweden," in J.C. Fout (ed.), *Forbidden History: The State, Society and the Regulation of Sexuality in Modern Europe* (Chicago: University of Chicago Press, 1992), p. 63.

96. Frances Dolan, *Dangerous Familiars: Representations of Domestic Crime in England 1550-1700* (Ithaca, NY: Cornell University Press, 1994), see especially pp. 175-93.

97. Dolan, *Dangerous Familiars*, pp. 190-94.

98. Owen Davies, *Witchcraft, Magic and Culture 1736-1951* (Manchester: Manchester University Press, 1999), pp. 86-99.

99. C. Ewen, *Witch Hunting and Witch Trials* (London, 1929) p. 68, cited in Currie, "Crimes Without Criminals," p. 354. The description is that of Matthew Hopkins.

100. Hester, *Lewd Women*, p. 130.

101. Julia Kristeva, *Powers of Horror: An Essay on Abjection*, trans. L.S. Roudiez (New York: Columbia University Press, 1982).

102. Alison Young, *Imagining Crime* (London: Sage, 1996), p. 11. See also, generally, pp. 11-15.

103. Paul Oppenheimer, *Evil and the Demonic: A New Theory of Monstrous Behaviour* (New York: New York University Press, 1996), p. 95.

104. Simon Williams and Gillian Bendelow, *The Lived Body: Sociological Themes, Embodied Issues* (New York: Routledge, 1998), p. 120. For an excellent general introduction to the ideas expressed here see Elizabeth Grosz, *Volatile Bodies* (Bloomington: Indiana University Press, 1994).

105. For an in-depth treatment of this topic see Kristeva, *Powers of Horror*.

106. William Miller, *The Anatomy of Disgust* (Cambridge, MA: Harvard University Press, 1997), p. 154.

107. Lyndal Roper, *Oedipus and the Devil*, p. 25.

108. Mary Douglas, *Purity and Danger: An Analysis of the Concepts of Pollution and Taboo* (London: Routledge and Kegan Paul, 1966).

109. See Bordo, *Unbearable Weight*, pp. 10 ff.

110. See, for example, the work of Susan Bordo, *Unbearable Weight*, and the collection *Anatomy of Gender: Women's Struggle for the Body*, eds. D. Currie and V. Raoul (Ottawa: Carleton University Press, 1992).

111. Michel Foucault suggests that he means by this a movement "toward a definition of the specific domain formed by relations of power, and toward a determination of the instruments that will make possible its analysis." See *History of Sexuality* (New York: Pantheon, 1978), p. 82.

112. Although Foucault does not attempt a definition of this form of power, it is linked to the notion that "power acts by laying down the rule." Power under this account resides in the monarch (or legislator) and operates "through the statement of the law and the operation of taboos" (*History of Sexuality*, p. 85). Western monarchies since the middle ages established themselves, and represented their power through law. Foucault suggests that this exercise of power was something of an obfuscation.

113. Foucault, *History of Sexuality*, p. 82.

114. Foucault, *History of Sexuality*, p. 93. He goes on:

> Power's conditions of possibility ... must not be sought in the primary existence of a central point, in a unique source of sovereignty from which secondary and descendent forms would emanate; it is the moving substrate of force relations which, by virtue of their inequality, constantly engender states of power, but the latter are always local and unstable. The omnipresence of power: not because it has the privilege of consolidating everything under its invincible unity, but because it is produced from one moment to the next, at every point, or rather in every relation from one point to another. Power is everywhere; not because it embraces everything, but because it comes from everywhere. And "Power," insofar as it is permanent, repetitious, inert, and self-reproducing, is simply the overall effect that emerges from all these mobilities, the concatenation that rests on each of them and seeks in turn to arrest their movement.

115. Foucault, *History of Sexuality*, p. 89.

116. Smart, *Feminism and the Power of Law*.

117. Brauner, *Fearless Wives and Frightened Shrews*, p. 4.

118. Brauner, *Fearless Wives and Frightened Shrews*, pp. 5-7.

119. Margaret Murray, *The Witch-Cult in Western Europe* (Oxford: Oxford University Press, 1962).

120. Roper, *Oedipus and the Devil*.

121. Levack, *The Witch-Hunt in Early Modern Europe*, p. 78.

122. Levack, *The Witch-Hunt in Early Modern Europe*, p. 78.

123. This is a phrase I heard used by Maureen Cain. For me it captures something of the essence of women existing beyond male control, be they lesbian, or living an existence without male partners.

124. Some recent work suggests that the model of the witch as a poor, elderly woman does not work for Finland, or Iceland, where men accused of witchcraft might be viewed as having participated in shamanistic practises. See Peter Burke, "The Comparative Approach to European Witchcraft," in B. Ankarloo and G. Henningsen (eds.), *Early Modern European Witchcraft* (Oxford: Clarendon Press, 1990), pp. 440-41.

125. Monter, "Protestant Wives, Catholic Saints," p. 213.

# Bibliography

Achterberg, J. *Woman as Healer*. Boston: Shambhala Publications, 1990.

Baigent, M., and R. Leigh. *The Inquisition*. London: Viking, 1999.

Barstow, A.L. *Witchcraze*. San Francisco: Pandora, 1994.

Boguet, H. *An Examen of Witches*. New York: Barnes and Noble, 1971.

Bordo, S. *Unbearable Weight: Feminism, Western Culture and the Body*. Berkeley: University of California Press, 1993.

Brauner, S. *Fearless Wives and Frightened Shrews: The Construction of the Witch in Early Modern Germany*. Amherst: University of Massachusetts Press, 1995.

Burke, P. "The Comparative Approach to European Witchcraft." *Early Modern European Witchcraft*. Eds. B. Ankarloo and G. Henningsen. Oxford: Clarendon Press, 1990. 435-41.

Bynam, C. Walker. *Fragmentation and Redemption*. New York: Zone Books, 1991.

Calvin, J. *Institutes*. Louisville, KY: Westminster, 1989.

Chamberlain, M. *Old Wives Tales: Their History, Remedies and Spells*. London: Virago Press, 1981.

Clark, A. *The Working Life of Women in the Seventeenth Century*. London: Routledge, 1992.

Clark, S. *Thinking with Demons: The Idea of Witchcraft in Early Modern Europe*. Oxford: Oxford University Press, 1997.

Cohn, N. *Europe's Inner Demons: An Inquiry Inspired by the Great Witch Hunt*. New York: Basic Books, 1975.

*Corpus Juris Civilis*, Codex 9, Tit. 18.

Currie, D., and V. Raoul, eds. *Anatomy of Gender: Women's Struggle for the Body*. Ottawa: Carleton University Press, 1992.

Currie, E. "The Control of Witchcraft in Renaissance Europe." *The Social Organization of Law*. Eds. D. Black & M. Mileski. New York: Seminar Press, 1973.

——. "Crimes Without Criminals: Witchcraft and its Control in Renaissance Europe." *Law & Society Review* 3(1968): 7-31.

Daly, M. *Gyn/Ecology*. Boston: Beacon Press, 1978.

Davies, O. *Witchcraft, Magic and Culture 1736-1951*. Manchester: Manchester University Press, 1999.

Dinnerstein, D. *The Mermaid and the Minotaur: Sexual Arrangements and Human Malaise*. New York: Harper and Row, 1976.

Dinshaw, C. *Getting Medieval: Sexualities and Communities, Pre- and Postmodern*. Durham, NC: Duke University Press, 1999.

Dolan, F. *Dangerous Familiars: Representations of Domestic Crime in England 1550-1700*. Ithaca, NY: Cornell University Press, 1994.

Donnison, J. *Midwives and Medical Men: A History of the Struggle for the Control of Childbirth*. London: Historical Publications, 1988.

Douglas, M. *Purity and Danger: An Analysis of the Concepts of Pollution and Taboo*. Harmondsworth: Penguin, 1970.

Dworkin, A. *Woman-Hating*. New York: Dutton, 1974.

Ehrenreich, B., and D. English. *Witches, Midwives, and Nurses: A History of Women Healers*. Old Westbury, NY: Feminist Press, 1973.

Ewen, C. *Witch Hunting and Witch Trials*. London: Barnes and Noble, 1971.

Faith, K. *Unruly Women*. Vancouver: Press Gang Publishers, 1993.

Foucault, M. *History of Sexuality*. New York: Pantheon Books, 1976.

Fowler, J., and J. Bromall. *Midwives in History and Society*. London: Croom Helm, 1986.

Ginzburg, C. *Ecstasies: Deciphering the Witches' Sabbath*. New York: Pantheon Books, 1991.

Green, M. "Women's Medical Practice and Health Care in Medieval Europe." *Signs* 14.2(1989): 434-73.

Grosz, E. *Volatile Bodies*. Bloomington: Indiana University Press, 1994.

Hester, M. *Lewd Women and Wicked Witches*. London: Routledge, 1992.

——. "Patriarchal reconstruction and witch hunting." *Witchcraft in Early Modern Europe*. Eds. Barry, Hester, and Roberts. New York: Cambridge University Press, 1996.

Hole, C. *Witchcraft in England: Some Episodes in the History of English Witchcraft*. Totowa, NJ: Rowman and Littlefield, 1977.

Horsley, R. "Who Were the Witches? The Social Roles of the Accused in the European Witch Trials." *Journal of Interdisciplinary History* 18(Spring 1979): 689-715.

Kristeva, J. *Powers of Horror: An Essay on Abjection*. Trans. Leon S. Roudiez. New York: Columbia University Press, 1982.

Larner, C. *Witchcraft and Religion: The Politics of Popular Belief*. New York: Blackwell, 1985.

——. *Enemies of God: The Witch-hunt in Scotland*. London: Chatto and Windus, 1981.

——. "Crimen Exceptum? The Crime of Witchcraft in Europe." *Crime and the Law: The Social History of Crime in Western Europe since 1500*. Eds. V.A.C. Gartell, B. Lenman, and G. Parker. London: Europe Publications, 1980.

Levack, B. *The Witch-Hunt in Early Modern Europe*. London: Longman, 1987.

Liliequist, J. "Peasants against Nature: Crossing the Boundaries between Man and Animal in Seventeenth and Eighteenth-Century Sweden." *Forbidden History: The State, Society and the Regulation of Sexuality in Modern Europe*. Ed. J.C. Fout. Chicago: University of Chicago Press, 1992. 57-88.

Macfarlane, A. *Witchcraft in Tudor and Stuart England: A Regional and Comparative Study*. London: Routledge and Kegan Paul, 1970.

Merchant, C. *The Death of Nature: Women, Ecology and the Scientific Revolution*. London: Harper and Row, 1980.

Midelfort, H.C. *Witch-Hunting in Southwestern Germany 1562-1684*. Stanford: Stanford University Press, 1972.

Miller, W.I. *The Anatomy of Disgust*. Cambridge, MA: Harvard University Press, 1997.

Monter, W. "Protestant Wives, Catholic Saints, and the Devil's Handmaid: Women in the Age of Reformations." *Becoming Visible: Women in European History*. Eds. R. Bridenthal, C. Koonz, and S. Stuard. Boston: Houghton Mifflin, 1987. 203-19.

Muchembled, R. "Satanic Myths and Cultural Reality." *Early Modern European Witchcraft*. Eds. B. Ankarloo and G. Henningsen. Oxford: Clarendon Press, 1990. 139-60.

——. "The Witches of the Cambresis: The Acculturation of the World in the Sixteenth and Seventeenth Centuries." *Religion and the People, 800-1700*. Ed. J. Obelkevich. Chapel Hill: University of North Carolina Press, 1979. 221.

Murray, M. *The God of the Witches*. London: Oxford University Press, 1981.

——. *The Witch-Cult in Western Europe*. Oxford: Oxford University Press, 1962.

Oppenheimer, P. *Evil and the Demonic: A New Theory of Monstrous Behaviour*. New York: New York University Press, 1996.

Perkins, W. *Discourse of the Damned Art of the Witchcraft*. Cambridge, 1608.

Purkiss, D. *The Witch in History*. London: Routledge, 1996.

Robbins, R. *The Encyclopedia of Witchcraft and Demonology*. London: Spring Books, 1959.

Roper, L. *Oedipus and The Devil: Witchcraft, Sexuality and Religion in Early Modern Europe*. London: Routledge, 1994.

Rowland, R. "Fantastical and Devilishe Persons: European Witch-Beliefs in Comparative Perspective." *Early Modern European Witchcraft*. Eds. B. Ankarloo and G. Henningsen. Oxford: Clarendon Press, 1990. 161-90.

Sanders, A. *A Deed Without a Name: The Witch in Society and History*. Washington, DC: Berg Publishers, 1995.

Sharpe, J.A. *Instruments of Darkness: Witchcraft in England, 1550-1750*. London: Hamish Hamilton, 1996.

Smart, C. *Feminism and the Power of Law*. London: Routledge, 1989.

Summers, M., ed. and trans. *The Malleus Maleficarum of Heinrich Kramer and James Sprenger*. London: Arrow Books, 1971.

Thomas, K. *Religion and the Decline of Magic*. London: Weidenfeld and Nicolson, 1971.

Torjesen, K. *When Women were Priests: Women Leadership in the Early Church Scandal of their Subordination in the Rise of Christianity*. San Francisco: Harper, 1993.

Towler, J., and J. Bromall. *Midwives in History and Society*. London: Croom Helm, 1986.

Trevor-Roper, H. *The European Witch-Craze of the Sixteenth and Seventeenth Centuries and Other Essays*. New York: Harper and Row, 1969.

Waler, G. "Witchcraft and History." *Women's History Review* 7.3(1998): 423-32.

Wiesner-Hanks, M. *Christianity and Sexuality in the Early Modern World: Regulating Desire, Reforming Practice*. London: Routledge, 2000.

Williams, S., and G. Bendelow. *The Lived Body: Sociological Themes, Embodied Issues*. New York: Routledge, 1998.

Young, A. *Imagining Crime*. London: Sage, 1996.

# PART III

*Social Location and the Application of Law*

# 6

## The Farmer Takes a Wife and the Wife Takes the Farm: Marriage and Farming

### Susan T. Machum

When a woman marries a farmer, she is entering a different social, economic, and political arena from her urban counterpart who marries a worker or a professional. According to Weitzman, when two people marry they enter into a legal contract which may be spoken or unspoken. The traditional, urban marriage contract embodies four provisions:

1. The husband is the head of the household;
2. The husband is responsible for support;
3. The wife is responsible for domestic services; and
4. The wife is responsible for childcare, the husband for child support. (Weitzman, 1981:2)

These provisions have traditionally formed the basis for resolving legal conflicts between husbands and wives.

Farm women find themselves in a far more complex marriage contract than Weitzman suggests. Since, traditionally, family farms did not separate the farm enterprise from the family household, farm wives were responsible not only for the normal domestic responsibilities but also for a wide variety of on-farm work (Smith, 1973). Through marriage, a farm wife became directly or indirectly involved in the success or failure of the farm enterprise. By extending her household labour to include such activities as growing, canning, and freezing vegetables as well as raising chickens, and so on, a farm wife effectively subsidized the farm unit by reducing the cash needs of the family. Additionally, her outdoor work in the barn and in crop production meant more could be produced for market or family consumption without extra labour costs. If the farm succeeded she had a home and an income; if it failed she lost both. In many cases, the converse was also true. If the marriage failed and a woman withdrew her labour, the family farm would also fail (MacInnes and MacLaren, 1992). Women who marry farmers do not just marry the farmer, *they marry the farm*. And as one farm woman said, "No two men in their right minds would dream of committing themselves to farming together under such an unequal arrangement much less for a lifetime" (Match, 1981:48).

Research on farm women makes it clear that they do a triple day of work compared to their urban counterparts' double day (Ceboratev *et al.*, 1986; Ghorayshi, 1989; Graff, 1982; Koski, 1982; Reimer, 1986; Shaver, 1990; Smith, 1987; Willick, 1982). They work at jobs off the farm, directly on the farm in production, and they do the reproductive work of child bearing and rearing and the accompanying household chores. Thus, farm women's work is basically divided into three components: off-farm work, on-farm work, and domestic work.[1] The first and last categories include the same range of domestic labour and out-of-home paid labour (or small-business activities) shared with urban women. The on-farm component can be divided into two aspects: work in the production process of the commercial commodity; and work done on the farm to either substitute for, or provide cash for, store-bought inputs.

Farm women are not working a triple day because they want to; they are doing it because it is the only way their households and the farm enterprises in which they are entwined can survive. The problem is that not only are these women working extraordinarily hard, but they seldom seem to be the beneficiaries of their own labour. If the women doing the work are not the direct beneficiaries of their own work, then who is? How can we understand these women's exploitation, and the role of the legal and social order in establishing and maintaining it?

Women's work in producing the commodity sold by the farm is often crucial to the success of the farm business (MacInnes and MacLaren, 1990; Reimer, 1986; Ghorayshi, 1989). Likewise, when farm wives engage in tasks that reduce the cash needs of the household, they are in fact supporting the farm enterprise, since, without this work, the family unit would have to rely on a larger income from the farm business operation. Farm wives frequently engage in a range of production activities like growing gardens, canning and freezing fruits and vegetables, baking bread, quilting, sewing, and other activities which constitute the production of what are usually inputs into the domestic labour of modern urban women (Reimer, 1986). Yet, as Brown points out,

> Despite the multitude of tasks performed by farm women,
> and the value of their contribution ... women themselves
> don't always see their own worth, often because they are
> working without pay in a society which equates worth with
> pay. (1980:11)

While women's off-farm work for a wage or salary is clearly productive
(because it produces profit for their employers like all other workers'
labour), in the farm enterprise off-farm wages also become a subsidy to the
farm enterprise. Farm women's wages can either subsidize the farm enterprise directly by financing the cost of the farm operation, or indirectly, by
covering household costs, which permits the farm operation to continue
when it could not otherwise provide an adequate standard of living for the
farm family.

Since farm wives' direct and indirect contributions to the farm enterprise do not fit into standard economic productivity calculations like Gross
National Product (GNP), their work is often undervalued and taken for
granted by family members, courts, the Canadian government, and
agribusiness. In even the recent past, this invisibility of farm wives' contributions has been most apparent when their marriages dissolved either
through separation, divorce or death. It was then that farm women were
shocked to find that their work did not entitle them to any ownership of
the farm enterprise to which they had devoted their lives. In the case of the
death of their husbands, many farm women discovered they were not partners in the farm enterprise, but only heirs to it along with their children.
They did not own part of the farm enterprise any more than their children
did. They were entitled to one-third while their child or children were
awarded the remaining two-thirds of his property. If a farm wife chose to
continue farming after her husband's death, she faced many obstacles.

One woman I interviewed,[2] Barbara,[3] recalled the opposition she
received from family members, the bank manager, and the community
when, after her husband's unexpected death in early 1970, she decided to
work the family farm on her own. She had to have her brother-in-law
accompany her to the bank to discuss financial transactions with the bank
manager since the bank manager "wouldn't talk to a woman." She also
had to do most of the work on her own since her children were too young
to help. And despite working the farm alone for five years after her husband's death, she was still entitled only to one-third of the family farm
property when she decided to sell the farm in 1975. Two-thirds of her

intense labour now became part of her children's inheritance. Even after his death, her husband's estate became the direct beneficiary of her labour. Furthermore, during the time she worked the farm alone, Barbara had to keep careful records of the farm's transactions in order to keep the children's inheritance intact and separate from her own.

A well-known instance of how farm women's labour was subsumed by their husband is the infamous case of Irene Murdoch, where courts dealt with separation and divorce between a married couple who were farming together prior to their marriage breakdown. Between 1969 and 1974, Irene Murdoch went all the way to the Supreme Court of Canada, trying to establish her right to a share of the farm property that she and her husband had developed during their 25 years of marriage (Atcheson *et al.*, 1984; Hale, 1990). Their 480 acres of ranch property were held solely in her husband's name. Yet it was well documented in the legal proceedings that she had made a substantial contribution to the running of the ranch by

> haying, raking, swathing, moving, driving trucks and tractors and teams, quieting horses, taking cattle back and forth to the reserve, dehorning, vaccinating, branding, and doing anything else that was to be done. [She] worked outside with [her husband], just as a man would, doing anything that was to be done. (Atcheson *et al.*, 1984:26)

Moreover, she maintained the ranch alone for five to eight months of each year when her husband left to work for the Canadian Forestry Service (Weitzman, 1981). In 1974, the Supreme Court of Canada denied her a share in the ranch on the grounds that she had only done "what any ranch wife would do" (Atcheson et al., 1984:26; Hale, 1990; Weitzman, 1981:69).

Despite the magnitude of her direct contribution to the farm enterprise, Irene Murdoch was awarded support of only $200 a month for the 25 years of labour she had put into the farm (Weitzman, 1981:69). The court decided that for 25 years she had worked as a ranch hand, managed the day-to-day operations of the Murdoch ranch, and maintained the household essentially as a volunteer. She was not paid a wage for her labour and in the end she did not own the property she had helped improve and accumulate. The fruition of her work did not belong to her; it was appropriated by her husband, and this appropriation was endorsed by the state. According to Weitzman (1981:69), the judge justified the order in this way:

> The land was held in the name of Mr. Murdoch at all times.
> The cattle and the equipment were also held in his name;
> income tax returns were filed in his name; no declaration of
> partnership was ever filed ...; and I, therefore, do not form the
> conclusion that the [Murdochs] were partners, or that a rela-
> tionship existed that would give [Mrs. Murdoch] the right to
> claim as a joint owner in equity in any of the farm assets.

In fact, the trial judge went even further by declaring that Irene Murdoch had simply "done the work of any ranch wife and that [her labour] did not create any interest in the lands" (Atcheson *et al.*, 1984:26). While the judges used the traditional marriage contract to establish Mrs. Murdoch's "domestic responsibilities," as a farm wife her responsibilities clearly extended beyond the doorstep of the family homestead. In this case, farm labour was considered to be nothing more than a farm wife fulfilling the "domestic service responsibility" identified by Weitzman.

The Murdoch case became a *cause célèbre* for the Canadian women's movement. It motivated researchers to begin documenting what farm women actually do, by engaging in extensive time-budget studies (Ceboratev *et al.*, 1986; Koski, 1982; Smith, 1987). It spurred Canadian women's groups to demand changes in family law to establish joint own-ership for assets accumulated during the marriage (Atcheson *et al.*, 1984; Hale, 1990; Weitzman, 1981). Women's groups argued that farm women's lives would be fundamentally transformed through legal equality with their husbands in all political, economic, and social interactions. Women also needed child-care facilities, training programs, equal access to credit, health, and safety programs, job opportunities, and new government tax regulations for greater equality with men (see the Canadian Advisory Council on the Status of Women, 1987). Their analysis was that farm women needed equality of opportunity with farm men and urban women. By eliminating sexism and providing an urban level of services and oppor-tunities, farm women would achieve independence and escape exploita-tion. This, they believed, would free women from the most oppressive relationships in which they found themselves. As a result of their work, between 1974 and 1981 all Canadian provinces (with the exception of Quebec, which had already instigated such changes) changed their statutes regarding family or matrimonial property (Atcheson et al., 1984; Weitzman, 1981).

State policy has tended to reinforce the inequity of their situation by treating farm women's work as not "real work" at all. Traditionally, farm women's work, even in the commercial production process, was considered a domestic service to her husband. It was both owed to him and, by a twist in logic, supposedly given freely to him as an act of love. Farm women were not expected to be paid wages for their work (and, as we have seen, their labour created no "sweat equity" as business partners). As the 1969 Farm Tax Guide put it in instructions to (male) farmers: "Wages to your wife cannot be allowed as a deduction from [farm] income" (Farm Tax Guide, 1969) in the same way other labour costs can be deducted as a business expense. On the other hand, wages paid to hired hands, and even to the family's children (Farm Tax Guide, 1969; McNair, 1981:91), were allowed to be treated as real costs of production and could be deducted as a business expense. By a similar logic, a wife's work in farm production did not entitle her to unemployment insurance nor to Canada Pension for her old age. Officially, whatever labour she performed for the farm was not "work" in any legal sense. Given the marriage contract and the Murdoch case we can see that she was expected to labour, but her labour didn't count as work: a farm wife was a mandatory volunteer in this scheme.

Such discrimination against farm women is far more than reflexive sexism. By so arranging the tax system the state was able to require women's work while denying the same tax and pension benefits to farm women as given to other working people. The state treated the personal (sexual) commitment of the wife to the husband as also a labour agreement to the farm enterprise. At the same time, government policy was increasingly targeting farm wives for agricultural training programs, claiming that they were "an untapped management resource" (New Brunswick, October 1972).

Changes in the state's treatment of farm women's work has been slow in coming. While by the 1993 tax year one could deduct spousal wages from a male farm income (Farming Income Tax Guide, 1993), this was only if one's spouse was not a partner in the farm. Not surprisingly, only 9 per cent of all types of farm have partnership agreements or incorporation documents, yet 45 per cent of farm women say they are "partners" with their husbands (Canada, 1991:2). Only one person is able to pay into the Canada Pension Plan (CPP) for each farm — and this person has usually been the male. This tax policy led accountants by the late 1980s to advise farm women to take a salary for the work they were doing in keeping the farm's accounts (daily book-keeping) in order to pay into CPP (Income Tax Guide and Canada, 1991). This was now possible due to the changes made to the Income Tax Act in 1981 allowing wives to be paid a salary for farm work (Bruners, 1985:18). But the flaw with this particular strategy is that it requires that a farm woman not be a legal partner but rather an employee of the farm.

Despite the positive changes in women's political and socioeconomic status in society as a whole, farm women's positions have not improved as much as those supporting law reform might have expected. Farm women are still working extraordinarily hard and reaping little reward for it. Why? These attempts at legal reform to ameliorate farm women's plight, I would argue, did not address the political economy within which farm enterprises operate. To fully appreciate farm women's situation, we need to examine the impact of agribusiness and government policy on the family farm household.

## The Political Economy of Agriculture: Agribusiness and the State

It is impossible to understand the patterns of women's work or to ascertain who benefits from the fruits of that labour without knowledge of the conditions under which contemporary farming occurs. Farming is no longer an independent economic activity. It has been subsumed by corporations as a subordinate component within what the federal government calls the *agri-food system* (Canada, 1981), what most people refer to as *agribusiness*. Agribusiness refers to the system whereby large corporations control the production of food from the level of farm inputs, such as seeds and fertilizer, through the level of distribution and marketing of processed food products, such as frozen pizzas and french fries. All commercial farms have been integrated to one degree or another into the agri-food system, as outlined in Figure 1. In some ways, agriculture as an industry has very little to do with farming anymore. Within the agri-food system, farm enterprises are simply providing raw materials to the processing industry, which in turn markets a finished food product. The industrial inputs to farming — machinery, fertilizer, and chemicals — are also purchased from agribusiness corporations. The large national banks provide the credit which makes modern farming possible and ensures a healthy profit for the banks from the loans taken out by farm families.

Nowhere has this system of vertical integration been more thoroughly pursued than in the case of potato production in New Brunswick's Upper

*Figure One: Agribusiness*

| Industrial Inputs | Industrial Raw Materials | Finished Products |

St. John River Valley (see Figure 2). McCain Foods Limited controls production from the input level to the distribution level, and has built a multinational vertically integrated empire. The newspaper headlines repeatedly express McCain's "strategy for success" — takeovers, accumulation, and profit (Branch, 1983; Bruce, 1973; Bueckert, 1977; Dearborn, 1981; Nielson, 1979; Surette, 1977; Watkins, 1982). By the late 1980s, McCain's expanded from one french fry plant in Florenceville, N.B. in 1957 to operations in 20 countries on three continents (Godfrey, 1990). They are promoted by the state and the business media as local business "heroes" (Godfrey, 1990; Watkins, 1982). But what is not talked about is how farmers and their families have paid the price for McCain's success (MacFarlane, 1987; McLaren, 1977; McLaughlin, 1987; Senopi Consultants, 1980; Stewart, 1974).

Since everything in agriculture is controlled by vertically integrated agribusiness corporations interested in profits, not food, their goal is to produce a marketable food product for the consumer at the highest profit to themselves. In real terms, this has meant that farmers regularly pay more for their inputs from agribusiness than they recover from their sales to agribusiness. In other words, the costs of farming are usually greater than the income from farming. This phenomenon, known as the cost-price squeeze, has been suggested by many as the reason why family farms are disappearing[4] (MacFarlane, 1987; McLaren, 1977; McLaughlin, 1990; Koski, 1982; Pugh, 1989; Senopi Consultants, 1980; Stewart, 1974).

The state has not been an idle bystander to the phenonenon of the shrinking farm community. Indeed, its policies and practices have rein-

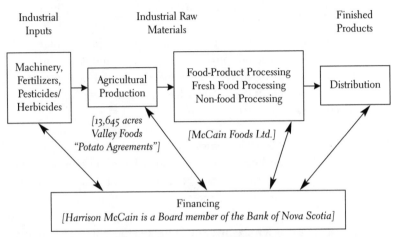

Figure Two: Agribusiness and McCain's:
Controlling Potato Production in the Upper St. John River Valley

Potatoes are grown on McCain land (Valley Farms Ltd) enriched by McCain fertilizer (McCain Fertilizers Ltd) using McCain seed (Foreston Seed Co. Ltd). Harvesting is done with McCain machinery (Thomas equipment Ltd) and the harvested potatoes are either stored in McCain facilities (Careleton Cold Storage Co. Ltd), send to McCain's plant for processing (McCain Foods Ltd) or sold fresh. In the latter case, the potatoes are handled by McCain shippers (McCain Produce Co. Ltd) which use McCain trucks (Day of Ross Ltd) to move them to McCain storage facilities (Bayside Potatoport Ltd) at the point of shipping. The processed potatoes can similarly be moved in McCain trucks (M&D Transfer Ltd) for shipment abroad where one of McCain's sales distribution systems (McCain International Ltd) handles the marketing. [Senopi Consultants, 1980:34-5]

forced the cost-price squeeze. The state has been an active party to the process of concentration of ownership and reduction in the number of farming families, while trying to pretend that it has worked in favour of the preservation of the "family farm." It has deliberately manipulated the notion of the "family farm," which most people think of as a family farming together in order to make a livelihood for themselves. The state has actively sought to confuse people about its intention to promote the accumulation of capital at the expense of traditional family farms by changing the meaning of the term to represent a family-owned business focused on the production of cheap inputs to food processors for the corporations' greatest possible profit. The state's agenda to muddy the waters has occasionally been made explicit, as in this statement from the New Brunswick Department of Agriculture:

> Alarmist stories about the impending disappearance of the family farm, vertical integration, and the take-over of the farming business by large corporations have little foundation in New Brunswick. It appears the family farm is likely to remain the basic form of production unit. *The concept and philosophy of the family farm is to be preserved, but its connotation must be altered* [emphasis added]. To preface a program by the title "family farm" does not define the issue at hand. (New Brunswick, 1974)

However, the McCains do not want to take over the bulk of farm production themselves on huge corporate farms where hourly workers and salaried managers do the work on corporate-owned land. While such plans were once on the agribusiness agenda, they proved quite unprofitable in the northern part of North America (ARS, 1974-1977). First, corporate farming would involve a huge investment in land in a climate where field crops grow for only a few months a year. And second, no hired workforce will work as doggedly for as little as the farm family which thinks it is farming for itself: "Agribusiness corporations have indirectly admitted that they cannot pay anyone to work for them as cheaply as a farmer, his wife and children would work for a family farm" (Carey, as quoted in Smith, 1979). As we shall see, the issue at hand for the state and capital is how to build family-owned capitalist farming businesses to meet the needs of the agrifood system. Such a policy has meant insecurity, misery, and bankruptcy for many family farms.

The common agenda of the state and capital has been to promote the accumulation of capital in processing industries and to a lesser extent in what McLaughlin (1990)[5] calls *corporate family farms*. With the adoption in the mid 1960s of the mechanical harvester instead of hand pickers to harvest the potato crop, it was at last possible for farms to expand and capitalize at an accelerated rate in order to "get big" and try to bring down the costs of potato production. By modernizing and expanding, Farm A could more vigorously compete with Farm B, and as a result, the differentiation between family-owned potato operations became more acute.

The state, through the Department of Agriculture, encouraged and supported this differentiation. They wanted "efficient, mechanized, family farm businesses" instead of "inefficient, non-mechanized, family welfare operations" (New Brunswick, 1977). The state's ideal was to have a smaller number of larger, "better managed" capitalist farm businesses to supply raw materials to the processing industry (see n.5). The traditional family farm was seen as resembling a family-run corner store: it was inefficient and obsolete compared to the modern supermarket or the large, heavily mechanized corporate family farm. Consequently, traditional family-farm operations which sustained a modest but secure way of life for the farm family would disappear, as they produced poor economies of scale and were inefficient "welfare" operations (New Brunswick, 1962:170-71).

The state's declared goal was for family farms to provide an "urban" standard of living and a prosperous business climate for the few farms that would remain. To do this, farms had to provide a "reasonable return on investment," which could only be accomplished by changing the philosophy of farming from a "way of life" to a profit-oriented business venture. Driving small, traditional farms out of farming became the thinly veiled goal of government policy (see New Brunswick, 1974, 1977, 1987, 1988).

As the state pursued this goal, "successful" farms were no longer to be those that provided a secure way of life for the farm families, but rather growing, "successful" businesses operating within the agri-food system, merely one link in a much larger socioeconomic system whose goal is to produce not food but profits. To work effectively within and contribute to this overall system, "family farm" operations needed to be 'efficient' production units. This vision of farming is clearly advanced in the following statement from the New Brunswick Department of Agriculture's Planning and Development Branch in 1977:

> It is urgently necessary to provide an economic climate in which farmers can expand their operations and, in which producers can develop the skills and command of resources to join the cadre of large scale and efficient producers. The thrust of the policies of the Department of Agriculture, particularly in meeting market needs must be with aiding the commercial farmer and the efficient producer, and in adding to the numbers of such operators. The future of agriculture must be oriented towards rationally managed, profit-oriented businesses. Farm mergers and consolidation of holdings result in larger farm-units not only for increased production efficiency, but also to structure units that are large enough to afford better management. As the size of units increase, the financial requirements increase in complexity, and the ease of entry into commercial farming is cut drastically.

> Furthermore, as agriculture is encouraged to rationalize its management processes and organizational structure, a more clear separation of welfare and commercial farm policy and programs will emerge. (New Brunswick, 1977:14)

In the eyes of state policy, only the corporate family farm was an economically viable form of production. Maintaining the small, commercial family farm was "in direct conflict with the goals of the agricultural sector" (ARS, Task Force #5,1977:9), since they did not fill a large enough percentage of the agri-food system's needs — producing raw materials and consuming farm inputs. Driving small, traditional family operations out of business was easily accomplished given the enormous pressures created by the cost-price squeeze on farms. The larger, more capitalized and specialized the farm operation is, the more locked into the agri-food system the operation becomes.

Once farm operations are specialized in potatoes it is virtually impossible to move in and out of production. They are trapped because, with the exception of the tractors and equipment for soil preparation, cultivation and spraying, everything else in a highly capitalized operation is geared specifically to potato production. As Ouellette argues, "the capital and operating costs of such machinery must, therefore, be allocated exclusively to this crop" (Oullette, 1971:100). The very costs of buying and operating machinery force farmers to further increase their level of production and debt. According to Murphy, to economically justify a harvester and the other equipment it entails, farms "must plant at least 70 acres of potatoes" (1982:127).

In contrast, a potato farmer was historically part of mixed farming, using his own manure to fertilize his fields, and his own labour to prepare soil for planting with his own seed potatoes. Today's large-scale, mono-crop potato farmer needs chemical fertilizers, lime, and a host of machines to cultivate his fields for the potato seed he purchases. To buy the inputs to plant the crop, it is often necessary to obtain an operating loan from the bank, or the state, or to buy it on credit from fertilizer or seed companies. Today, even before the crop is in the ground, the farm enterprise is in debt (McLaren, 1977; Murphy, 1982; Senopi Consultants, 1980; Stewart, 1974). The cost-price squeeze and debt create a permanent state of financial crisis and insecurity for the farm family, even the "successful farms":

Debt and the cost-price squeeze frequently result in the farm enterprise not being able to financially support itself. The labour of neither the farmer nor the farmer's wife, partner or children is garnering enough money to flourish. In short, the farm enterprise is not making enough money to support itself and the farm household. As a result, the farm family is often facing some sort of financial crisis and/or bankruptcy. (Pugh, 1991:32)

The farming crisis in the early 1980s was a consequence of banks foreclosing on farm loans and refusing to provide farms with operating capital. Many farms disappeared, yet farm debt continued to rise:

Farm debt rose dramatically from $4.4 billion in 1970 to $18.134 billion in 1981 and $22.13 billion in 1985, largely as a result of record high interest rates. In 1990, the level of farm debt stands at $21.2 billion, even after millions of dollars have been unofficially written off by creditors through farm foreclosures. The overall debt is now borne by far fewer farm operators, making the average farm debt load higher now than in 1985. (Pugh, 1991:32)

The agri-food system is so efficient at driving farmers out of business that it presents a problem for the agribusiness corporations and the state. They do not want to put all farmers out of business. If they did, the corporations would have to do all the farming themselves, which would be much more costly than the current arrangement of buying the raw product from the farmer. For example, the McCains are very explicit about their dependence on potato farms:

The farmers are not going broke, and we don't want them to go broke. If they go broke, McCain goes broke and vice versa. (a McCain's spokesperson as quoted in Branch, 1983:11)

According to the McCains, the real reason farm families are struggling to make a living is not the cost-price squeeze that results from vertical integration, but business inefficiency:

> It is unadulterated rubbish to suggest that farmers have their
> backs to the wall. They are comfortable, not rich. With a per-
> ishable product, you can not avoid price peaks and valleys....
> In my opinion, the only long-run solution to better returns to
> the grower is for them to do a better job; to produce better
> quality and reduce their costs. That is a much better solution
> in my mind than for them to rely on a marketing board and
> artificially rigged prices. (a McCain's spokesperson as quoted
> in Bueckert, 1977:12)

This "better management" philosophy is espoused by both agribusiness
and the state as the key for successful farming (New Brunswick, 1974). The
gospel of mechanization, efficiency, and better management has been vigorously promoted by the agricultural schools, which are primarily funded
by the state and agricultural industries. Students were and are still encouraged to go home and bring their "backward" farms into the present century by mechanizing, specializing production, and using volumes of
chemical and toxic inputs to increase yields per acre (Advisory Committee
on Potatoes, 1990b). They are schooled to believe that this formula and
good management will produce a booming business. The attraction, of
course, is the promise of boom. What everybody always leaves out are the
far more frequent occasions of bust.

In fact, most farms that attempted to engage in the capital accumulation cycle went bust. They expanded production, bought machinery, and
extended their credit, but were unable to receive enough revenue from
farm sales to pay their costs of production. A relative few — the surviving
corporate family farms — were more successful and continue to operate
within the cycle of investment/production/profit/expansion, and sustain
the elusive promise of "success." Still others, much to the Department of
Agriculture's dismay, continue to survive by avoiding the capital accumulation cycle as much as possible. These latter farms, the state-maligned
"welfare farms," have avoided loans for bigger and newer harvesters, bulk
bodies and trucks, and larger tractors by continuing to harvest with older
harvesters, or pickers, baskets, and barrels.

But, every year, it gets harder to maintain the latter survival strategy. As
old machinery has to be replaced with new, as the regional schools push
to eliminate the "potato break"[6] in favour of urban timetables, and as the
price for potatoes does not improve, commercial family farms are pushed
toward bankruptcy by the same cost-price squeeze that their rivals, the cor-

porate family farms, face. Some family farms, partly encouraged by finance programs and endless state pressure, conform to state policy and become corporate family farms. Others band together, expanding production and sharing the cost of machinery to operate as much like corporate family farms as they can without relying on wage labour, and spread the labour demands and risks across household enterprises. Still other family farms stubbornly refuse to "get big and go bust" like their neighbours.

## Farm Women's Work and the Political Economy of Agriculture: A New Brunswick Example

My study of women's work on potato farms in northwest New Brunswick, in the so-called "potato belt" of the province, indicated that two distinct patterns of commercial family-owned farms exist. One is the relatively traditional low-mechanized family farm. Women on these farms are struggling to maintain a way of life against enormous pressures tending to drive them into bankruptcy and out of farming. Women on the far less numerous but larger and highly mechanized "corporate family" farms are working to expand their farm operations into a more efficient business enterprise. In interviews, many women explicitly said that "the farm comes first." Household tasks were always secondary to on-farm work, and only off-farm work took precedence over the demands of the farm enterprise. As Cebotarev, *et al.* have noted, "The majority of farm women are not engaged in off-farm work for self-actualization or other social purposes, but out of concerns for the well-being of the family and survival of the farm." (1986:14). What farm women do and how their work is organized depend on the type of farm operation in which they are involved.

### LOW-MECHANIZED FARMS

Farm women on today's low-mechanized potato farms are heavily involved in the potato production process to sustain the farm enterprise. Others work full-time, off the farm, in order for the family not to draw an income from the farm enterprise. However, it is the exception for women in low-mechanized farms to take the latter option; instead, most intensify their work efforts on the farm.

In many ways, low-mechanized potato farms are similar to commercial farms of the 1950s and early 1960s. Their scale of production has increased because they have tractors, plows, disc harrows, sprayers, and trucks but they continue to rely on hand-pickers using baskets and barrels to harvest the crop. In so doing they keep their debt load low compared to highly mechanized operations, and they minimize environmental damage. Low-mechanized operations are deliberately avoiding expansion and minimizing debt in order to avoid being crushed by the cost-price squeeze. Women on such farms would say, "we try to pay as we go." For example, Belinda said, "you may not always have what you want, but you know it's yours and not the bank's."

Women on low-mechanized farms not only work regularly in the potato production process, but, lacking off-farm wages, they make their own bread, have larger vegetable gardens than women on high-mechanized farms, pick fiddleheads because "they are free," keep chickens and sell eggs, knit and sew the family's clothing, and can and freeze products that urban people and women on high-mechanized farms buy. Women's contributions to the farm enterprise include going for replacement machinery parts, cutting potato into seed, helping with the harvest by picking potatoes, and doing the farm book-keeping. Amanda recounted:

> As a rule I drive a truck or tractor all day. I go for the pickers, haul potatoes, get parts. My days are quite disrupted. There's no real schedule except getting meals.

Women who do not have paid employment continue to have huge vegetable gardens, growing and processing their family's foodstuffs. Cindy said:

> I have a garden, go pick berries and prepare enough frozen vegetables, pickles and jams for the winter — at least 400 quarts or more a summer. I pick fiddleheads too, in the spring, it's free so why not take advantage of it? Last year I didn't grow a garden (due to an injury) and found a big increase in household costs. I don't really want to do this stuff, but I just do it. Really I think a farmer's wife has three times as much work to do [as urban women].

Meanwhile, Cathy admitted:

> Since I went back to work I do less gardening and stuff. For one thing I couldn't afford to buy foodstuffs before. Now I

don't have to bargain for a monthly allowance, so I can spend
my money as I please.

Bertha keeps 199 hens because if she has 200 she needs an egg quota.
She sells eggs to four stores and people constantly drop in to buy them,
which means she always has to be able to come to the door or risk losing
a sale. This money is used for household things and not the farm:

> I use the egg money for household living, to get groceries, for
> everyday expenses, pocket money, the telephone bill or a pair
> of shoes, whatever's needed. It's my money, it does not go into
> the farm.

All the women reported that they knit, and Cindy and Belinda sew and
make all their family's clothes. Cindy (who is on a medium-mechanized
farm) makes and sells crafts at local craft markets to generate "extra" cash
to use for household expenses. This work is more flexible than paid
employment would be, so she can do whatever work needs to be done on
the farm and avoid the problem of trying to find a baby-sitter, which she
would need if she worked off the farm.

If women are intensifying their on-farm work, the tendency is for the
household and enterprise to operate from one bank account. When
women have their own income, a distinction is drawn between family
expenses and the farm enterprise, just as in high-mechanized operations.
Since the farm does not have to provide a living for the family, it can continue to operate without making a decent return to labour. Cathy said:

> The last thing on the priority list is home. When money goes
> into the house instead of the farm there are a lot of guilty feel-
> ings. We can't afford brand name clothes so our kids wear
> hand me downs.

In other words, the farm household is working very hard for very little to
provide cheap industrial raw materials to food processors.

HIGH-MECHANIZED FARMS

As farms mechanize and increase in size, women's work changes. A
distinct difference between women's work on high-mechanized and low-

mechanized operations is the management role that high-mechanized farm women have assumed. Whereas, before the mechanical potato harvester was widely used, women were cooking for picking crews and counting tags, they are now driving the harvester or managing harvester crews of (four to eight people). They constantly answer the telephone and spend at least half a day per week doing finances and payroll.

This change is not surprising given the direction that state policy took in the 1970s. The state believed farm women could play an important role in the modernization process of family-farm operations. In *Agricultural Training for Farm Wives*, a document prepared by the Planning and Development Branch of the New Brunswick Department of Agriculture and Rural Development (October, 1972), the government's goal of having farm wives act as farm managers is made clear:

> It is obvious that New Brunswick farm firms need all the good management help they can get and wives offer a potential solution. Most farm wives are an untapped management resource ... Farm wives are capable of learning, and with the introduction of modern labour saving devices in the farm home and the changing role of women in society, they are becoming more and more available for training opportunities. We should not let this opportunity to improve the management team on New Brunswick farms go unexploited.

Clearly farm women on today's corporate family farms have felt this pressure, since so many of them are playing an active role in farm management and commodity production.

Cindy's on-farm commodity production in growing potatoes is typical of the women on high-mechanized farms, even though they have a medium-mechanized operation:

> I help cut, plant and grade the seed and supervise other workers. I used to work on the harvester but now I go for parts if things break down. We have found that things are smoother if I am in the house to answer the phone or I am able to run the errands.

Carla referred to herself as the "Girl Friday" while Belinda said she was the "Errand Lady." Belinda admitted she always gets the driver's job, and has even had to drive the harvester, which she said was "hard on the head — I had no instructions and I wasn't sure what I was doing but I had to do it because there was nobody else to do it." Andrea knows how all the machinery works but will not run it. She told me,

> I could demonstrate any machine but not run it. I will work on the potato seed cutter and I have worked on the harvester with the crew. I used to drive the truck sometimes or the tractor when we were picking rocks, but I haven't driven a machine for working. I do these things when I have to, not because I want to — I basically help out when necessary.

In short, these work activities of farm women which directly contribute to the commodity production are not their preferred work. They do this work because it is necessary for the success of the farm operation. If they do not make themselves available to pinch-hit, run errands, and cut costs, the farm enterprise will be less profitable. Consequently, women on high-mechanized farm operations continue to grow and process food. It is one way they can subsidize the household enterprise without taking surplus from either their businesses or the farm business. As Carla noted, having a large garden and freezing vegetables "takes quite a bit off the grocery bill." Finances and book-keeping are very complicated on high-mechanized farms, so women report spending as much as half a day per week doing payroll, organizing accounts, paying bills, and balancing accounts and preparing deposits. Women on high-mechanized farms not only seem to like this "business work" more than women on low-mechanized farms, but they also take on responsibilities to keep abreast of government programs for which their farm may be eligible.

While low-mechanized farms are generally operating with one bank account or the philosophy that the household enterprise is combined, women in high-mechanized operations draw a clear distinction. They refer to the household as separate and distinct from the farm "business" enterprise. They take salaries for their on-farm work in potato production and for book-keeping and tend to see the household as their prime responsibility. The gendered division of labour becomes more pronounced as women on high-mechanized farms take full responsibility for housework. Andrea said, "my husband is running the business, he doesn't have time for housework," and Cindy said, "I probably help him more than he helps me."

Women on high-mechanized farms spend a lot of their time in commodity production or running their own businesses. Andrea's, Annette's, and Carla's farms had the biggest potato acreage amongst my interviewees, and they all ran their own businesses. Carla's business is farm related but the other two are not. They all run their businesses out of their own home so they can "run errands, go for parts or do whatever needs to be done," as Carla said. Their businesses provide them with their own income independent of the farm; at the same time, it gives them the flexibility to help on the farm on those occasions when they are needed to pinch hit.

The finances on high-mechanized operations are more complicated than those on low-mechanized operations since most of the former have taken substantial loans to expand and operate. Large loans and high interest rates create a huge amount of financial stress. The cash income typical of women on high-mechanized farms allows them the option to buy foodstuffs that low-mechanized farm women are supplying to the household. Their off-farm income gives them greater independence from the ups and downs of the farm enterprise, is used to maintain and improve the family household, and provides a reserve for meeting urgent household and farm enterprise requirements. Thus women on high-mechanized operations, like those on low-mechanized farms, are subsidizing the farm enterprise. Their off-farm work enables family farms to expand or survive during high interest rates and the everpresent cost-price squeeze without giving a reasonable return on labour to the family household.

The distinction between these farm types and women's work is indicative of whether or not they are farming for a living or pursuing a profit in order to accumulate capital. The first is a goal typical of the classic petit-bourgeois farm, whereas the second is characteristic of ambitions to emulate corporate farming. Low-mechanized household enterprises represent real resistance to state policy promoting "get big or get out."

## Conclusion

As we have seen, one must consider three dimensions to farm women's economic exploitation:

1. Inequities in family law;
2. Inequities in how the law, regulation, and policy circumscribe the role of wives as "partners" with their husbands in the family farm; and

3. Inequities in the organization of the whole agribusiness sector, i.e., in the organization of the agri-food (agribusiness) sector, supported by the legal and policy framework [of the state] which promotes capitalist development.

Before 1981 in New Brunswick, marriage laws and customs meant that farm wives were not the direct beneficiaries of their labour. The courts, legal documents, and banks considered men the heads of the household and sole owners of family property. Regardless of how many hours farm women worked or whether they worked in the barn, on the fields or in the vegetable garden as much or more than their husbands, upon the death of their spouse, separation or divorce farm women were at best only entitled to one-third of the family property (Smith, 1973). Since farm women were never awarded an equal share in farm and household property upon dissolution of their marriages, regardless of their work contributions, husbands were direct beneficiaries of their wives' labour. While changes in matrimonial property laws have benefitted farm wives, their situation has not substantially improved.

In spite of moves toward more formal legal equality with their husbands, farm women are still working long hours, essentially as volunteers in the family farm enterprise. Changes in family property laws did not address the day-to-day inequities that farm women face compared to other workers. These inequities must be understood in terms of the particular organization and troubled state of contemporary farming and the work burdens that the agri-food system and the state, through its support of corporate agriculture, impose on farm families, particularly farm wives. Farm wives' arduous work load, economic insecurity, and lack of reward are just as much the outcomes of the organization of farming as they are of the inequitable and inegalitarian marriage contracts.

Farm women's labour has been instrumental in enabling farm enterprises to survive, since without it the enterprise does not make enough income to match its real costs. The cost-price squeeze has meant that farm women are not really working for themselves or their families but for the bank and large corporations. Farm women's work enables agribusiness profits to be as large as they are.

Clearly the situation of farm women needs to be understood within the wider context of agribusiness and state policy of which they are a part. Farm women have been and are responding to the needs of the farm enterprise. State policy and popular mythology leads them to believe they are all in the same boat, but they are not. Researchers need to recognize the differences between farm women and urban women and amongst farm women themselves to fully appreciate farm women's contributions to the household enterprise and agriculture. Only then will the source of farm women's exploitation be addressed and more fundamental and long lasting changes assured.

To further our understanding of farm women's work, we will have to develop a theoretical approach that accounts for the real social relations of production within farm enterprises. It is ridiculous to ascribe farm men's labour as productive when women's labour is classified as "unproductive," "invisible," "indirect," and merely reproductive. Farm women do much more than simply raise children, clean the house, and cook meals. They are participating in commodity production, the production and processing of foodstuffs, and managing and financing the household enterprise. If the concept of productive work cannot include these activities, it must be rethought. We will never successfully understand why farm women do what they do until we adjust our theoretical suppositions. We need a new language and new ideas which appreciate the real, productive character of farm women's work.

Research on improving the lives of farm women has pursued an urban liberal agenda. Liberal notions of equality and opportunity assume that rural women should want to emulate their urban counterparts and seek "liberation" from the restrictive life on-farm. Researchers in this genre have emphasized the need for childcare in rural areas, equating improving women's status and equality with increasing off-farm employment. To improve farm women's lives, perhaps a more valuable goal would be for research on farm women to make clear the need to pressure consumers and the government to promote fairer prices at the farm gate and in the supermarkets, in order to truly reflect the real costs of food production. Farm women are not working a triple day because they want to; they are doing it because it is the only way their household enterprises can survive. When women's work, not to mention children's, is considered, the gap between production costs and the prices paid by processors and distributors becomes even more odious. At the moment, the real beneficiaries of farm women's labour are not the women themselves or farm families but the banks, supermarkets, and food processors. There is no free lunch: Canada's farm women and their household enterprises are footing the bill.

# Notes

1. Shortall (1993) argues that farm women do a quadruple day when one considers community and volunteer work. This would, of course, mean that urban women are engaged in a triple day rather than the double day so frequently attributed to them, since they too are engaged in such work.

2. The research in this paper was conducted as part of my MA thesis (Machum, 1992). In the summer of 1990, I interviewed twelve women who were or had been involved in farms growing potatoes, and three key informants. The women interviewed fell into three time periods: those who began farming before McCain Foods Limited started their french fry operation in 1959; those who began farming during the transition years (i.e., between 1960 and 1975), and those who began farming after 1975. This was necessary in order to study the impact of the changing agricultural industry on farm women and their work.

3. For purposes of confidentiality, the names used here are pseudonyms and not the respondents' real names. Women who fall into the first time period (see note 2) have names beginning with the letter A; those in the second have been given names beginning with the letter B, while those falling into the last time period have been given names starting with letter C.

4. According to Murphy (1982) the major exodus from farming in New Brunswick occurred between 1951 and 1961, when the farm population shrank from 29.1 to 10.6 per cent of the population and 14,645 farms disappeared. In Carleton, Victoria, and Madawaska counties where potatoes are principally grown today, the number of farms fell from 4,735 in 1951 to 875 in 1991 (from a phone interview with Statistics Canada).

5. My research has utilized the typology of farm types identified by McLaughlin (1990), since his analysis stems from a study of the New Brunswick community my research work examines. Unlike other models, his conception acknowledges the household as part of the farm enterprise unit and adopts clear and concise language for placing the family within the changing relations of farming. He identifies four types of farms with varying forms of production: the hobby/subsistence farm, the family farm, the corporate family farm, and the corporate farm. The first two types involve independent commodity production while the last two engage in capitalist production.

Hobby/Subsistence farms are residual farms not engaged in commodity production for commercial sale. These farm units have no interest in or impact on the market. Most of these operations have at least one person engaged in off-farm labour as the farm does not provide them with a living.

Family farms are petit-bourgeois operations trying to maintain a "way of life" while keeping the assets they have built up over the years. They rely largely on family labour and are engaged in commercial commodity production.

Corporate family farms are small capitalist operations that are family owned and operated but dependent on wage labour. They represent small capitalist enterprise in farming and think of themselves as businesses in farming. They are engaged in the effort to expand their operations to create a self-sustaining cycle of capital accumulation. This group is the most important group for policy makers, and tends to be the most influential in "mainstream" farm organizations (like Federations of Agriculture) and in state policy formation.

Corporate farms are corporate owned and operated. Farmers are hired as managers and workers with wage relations like any other business. They do not participate in decision-making but execute company plans. Because corporate farms employ only wage labour, they are not part of the "family farm" sector. They are factories-in-the-field.

The difficulty with most farm typologies is that outside the instances where family members are paid a wage, they ignore family member's (i.e., women's and children's) work contributions to each farm operation. The farm enterprise is treated as one unit which presumes that political, social, and economic issues are equal for each participant. Consequently, using farm enterprises and wage labour as the basis for discussion leads to a structural transformation argument which is blind to the internal work organization of the household and blind to gender issues. The omission of women's contribution is particularly important in examining the commercial family farm and the corporate family farm, the focus of the case study at the heart of this paper. Since the hobby/subsistence farm unit does not derive its livelihood from agricultural production, the impact of structural changes in agriculture is deemed to be minimal for the survival and operation of family households. Consequently, farm enterprises organized as hobby/subsistence production units are not part of this study. Likewise, corporate farms do not engage family farm households in production and were therefore beyond the scope of my study.

6. Schools in the area have traditionally gone back in August in order to give students three weeks off at the end of September and beginning of October to participate in the potato harvest. As schools become consolidated on the regional level and ties with the farm community continue to decrease (in part because of the declining farm population) there is continuing pressure year after year for schools to eliminate the "potato break" and conform to a more urban timetable.

# References

Abel, H. (1975). "Adaptation of the rural family to change." In P. Wakil (ed.), *Marriage, family and society*. Scarborough: Butterworth and Company. 367-77.

Advisory Committee on Potatoes (1990a). *Atlantic Canada potato guide*. Fredericton: Atlantic Provinces Agricultural Services Co-ordinating Committee.

Advisory Committee on Potatoes (1990b). *Potato crop: variety, weed and pest control recommendations 1990 for the Atlantic Provinces*. Fredericton: Atlantic Provinces Agricultural Services Co-ordinating Committee.

Agricultural Resources Study (ARS). (1974-1977). Archival files pertaining to statistics, family farms, corporate farms, education programs and the proposed potato agency. Excerpts from *Hard Tomatoes, Hard Times*. Fredericton: New Brunswick Provincial Archives.

Atcheson, M.E., M. Eberts and B. Symes, with J. Stoddart, (1984 October). *Women and legal action: precedents, resources, and strategies for the future*. Ottawa: Canadian Advisory on the Status of Women.

Branch, S. (1983, January). "McCain Foods Limited: regional, national and now multinational." *The Atlantic Advocate* 8-13.

Brown, R.G. (1980, November). "Farm women: Alternatives are needed to preserve a way of life." *Briarpatch* 10-11.

Bruce, H. (1973, November). "Meet the McCains of New Brunswick." Great families of Canada: First of a series. *Maclean's* 95-103.

Bruners, D. (1985). "The influence of the women's liberation movement on the lives of Canadian farm women." *Resources for Feminist Research/ Documentation sur la Recherche Feministe* (RFR/DRF), 14 (3):18-19.

Bueckert, D. (1978). "The McCain Phenomenon." *Atlantic Advocate*. 22-26.

Busque, G. (1987). "The needs and resources of farm women." In Canadian Advisory Council on the Status of Women (ed.), *Growing strong: Women in agriculture*. Ottawa: CACSW. 13-47.

Canada (1993). *Farming Income Tax Guide*.

Canada (1981). *Canada's agri-food system: An overview*. Ottawa: Agriculture Canada.

Canada (1981, January). *Farm women and agriculture: An overview of issues* (first draft). Ottawa: Farm Women's Bureau, Policy Branch, Agriculture Canada.

Canada (1969). *Farming Income Tax Guide 1969.* Ottawa: Queen's Printer.

Canadian Advisory Council on the Status of Women, ed., (1987). *Growing strong: Women in agriculture.* Ottawa: CACSW.

Cebotarev, N., W.M. Blacklock, and L. McIssac (1986). "Farm women's work patterns." *Atlantis* 11 (2):1-22.

Ceboratev, N. and F. Shaver (1982). "Women in agriculture and rural societies." *RFR/DRF* II (1):1-2.

Clow, Michael (1987). "Understanding the assault on the environment: Agriculture and forestry as a case study." *Paper presented at the Canadian Sociology and Anthropology Association Annual Meeting.* Hamilton: McMaster University.

Dearborn, D. (1981, January 3). "McCain heats up the economy of the village." *Financial Post.*

Ghorayshi, P. (1989). "The indispensable nature of wives' work for the farm family enterprise." *Canadian Review of Sociology and Anthropology* 24 (4):571-95.

Godfrey, J. (1990). "The outstanding CEO of 1990 (Harrison McCain)." *The Financial Post Magazine* (special issue) 8-15.

Graff, L. (1982). "Industrialization of agriculture: implications for the position of farm women." RFR/DRF II (1):10-11.

Hale, S. (1990). *Controversies in Sociology: A Canadian Introduction.* Toronto: Copp Clark Pitman.

Koski, S. (1982). "The employment practices of farm women." Winnipeg: National Farmers Union.

MacFarlane, C. (1987, March). "Agri-business means goodbye to small New Brunswick farms." *Anti-Poverty News* 1 (2):4-5.

Machum, S. (1982). *The impact of the structural transformation of agriculture on women's work: on-the-farm, off-the-farm and in the household: A New Brunswick case study.* Unpublished MA thesis, Dalhousie University, Halifax.

MacInnes, D. and MacLaren, J. (1992, March). Inferences on women's networks as related to the women's role in the Antigonish Movement. Paper presented at the Annual Meeting of the Atlantic Sociology and Anthropology Association, Halifax, Nova Scotia.

Match. (1981, Summer). *Women and Agriculture: Resource Kit on Rural Women on Third World Countries and Canada.* Ottawa: International Centre.

McLaren, K. (1977, March). "Farmers, feds and fries: potato farming in the St. John Valley." *Round One* (7):1-8.

McLaughlin, Darrell. (1990). *A critical review of rural sociology in advanced industrial societies.* Unpublished BA thesis, St. Thomas University, Fredericton, New Brunswick.

McLaughlin, D. (1987). "From self-reliance to dependence: Agribusiness and the politics of potatoes in New Brunswick." In G. Burrill and I. McKay (eds.), *People, Power and Resources.* Fredericton: Acadiensis. 30-35.

McNair, D.K. (1980). *Taxation of Farmers and Fishermen.* Toronto: Richard de Boo. Ltd.

Murphy, Tom (1986, September). "From family farming to capitalist agriculture: Food production, agribusiness and the state." Paper presented at the Atlantic Canada Studies Workshop, Fredericton: University of New Brunswick.

New Brunswick (1989). *Agricultural Statistics: 1989.* Fredericton: Province of New Brunswick.

New Brunswick (1988, February). *Goals and Objectives for the New Brunswick Department of Agriculture.* Fredericton: Department of Agriculture.

New Brunswick (1987, June). PROFARM: *Programs to help New Brunswick agriculture grow.* Fredericton: New Brunswick Department of Agriculture.

New Brunswick (1985). *Agricultural Statistics: 1985*. Fredericton: Province of New Brunswick.

New Brunswick (1977, November). Report of the Agricultural Resources Study. Fredericton.

New Brunswick (1974, September 1). Family improvement program, evaluation 1974. Fredericton: Planning and Development Branch, New Brunswick Department of Agriculture and Rural Development.

New Brunswick (1972, October). *Agricultural training for farm wives*. Fredericton: Planning and Development Branch, New Brunswick Department of Agriculture and Rural Development.

New Brunswick (1962). *Report of the Royal Commission on the New Brunswick Potato Industry*. Fredericton: Printer of the Queen's Bench.

Nielson, R. (1979, December). "McCain's equals spud power." *Atlantic Insight* 56-61.

Ouellette, G. (1971). "The New Brunswick potato industry: An analysis." Fredericton, New Brunswick Department of Agriculture.

Pugh, T. (1992, January/February). "Index on farming." *Canadian Forum* LXX (806):32.

Pugh, T. (1991, December). "Index on farming." *Canadian Forum* LXX (805):32.

Pugh, T. (1989, April). "Agriculture and the corporate agenda." *Briarpatch* 18 (3):7-11.

Reimer, B. (1986). "Women as farm labour." *Rural Sociology* 51 (2):143-55.

Senopi Consultants Ltd. (1980). *A report on the situation of New Brunswick potato farmers*. Winnipeg: The National Farmers Union.

Shaver, F. (1990). "Women, work, and transformations in agricultural production." *Canadian Review of Sociology and Anthropology* 27 (3):341-56.

Shortall, S. (1993). "Canadian and Irish farm women: Some similarities, differences and comments." *Canadian Review of Sociology and Anthropology* 30 (2):172-90.

Smith, D. (1979, September). *Women's inequality and the family*. Unpublished working paper. Toronto: OISE.

Smith, D. (1973). "Women, the family and corporate capitalism." In M. Stephenson (ed.), *Women in Canada*. Toronto: New Press.

Smith, P. (1987). "What lies within and behind the statistics?: Trying to measure women's contribution to Canadian agriculture." In Canadian Advisory Council on the Status of Women (ed.), *Growing Strong: Women in Agriculture*. Ottawa: CACSW. 130-95.

Stewart, W. (1974). "Old MacDonald had a farm; now it belongs to McCain's." In W. Stewart, *Hard to Swallow*. Toronto: MacMillan. 54-63.

Surette, R. (1977, February). "New Brunswick: Politics is McCain's business." *Last Post* 10-11.

Watkins, L. (1982, May/June). "A star in the business sky: After 25 years, McCain's is the world's largest french-fry maker." *Atlantic Business* 33-43.

Weitzman, L. (1981). *The Marriage Contract: A Guide to Living with Wives and Spouses*. New York: The Free Press.

Willick, L. (1982, May). "Labour and conditions of farm women often overlooked in agriculture equation." *Briarpatch* 22-23.

# 7

## Medico-legal Expertise and Industrial Disease Compensation: Discipline, Surveillance, and Disqualification in the Era of the "Social"[1]

### 'NOB' DORAN

Recent Canadian research in the sociology of law (Boyd, 1986; Brickey and Comack, 1986; Currie and Maclean, 1986; Caputo *et al.*, 1989; Comack and Brickey, 1991) has been primarily concerned with providing a critical, usually Marxist-informed perspective on law and the state so as to demonstrate its coercive character. Moreover, as much of this work has been concerned with criminal law (Maclean, 1986; Fleming, 1985; Comack, 1986; Hopkins, 1986; Mandel, 1986), this allows for the relatively straightforward assessment of law as a form of coercive social control.[2] However, such analyses have difficulties with the administrative law that grew spectacularly with the rise of the welfare state, as this legal form prioritized neither the general liberal emphasis on the rule of law (Dicey, 1885; Hayek, 1944, 1972; Raz, 1977), nor the Marxist emphasis on punitive social control.[3] As a result, administrative law has been somewhat neglected by both Marxist and liberal perspectives, as it fits uneasily within their conceptual frameworks.[4]

In contrast, this paper will examine one example of an administrative law system, workers' compensation, to demonstrate some problems with this critical sociology of law and to suggest an alternative means of explanation. In the first half of the paper, I discuss some theoretical difficulties the political economy approach has with fully comprehending the emergence and specificity of workers' compensation. By focussing on the historical displacement of the prior, purely legal system of employers' liability into the contemporary medico-legal system of no-fault compensation, and by outlining the resulting re-organization which moved the problem out of the law courts and into an administrative-scientific bureaucracy, I highlight the existing explanatory weaknesses regarding this change. I then go on to suggest how recent post-structuralist and feminist theorizing on law might be more usefully applied to analyse this particular transformation in the treatment of work-related disabilities.

In the second half, I briefly illustrate some of the constitutive elements of this modern displacement of law. By examining how one Canadian workers' compensation board handles industrial disease claims, I show not only how such claims are decided but also how disabled workers are disciplined, surveyed, and disqualified in the process. Furthermore, I suggest that organized labour (at least in Alberta), despite its apparent oppositional resistance to the compensation system, and despite its preferred theoretical status within the political economy tradition, also serves to help disqualify the embodied experience of disabled workers. Finally I suggest that any adequate analysis of this disqualification of workers' voices must also address the historical specificity of this rise of medico-legal expertise and its simultaneous transformation of a prior working-class cultural experience.

## Theoretical Issues and Legal Paradigms

Workers' compensation legislation was specifically introduced into the Anglo-American legal system to solve the tangled problems of dealing adequately with workplace injuries under the common law (Piva, 1975; Hanes, 1968; Guest, 1981; Risk, 1981). Throughout the nineteenth century, workers who suffered injury at the workplace had recourse to a number of possible, but usually inadequate, options. Many were enrolled in friendly societies and could receive payments based on their membership (Gosden, 1961, 1973). Others, less fortunate, might have to rely on the "parish" — that is, they could obtain relief under the Poor Law (Cunningham, 1817:21). A few might have been lucky enough to obtain some monetary compensation from their employer (Dodd, 1968 [1842]:119), while a very small minority attempted to use the courts of law (Bartrip and Burman, 1983).

Tucker's (1984a) analysis of employers' liability in Ontario between 1861 and 1900 provides a thorough overview of these difficulties of common law that workers faced in this period. Although an employer had formal responsibility for workers in his care,[5] judicial decisions through the course of the nineteenth century produced the "unholy trinity" of defences that were regularly used to ensure that employers were rarely found culpable of neglecting that responsibility. Thus workers were frequently judged to have "voluntarily assumed the risk" of their employment, or to have demonstrated "contributory negligence" with respect to their accident, or that their injury was caused by the negligence of a "fellow servant" rather than that of their employer (Tucker, 1984a:216-20; Bartrip and Burman, 1983:103-25; Ingman, 1978). Although these decisions could probably be easily formulated within an instrumental Marxist approach (Marx and Engels, 1967[1846]; Panitch, 1977; Miliband, 1969) which typically sees modern law as a relatively straightforward mechanism for capitalist domination, Tucker's analysis is much more subtle. Specifically, he analyses legislative reform and subsequent changes in judicial interpretation that occurred in the latter half of the nineteenth century. This statutory reform of the common law resulted in an 1886 statute in Canada (Tucker, 1984a:235), and an 1880 reform in England (Bartrip and Burman, 1983:149), both of which led to more favourable judicial decisions for workers seeking legal redress. As a result, Tucker argues that one should understand these legal changes as better exemplifying a structuralist Marxist (Poulantzas, 1973, 1978) rather than an instrumentalist Marxist approach. Obviously, these and similar reforms were not passed for the direct benefit of a capitalist class, and thus they exemplify the "relative autonomy" of the law and the state (Walters, 1982, 1983, 1985; Tucker, 1984b; Colwill, 1987) within a capitalist society.

Unfortunately, Tucker's analysis ends just before the introduction of workers' compensation legislation in Canada. Consequently, he does not see the paradigmatic shift (Kuhn, 1962; Foucault, 1970) in the legal response to workplace injuries which this heralded. That is, employers' liability legislation changed to workmen's compensation legislation.[6] Most researchers have not examined the significance of this change in terminology, and have concerned themselves with evaluating compensation legislation in terms of how it improved upon employers' liability legislation (Horovitz, 1944; Somers and Somers, 1954; Pritt, 1970; Kessler, 1941; Mallalieu, 1950; Piva, 1975; Chambliss, 1986; Reasons, Ross and Patterson, 1981; Bale, 1989). Little attention is paid to the qualitatively different legal machinery that was set up to replace the common-law system.

In Canada, this was more radically different than in the U.K. In fact, Canadian workers gave up their common-law rights in exchange for receiving compensation. Equally important, however, was the introduction of a "no-fault liability" principle. With the advent of compensation legislation, fault and culpability ceased to be issues. Lawyers were no longer needed. The state would now set up an administrative, bureaucratic, and medical system to replace the common-law machinery. No longer were decisions to be made by judges with lawyers at hand to represent injured workers; instead, commissioners were appointed to head the different provincial workers' compensation boards, and everyday decisions were put in the hands of skilled adjudicators. Further, as the adjudicative decision now concentrated on the issue of whether a disability was "arising out of and in the course of employment" (Bartrip, 1987:10), this allowed for the possibility of compensation for industrial diseases, if there were sufficient medical expertise to prove the case (Bartrip, 1987:26).

As this brief sketch suggests, workers' compensation embodies quite different principles of operation than employers' liability legislation. However, the critical analyses of workers' compensation (Chambliss, 1986; Reasons, Ross and Patterson, 1981; Bale, 1989; Berman, 1978; B. Smith, 1981; Colwill, 1987) have tended to ignore the specifics of these changes and have been content to analyse this bureaucracy from a perspective that typically sees compensation legislation in terms of the political struggle between capital and (organized) labour, or as part of the more general "legitimation" process of a "relatively autonomous" state for the purposes of long-term capital accumulation. As a result, both of these approaches reduce this institution to the playing out of class relations, without paying specific attention to the actual empirical details of contemporary workers' compensation. Furthermore, the accompanying rise to prominence of a medico-legal system of expertise (B. Smith, 1981; Bale, 1989), and of medicine more generally, is frequently commented on as ideological (Berliner, 1982; Elling, 1981; Figlio, 1978; Navarro, 1980), but rarely analysed in its own constitutive terms.

## Power/Knowledge and Modern Administrative Law

Foucault's work suggests a more promising means of analysing this specific displacement of common law into administrative law. His power/knowledge thesis not only provides a useful means of understanding the growth of administrative law, but also proposes a novel way of reconceptualizing the welfare state itself. Whereas Marxist understandings tend to reduce this phenomenon to the realm of the economic (Gough, 1979, Djao, 1983; Doyal, 1979; Moscovitch and Drover, 1987; O'Connor, 1973),[7] Foucault's work, and that of his students, insists on examining the constitutive elements of the "social" (Donzelot, 1979, 1980, 1988) as a topic of investigation in its own right. In particular, Foucault is interested in examining how modern power is expressly concerned with bodies. Unlike both the Marxist and liberal traditions which assume the body rather than analysing it, Foucault builds his theoretical work from a detailed understanding of the interaction between power and human bodies.

Specifically, Foucault understands the rise of the modern, therapeutic welfare state as marking a reversal in the traditional aims of the state. Whereas the original views of the state concerned themselves with obtaining and ensuring power for a "sovereign" or a "prince" (Foucault, 1980a, 1980b), this power was typically premised on the sovereign's ultimate right to take life. Although Marxist understandings of the modern state prioritize the state's economic role to different degrees (Jessop, 1980; Holloway and Picciotto, 1978; Fine, 1984; O'Connor, 1973), they generally agree on the state's typical role in the use of institutionalized violence against its citizens (Althusser, 1971; Poulantzas, 1978; Gramsci, 1971; Ratner, McMullan and Burtch, 1987).

In contrast, the welfare state is not so much premised on an ability to take life, but rather the will and desire to promote life. Increasingly, the state's traditional concern with allowing or disallowing life became residual. As Foucault asks rhetorically, "How could power exercise its highest prerogatives by putting people to death, when its main role was to ensure, sustain, and multiply life, to put this life in order?" (1980c:138). Foucault goes on to clarify the two poles of this new form of power, a power which fosters, rather than destroys, life. And it is here that he suggests the close connection between power and knowledge. *Biopower* identifies the state's concern with this power to foster life at the level of the social body, the level of population. In the eighteenth century, "one notes the emergence of demography, the evaluation of the relationship between resources and inhabitants, the constructing of tables analyzing wealth and its circulation: the work of Quesnay, Moheau and Sussmilch" (Foucault, 1980c:140). Thus, for Foucault, the emergence of demography, the economics of Quesnay, and the statistics of Sussmilch are all examples of these state sciences whose aim is to regulate and control the social body (Hewitt, 1983).

*Anatomo-politics* identifies the state's concern with the individual body rather than the social body, and is the other pole of this axis of power/knowledge. For Foucault, this is mainly concentrated upon issues of sexuality: "Between the state and the individual, sex became an issue, and a public issue no less, a whole web of discourses, special knowledges, analyses, and injunctions settled upon it" (1980c:26). Thus, medicine began to take over the management of sex in the nineteenth century, producing new "scientific" problems of sexuality (Frank, 1982; Arney and Bergen, 1984). For example, the act of sodomy becomes transformed into a "scientific identity"; that is, the "homosexual" is now created as a "pathology"; one who needs to be monitored, and regulated by the medical and other human sciences. Later, psychoanalysis emerges as the new "science of individual sexuality," and Donzelot's (1980) work shows in detail the interplay of the state and psychoanalysis in the control and regulation of "problem" families in the early twentieth century. By invoking these two axes of power over life, and insisting on the productive, not just repressive, nature of modern power, Foucault argues for the inseparability of modern power and modern scientific knowledge. It is not that a pre-existing power produces ideological knowledge, which can then be juxtaposed with the truth that a science, such as Marxism or psychoanalysis, can provide. Rather, Foucault's argument is that modern power produces regimes of truth in a constitutive fashion (Foucault, 1980a, 1980b). The two cannot be separated.

Furthermore, Foucault (1980c) suggests that his theory of power/knowledge demonstrates at least three major advancements over traditional liberal and Marxist views of law and the state. First, he argues that modern power may best be understood not in terms of "rights" but in terms of techniques. That is, the modern welfare state is not so much concerned with guaranteeing political or legal rights, but rather it uses certain techniques to promote its citizens' health and welfare. Thus techniques of insurance (Donzelot, 1988; Ewald, 1991), of rehabilitation (Garland, 1985b), of medicine (Armstrong, 1983), of tutelage (Donzelot, 1980), of scientific measurement (Rose, 1979; Garland, 1985a), of discipline (Garland, 1981), of bureaucracy (O'Neil; 1986) and so on, may all displace a traditional legal concern with individual or collective rights. For example, systems of national insurance, such as unemployment insurance in Canada (Finkel, 1977; Guest, 1981), or national health insurance in Britain (Gilbert, 1966; Fraser, 1973; Gregg, 1969) were both set up as measures through which the state could compulsorily (i.e., legally) force its citizens into contributing to their own well-being.

Second, modern power works by normalization rather than by law. Once again, Foucault is noticing the displacement of law and the creation of the "epistemologico-juridical" (1977:23) complex. In other words, the

modern century has been characterized by the inter-penetration of professional power and law, a combination that usurps the traditional legal
reliance on case and statute law alone and replaces it with a medico-legal
concern with normality and pathology. For example, juvenile delinquency
legislation was not so much concerned with punishing youths but rather
with finding "abnormal" children and families and rehabilitating them
(Meyer, 1982; Donzelot, 1980).

Third, modern power works not so much by punishing the population
but by controlling it. With the rise of the welfare state, the state took a
much more intrusive interest in its population, rather than merely seeking
to punish those who broke its criminal law (Burchell, 1979; Rose, 1979;
Garland, 1981). Even the criminal justice system, the pre-eminent state
institution concerned with "punishing," changed its philosophy from one
based largely on retribution to one organized around rehabilitation
(Foucault, 1977; Garland, 1985b; Wiener, 1987, 1990; Cohen, 1985).

However, Foucault did not only theorize contemporary understandings
of power and knowledge; he also paid specific attention to the particular
micro-techniques (1977:25) through which this power worked. In his seminal analysis of the emergence of the modern prison in the early nineteenth century, he identified two major techniques through which
"disciplinary power" worked. That is, he suggested that the discipline and
surveillance of bodies were constitutive elements of this modern power.
Through discipline, docile bodies (1977:138) were created which could be
made useful in a society whose economic structure was being re-organized
around the efficient use of labour. In addition, this power worked by a surveillance in which people were constantly watched. Foucault's notion of
panopticism elaborates this interplay of surveillance and discipline in the
modern prison. Not only were prisoners in their brightly-lit cells to be
watched by a guard in a central, darkened tower, but prisoners also monitored their own behaviour because they were never sure when they were
being watched. In addition, they were also subject to continuous discipline
that helped to "rehabilitate" them. In this sense, the panopticon was an
architectural masterpiece of modern power. Finally, its usefulness was not
confined to the prison but, rather, its principles have become extended to
other modern institutions such as hospitals, schools, and factories
(Foucault, 1977:228).

Nevertheless, Foucault's work has several problems that limit its direct
applicability. Most notably, although Foucault realized that his theory cannot be objective in any traditional sense of that word, he spent little time

clarifying the direction from which his own perspective emanated. That is, although Foucault adequately conceptualized the rise of disciplinary power, his work failed to acknowledge that the perspectival vision (Garland, 1990:152) he gave was from the viewpoint of the state itself, rather than from the perspective of those upon whom this power/knowledge was imposed. Recent feminist work, however, has attempted to improve upon Foucault's work by using a perspectival viewpoint originating from the embodied experience of those on whom this power/knowledge operates (Diamond and Quinby, 1988; Martin, 1982; Sawicki, 1986, 1991).

Carol Smart (1989), for example, has suggested that modern law needs to be understood in terms of its intimate relationship with the therapeutic professions. These "psy" professions (Donzelot, 1980) have established a regulatory control over the bodies of women and children in this century, because of their ability to speak the "truth" of these bodies and to disqualify the voices of those subordinated.[8] In other words, because women are outside these "official discourses" of truth, their experiential understandings are dismissed. Like Foucault's and other feminists' recent critique of scientific knowledge (Haraway, 1988; Harding, 1986a, 1986b; Jacobus, Keller and Shuttleworth, 1990; Keller, 1992), Smart is aware that traditional claims to scientific truth also involve a claim to power, and warns women to be cautious of embracing these discourses uncritically. Just as she is critical of nineteenth-century medicine's ability to enforce Draconian legislation against working class prostitutes because they were seen as carriers of "contagious diseases" (1989:94), she is also critical of the longstanding power of the psychoanalytic tradition to insist that "children lie and fantasize about sexual abuse" (1989:57) and is wary of more recent "scientific" developments that are now "pathologising the childless" couple (1989:110). In all cases, this "scientific" voice not only regulates and controls these bodies, but it also disqualifies the experience of those subjected to it. Thus, the great advancement of Smart's work over Foucault's is that although it too is perspectival in its nature, by beginning from the "subjugated knowledge" of women, she locates the experiential voice that is absent in Foucault (Hartsock, 1987, 1990a, 1990b). As Foucault's work has been widely criticized for leaving little room for human agency within its world of discourse (Smart, 1982; Hartsock, 1990b; Fine, 1984; Brown, 1987), Smart starts to redress that balance by introducing the subjugated voice of women, and how control over their own bodies is lost through this dependence upon the "psy" professions.

## Industrial Disease Compensation and Embodied Experience

The constitutive features of this displacement of law into medico-legal expertise can be easily demonstrated if we briefly examine workers' compensation practices regarding industrial diseases.[9] Specifically, workers' compensation boards (WCBs) display the Foucauldian notion of normalization and the related concerns with the discipline and surveillance of workers. For example, one primary mechanism by which this workers' compensation power/knowledge complex proliferates is the power of normalization: in this instance, the production of medico-scientific norms that are subsequently used to decide cases of industrial disease compensation. Unlike accidents at the workplace, the work-related nature of many diseases is seen to be difficult to prove for compensation purposes. Nevertheless, where such proof is available, compensation will be paid. Therefore, contemporary WCBs exhaustively use the expertise provided by medicine (X-rays, autopsies, etc.) and epidemiology (mortality statistics, morbidity tables, etc.) to help determine issues of workplace causation.

Epidemiological statistics, for example, have proved invaluable in the welfare-state era. Starting with the first mortality tables produced on workers in the nineteenth century (Neison, 1867; Ogle, 1885; Ratcliffe, 1850), these vital statistics were subsequently refined to show the correlations of mortality and morbidity with various demographic data, including occupations. Consequently, these norms of health and sickness are mundanely used by WCBs. For example, with respect to the diagnosis of respiratory diseases, WCBs often use such complex and involved tests as the following:

> (a) F.V.C. — (Forced Vital Capacity; (b) F.E.V. (1.0) — (Forced Expiratory Volume in one second; (c) D.L.C.O. (S.B.) — (Single Breath Diffusing Capacity for Carbon Monoxide); (d) Vo2 max. (Maximum Oxygen Uptake on Exercise [(Jones Protocol)]; (e) Arterial Blood Gas Pressures recorded at rest and exercise; (f) an E.C.G. (electrocardiogram) and a Haematocrit and/or Haemoglobin Determinations should always be part of the routine procedure. (WCB Alberta, 1983:7)

The use of such detailed and esoteric knowledge produces norms like the following:

> The normal or reference values for F.V.C. and F.E.V. (1.0) will be those proposed by the American Medical Association in their most recent edition of the Guides to the Evaluation of Permanent Impairment (Appendix #2) For the D.I.C.O. the criteria described in the report of the Disability Evaluation Committee of the American Thoracic Society (June 1982) will be used. For the maximal $Vo_2$, the normal value will be expressed as a percentage of predicted value, corrected for age and sex. (WCB Alberta, 1983:7)

These passages indicate how epidemiologically determined norms are intentionally put forward as a means of helping workers obtain compensation. In their specificity, they nicely illustrate the way in which workers' compensation is premised on a medico-legal expertise which decides cases based on this everyday usage of the "norm." Thus, workers will receive compensation for respiratory diseases like pneumoconiosis dependent upon whether they meet the appropriate scientific and legal criteria (Barth and Hunt, 1980), including disease requirements such as those listed above.

Yet this power/knowledge complex also displays the other aspects of discipline and surveillance which Foucault correctly identified as constitutive elements of this modern power. First, although these norms regarding industrial diseases are supposedly put forward in the workers' interests, they may still unintentionally operate to discipline workers attempting to obtain compensation. At the individual level, workers who do not fit the norm regarding exposure are subtly penalized. In essence, the norm acts to regulate the number of compensation claims allowed, such that individuals can now be evaluated and disciplined with regard to these norms, where distance from the norm is seen pejoratively. As a result, appeals must then be made to argue against this rule of the norm. In the case of one miner, his appeal resulted in the following decision:

> The independent specialists who examined you have certified to the Board that you are unfit for employment, but that the degree of disability attributable to your employment is not greater than that previously recognised by the Board. The previous assessment was that 20% of your disability was due to your employment.[10]

The onus then rests on those workers who dispute such findings to prove that they are "abnormal" in this regard, that they do have the illness despite what the statistical evidence suggests. As another miner, compensated for laryngeal cancer despite his distance from the norm, wrote,

> I write this letter to express my gratitude to the Manitoba Federation of Labour, the Alberta Federation of Labour, the Manitoba Workers' Advisor Program, the Occupational Health Centre of the Manitoba Federation of Labour, and other organizations and individuals for their help and solidarity during our 22 months of struggle for workers' compensation benefits.[11]

Second, these norms also lead to the surveillance of workers who are liable to come under the effects of this normalizing language.[12] Thus, occupational medical programs have been implemented to monitor the changing health of workers in "dangerous" occupations (Kaegi and Baynton, n.d.; Kaegi, 1978). The aim of such programs is to prevent miners, especially, from suffering the worst effects of the debilitating chest diseases that are so prevalent underground. Yet this is accomplished by the routinization of "medical surveillance."[13] So under the Alberta Fibrosis program,

> Alberta legislation requires any organization that employs people in jobs where they are exposed to silica, coal dust or asbestos fibres to provide their employees with: a two-part medical check up (chest x-ray and pulmonary function test) every two years, time off with pay for the check-ups. (Workers' health, safety and compensation, Alberta, n.d.)

But what is missed by this concern with the disciplining and surveillance aspects of the contemporary operation of this power/knowledge complex is the simultaneous disqualification of disabled workers' own experience of their bodies.[14] The following miner complains that his respiratory disease was originally diagnosed continually as bronchitis.

> the last year that I worked, I made seventy two hundred, but look at the shifts that I lost, you know, from my chest, I was half the time staying home. You come to see a doctor, uh,

> he'd say you've got a bad cold — bronchitis jeez, you had no,
> no help from nobody[15]

In the following comment, he complains that only 20% of his 100% disability from silicosis is seen by the board as being work-related:

> he said it's no use checking you up, he said because you're
> 100% disabled, he says we know that, you know, so there you
> were, you know, but it's not from the mine, only 20% from the
> mine. I've got every bloody thing here, I don't want to dig em
> up, but you can read all my records for some time, you know,
> yeah and he's got all the records too, so I was buggered[16]

Yet this miner's embodied experience told him that his silicosis was, in fact, caused by his workplace, rather than the smoking and pollution offered as the causally significant elements by the board:

> smoking, and pollution in the air, you know, so I fought that
> case, I went up, through every means we had, you know, and
> then I went to the ombudsman[17]

But comments such as the ones above are typically disqualified by the board, as they are not couched within the cultural frame of science. They do not rely on the expertise of medical science for their veracity, and thus they are generally ignored. Yet their veracity does not just lie in the subjective experience of disgruntled miners, but rather in the collective cultural experience of miners who have suffered these conditions. Usually this collective experience is tacit and unarticulated; however, in the following we see its explicit formulation:

> The docs keep telling me there's nothing wrong with the
> place where I work. I guess they're supposed to know it all
> because they've had a lot of education and everything. I'm no
> expert like they are, but I sure as hell know there's something
> wrong in that mill and the other guys are saying the same
> thing. One thing I know for sure — that place is killing us.
> (quoted in Navarro, 1986:141)

Just as important as the disqualification of these disabled workers is the contrasting situation with organized labour in Alberta. Not only is the voice of organized labour heard at the level of the state, but it is, in fact, closer to the discourse of state science rather than the embodied experience of these disabled workers.

Although recent Marxist theorizing has started to vehemently debate the theoretical status of the working class within the Marxist paradigm (Mouffe, 1983; Meiksins and Meiksins Wood, 1985; Palmer, 1990; Laclau and Mouffe, 1987; Baudrillard, 1983), actual empirical analyses of welfare-state institutions, beginning with Marx himself (1967), have generally tended to interpret the working class as an oppositional force to a capitalist class or a capitalist state, and have frequently analysed this working class as synonymous with organized labour and its political representatives (Gough, 1979; 1983; Swartz, 1977; Tucker, 1992; Navarro, 1978; Finkel, 1977). As a result, such analyses have been rather insensitive both to the embodied experiences of workers themselves[18] and to questions concerning the scientific discourse that organized labour has increasingly come to use today.

However, once we start examining this *frame* of organized labour's resistance rather than just its content, we see that it is acting more in line with the logic of modern state power/knowledge, rather than as an oppositional force. That is, when one examines the discourse of Alberta's organized labour since the introduction of worker's compensation legislation, one sees that it too came to speak this language of state science.[19] As early as 1927, a submission by the Mine Workers' Union of Canada to an Alberta special committee into workmen's compensation reflected this acceptance of medico-legal expertise, by requesting that

> the disease referred to as Miners (sic) Phthisis be changed to read (Anthracosis) it being declared by eminent Medical Authorities, that Miners Phthisis is not a recognised disease, but that Anthracosis is what it is intended to cover.

Fifty years later, however, organized labour was displaying a much greater familiarity with this scientific discourse of lung diseases. A submission by the United Mine Workers of America (UMWA) attempted to by-pass the usual reliance on epidemiological findings by suggesting an "automatic assumption" principle for older workers;[20] For workers with less than this requisite time in the mine, the UMWA proffered a sophisticated understanding of the methodological construction of the diagnosis of "coal workers' pneumoconiosis." It recommended

> that criteria be established for determining the presence of the disease ... establish medical criteria for all appropriate medical tests administered ... establish criteria for the techniques to be used to take chest roentgenograms (x-rays) ... establish ventilatory test criteria. (n.d.: 3-4)

The submission went on to formulate in detail how these tests should be operationalized:

> We recommend when applying roentgenograph criteria, that a subject of criteria are needed to define film quality and the means to obtain good films. The technique needed to provide a film to show the smaller nodules is very demanding. (n.d.:5)

Yet as a consequence of organized labour's acceptance of this discourse of epidemiology, a lay language of sickness based on the common cultural experience of disabled workers is largely ignored. At the level of official discourse in Alberta, organized labour displayed increasing scientific sophistication (Sentes, 1981), yet relegated this language to the margins. Although one could still find a few instances of the latter, as I did, they were typically outside the realm of official discourse.

## Conclusion: Going Beyond Disqualification?

In this paper I have attempted to illustrate how recent Marxist approaches to the study of law in Canada present significant problems in understanding the full specificity of workers' compensation. In contrast, Foucault's work on the rise of the "epistemologico-juridical complex" and its associated concerns with normalization, discipline, and surveillance seems to better explain the constitutive features of contemporary WCBs. Furthermore, by linking Foucault's work with recent insights emanating from contemporary feminism, I have suggested that this power/knowledge complex was also able to disqualify the voice of those workers who had actually experienced these workers' compensation practices regarding their industrial disease claims. Finally, I have suggested that the traditional voice of working-class resistance, organized labour, also spoke from within this contemporary power/knowledge complex and that as a result, the experiential understanding of disabled workers typically remained outside this official class-based resistance.

This last point, however, has received little attention so far in either Foucauldian or feminist literature. Despite Foucault's analytic advance-ment over Marxist analyses of law, and despite Smart's recognition of the accompanying disqualification of experiential voices resulting from this modern displacement of law by power/knowledge, neither of them had much to say about this apparent "codification" of the working class into this power/knowledge complex (Doran, 1987). That is, although Foucault's mature work (1977) was implicitly concerned with how power/knowledge was imposed on a working class in the nineteenth century, he said nothing about how that same class might eventually come to speak from within this power/knowledge complex. And although Smart's work was expressly con-cerned with the imposition of power/knowledge on embodied experience, the focus of her analysis was not the working class of the nineteenth cen-tury, but rather women in the late twentieth century.

Therefore, it seems that future research must seek to examine exactly what was occurring when power/knowledge was imposed on the working-class in the nineteenth century. In fact, the analysis suggested here points more in the direction of some type of historical incorporation and trans-formation of working class embodied experience rather than a simple dis-qualification. Whatever the final truth of this claim turns out to be, it seems necessary, at a minimum, that future analyses of administrative law must include both Foucault's awareness of power/knowledge and Smart's insistence on starting from embodied experience. It is to be hoped that the resulting "genealogy from below" will improve upon current explorations of the inter-penetration of class and power/knowledge (Levine, 1991; Ignatieff, 1978) by beginning that research from embodied experience and then reaching beyond to the historical structures that limit and constrain that experience.[21]

## Notes

1. Parts of this paper were originally presented at the Canadian Society of Sociology and Anthropology's annual meetings, Victoria, B.C., 1990, and this particular draft was completed in January 1994. Although this paper was originally intended as an examination into both the

origins and the contemporary practices of the Canadian workers' compensation system, recent mutations in the "social" (Donzelot [1984], Donzelet (ed.) [1991], Donzelot and Estebe [1994], Donzelot and Jaillet [1997]), combined with lengthy publication delays, suggest that it might be better understood today as a largely historical investigation.

2. See Chunn and Gavigan (1988) for a critical discussion of this viewpoint.

3. Recent Marxist work, however, has begun to formulate a grudging acknowledgment of the importance of this liberal notion of the rule of law. See Fine (1984) and Thompson (1975) for details.

4. However, administrative law now seems to be attracting some attention from sociological researchers in the field of law. See Caputo et al (1989:iv).

5. For an elaboration of this concept within the legal system in Britain, see Parliamentary Papers (1887).

6. Although a workmen's compensation act was passed in Ontario in 1886, the paradigmatic shift between employers' liability and workers' compensation legislation is usually recorded as being in 1914 with the passage of the Ontario legislation.

7. Of course, Marxism is not alone in this regard. Other perspectives also display their own typical styles of explanatory reductionism. For example, the Liberal approach stresses the political and its accompanying notion of "reform"; while the functionalist stresses a more abstract societal evolutionism. See Mishra (1977) for a general overview of these and other perspectives.

8. However, Smart is much more cautious than Foucault in accepting that there has been a total displacement of law by the power/knowledge complex. In her discussion of rape, she argues convincingly that traditional criminal law is quite capable of disqualifying women's voice, without the need for the intervention of the psy professions.

9. For a typical political economy approach to the problem of industrial disease, see Smith (1981). For an analysis that tries to incorporate some of Foucault's insights, but that concentrates on the historical construction of industrial disease, see Figlio (1982).

10. Alberta WCB letter to claimant, 21 June 1973, in the possession of the author.

11. Letter dated 25 October 1983, in the possession of the author.

12. This was perhaps most fully developed in Britain during this period. See Kaegi and Baynton (n.d.:V-20).

13. For specific discussion of the benefits of such "medical surveillance," see Kaegi and Baynton (n.d.), ch. V.

14. Although Leyton's (1978) work is exemplary in his close attention to the daily experiences of workers suffering from industrial disease, his analysis fails to explore the power relations that seem to underlie the "clash of cosmologies" which he, otherwise, so admirably describes.

15. Personal interview with claimant — Pete Youschuk.

16. Personal interview with claimant — Pete Youschuk.

17. Personal interview with claimant — Pete Youschuk.

18. One exception to this trend is the work of Walters (1982, 1983, 1985, 1988, 1991). Although her earlier work was greatly influenced by the structuralist Marxist framework and its emphasis on the role of organized labour, her more recent work has attempted to go beyond these limitations and to incorporate analyses of embodied health experiences.

19. Although the Alberta legislature has had a number of investigations into the problem of workers' compensation over the years (for example, 1948, 1955, 1965, 1969, 1976, 1980, 1984), the earlier ones are much clearer about the exact demands of organized labour with regard to compensation reforms.

20. This automatic assumption principle read as follows: "the problem of establishing 'causality' is much simplified by this provision in the legislation which adopts the automatic assumption principle. It provides for a presumption that pneumoconiosis was due to work in the mine when the miner works twenty or more years in the coal mining industry" (n.d.: 3).

21. Dorothy Smith's work in this area provides some useful methodological suggestions for beginning such research. Although not concerned with power/knowledge explicitly, throughout her career (1974a, 1974b, 1974c, 1978, 1981a, 1981b, 1987) she has attempted to begin from embodied experience but to link up with macro structures lying beyond that experience and largely textual in character.

# References

Alberta (1984). *Report of the Select Special Committee on the Workers' Compensation act and the occupational health and safety act.*

Alberta (1980). *Report of the Select Committee of the Legislative Assembly — Workers' Compensation.*

Alberta (1976). *Report of the Select Committee of the Legislative Assembly — Workers' Compensation.*

Alberta (1969). *Report of the Special Committee appointed May 14th 1968 to inquire into and make recommendations on the subject of Workmen's Compensation and the Workmen's Compensation Act,* sessional paper, No. 310.

Alberta (1965). *Report of the Special Committee appointed April 28th 1964 to inquire into and make recommendations on the subject of Workmen's Compensation and the Workmen's Compensation act,* sessional paper, No. 62.

Alberta (1955). *Report of the Special Committee appointed August 22nd, 1955 to inquire into and make recommendations on the subject of Workmen's Compensation and the Workmen's Compensation Act,* sessional paper No. 4.

Alberta (1948). *Report of the Special Committee appointed March 24th, 1947, to inquire into and make recommendations on the subject of Workmen's Compensation and the Workmen's Compensation Act,* sessional paper No. 52.

Althusser, L. (1971). *Lenin and Philosophy and Other Essays.* New York: Monthly Review Press.

Armstrong, D. (1983). *Political Anatomy of the Body.* Cambridge: Cambridge University Press.

Arney, W.R., and B.J. Bergen. (1984). "Power and Visibility: The Invention of Teenage Pregnancy." *Social Science and Medicine* 18 (1):11-19.

Bale, A. (1989). "Medicine in the Industrial Battle: Early Workers' Compensation." *Social Science and Medicine* 28 (11):1113-20.

Barth, P.S., and H.A. Hunt. (1980). *Workers' Compensation and Work-Related Illnesses and Diseases.* Cambridge, MA: MIT Press.

Bartrip, P.W.J. (1987). *Workmen's Compensation in Twentieth Century Britain.* Aldershot: Gower.

Bartrip, P.W.J. and S.B. Burman. (1983) *The Wounded Soldiers of Industry.* Oxford: Clarendon.

Baudrillard, J. (1983). *In the Shadow of the Silent Majorities.* New York: Semiotext(e).

Berliner, H. (1982). "Medical Modes of Production." In P. Wright, and A. Treacher (eds.), *The Problem of Medical Knowledge, Examining the social construction of medicine.* Edinburgh: Edinburgh University Press. 162-73.

Berman, D. (1978). "How cheap is a Life?" *International Journal of Health Services* 8 (1):79-99.

Boyd, N., ed. (1986). *The Social Dimensions of Law.* Scarborough, ON: Prentice Hall.

Brickey, S. and E. Comack, eds. (1986). *The Social Basis of Law.* Toronto: Garamond.

Brown, W. (1987). "Where is the Sex in Political Theory?" *Women and Politics* 7 (1):3-23.

Burchell, G. (1979). "A note on juvenile justice." *Ideology and Consciousness* 5:125-36.

Caputo, T.C., M. Kennedy, C.E. Reasons, and A. Brannigan, eds. (1989). *Law and Society: A Critical Perspective.* Toronto: Harcourt Brace Jovanovitch.

Chambliss, W. (1986). "On Lawmaking." In S. Brickey and E. Comack (eds.), *The Social Basis of Law*. Toronto: Garamond. 27-51.

Chunn, D.E. and S.A. Gavigan. (1988). "Social Control: Analytical Tool or Analytical Quagmire?" *Contemporary Crises* 12 (2):107-24.

Cohen S. (1985). *Visions of Social Control*. New York: Polity Press.

Colwill, J. (1987). "Politics, Social Policy and the State: the Reform of Workers' Compensation in the UK." *International Journal of the Sociology of Law* 15:281-308.

Comack, E. (1986). "'We will get some good out of this riot yet': The Canadian state, drug legislation and class conflict." In S. Brickey and E. Comack (eds.), *The Social Basis of Law*. Toronto: Garamond. 67-89.

Comack, E. and S. Brickey, eds. (1991). *The Social Basis of Law*. 2nd ed. Halifax: Fernwood.

Cunningham, J. (1817). *A Few Observations on Friendly Societies and their Influence on Public Morals*. London.

Currie, D. and Maclean, B. (1986). *The Administration of Justice*. Saskatoon: Social Research Unit, Department of Sociology, University of Saskatchewan.

Diamond, I. and L. Quinby, eds. (1988). *Feminism and Foucault*. Boston: Northeastern University Press.

Dicey, A.V. (1885). *Lectures introductory to the study of the Law of the Constitution*. London: Macmillan.

Djao, A.W. (1983). *Inequality and Social Policy*. Toronto: J. Wiley.

Dodd, W. (1968). *The Factory System Illustrated*. New York: Augustus M. Kelly. (Original work published in 1842)

Donzelot, J., ed. (1991). *Face à l'exlusion*. Paris: Esprit.

Donzelot, J. (1988). "The Promotion of the Social." *Economy and Society* 17 (3):395-427.

Donzelot, J. (1984). *L'invention du Social*. Paris: Fayard.

Donzelot, J. (1980). *The Policing of Families*. London: Hutchinson.

Donzelot, J. (1979). "The Poverty of Political Culture." *Ideology and Consciousness* 5:73-86.

Donzelot, J. and P. Estèbe (1994). *L'État animateur*. Paris: Esprit.

Donzelot, J., and M-C. Jaillet. (1997). "Europe, États-Unis: convergences et divergences des politiques d'insertion." *Esprit* Mai:70-89.

Doran, C. (1987, June). *Codifying Power: Are we trapped within its boundaries?* Paper presented at the Canadian Sociology and Anthropology Annual meetings, Hamilton, Ontario.

Doyal, L. (1979). *The Political Economy of Health*. London: Pluto.

Elling, R. H., (1981). "The Capitalist World-System and International Health." *International Journal of Health Services* 11 (1):21-51.

Ewald, F. (1991). "Insurance and Risk." In C. Burchell, C. Gordon, and P. Miller (eds), *The Foucault Effect*. London: Harvester Wheatsheaf. 197-210.

Figlio, K. (1982). "How does Illness mediate Social Relations? Workmen's Compensation and Medico-Legal Practices, 1890-1940." In P. Wright and A. Treacher (eds.), *The Problem of Medical Knowledge*. Edinburgh: Edinburgh University Press. 174-224.

Figlio, K. (1978). "Chlorosis and Chronic Disease in 19th-Century Britain: The Social Constitution of somatic illness in a capitalist society." *International Journal of Health Services* 8 (4):589-617.

Fine, B. (1984). *Democracy and the Rule of Law*. London: Pluto.

Finkel, A. (1977). "Origins of the Welfare State." In L. Panitch (ed.), *The Canadian State: Political Economy and Political Power*. Toronto: University of Toronto Press. 344-370.

Fleming, T., ed. (1985). *The New Criminologies in Canada: State, Crime and Control*. Toronto: Oxford University Press.

Foucault, M. (1980a). "Two Lectures." In C. Gordon (ed.), *Power/Knowledge: Selected Interviews and Other writings (1972-1977) by Michel Foucault*. Brighton: Harvester. 78-108.

Foucault, M. (1980b). "Truth and Power." In C. Gordon (ed.), *Power/Knowledge: Selected Interviews and Other writings (1972-1977) by Michel Foucault*. Brighton: Harvester. 109-33.

Foucault, M. (1980c). *The History of Sexuality, Volume 1: An Introduction*. New York: Vintage.

Foucault, M. (1977). *Discipline and Punish*. New York: Pantheon.

Foucault, M. (1970). *The Order of Things*. New York: Pantheon.

Frank, A. (1982). "The Anatamo-politics of Positive Prescription: Materials from the History of Masturbation." *Society for Critical Exchange Reports* 11:55-76.

Fraser, D. (1973). *The evolution of the British welfare state: a history of social policy since the Industrial Revolution*. London: Macmillan.

Garland, D. (1990). *Punishment and Modern Society*. Chicago: University of Chicago Press.

Garland, D. (1985a). "The Criminal and His Science." *British Journal of Criminology* 25 (2):109-37.

Garland, D. (1985b). *Punishment and Welfare*. Aldershot: Gower.

Garland, D. (1981). "The Birth of the Welfare Sanction." *British Journal of Law & Society* 8 (1):29-45.

Gilbert, B. (1966). *The Evolution of National Insurance in Great Britain: The Origins of the Welfare State*. London: Joseph.

Gosden, P.H.J.H. (1973). *Self-help; Voluntary Associations in the 19th Century*. London: Batsford.

Gosden, P.H.J.H. (1961) *The Friendly Societies in England 1815-1875*. Manchester: Manchester University Press.

Gough, I. (1983). "The Crisis of the British Welfare State." *International Journal of Health Services* 13 (3):459-77.

Gough, I. (1979). *The Political Economy of the Welfare State*. London: Macmillan.

Gramsci, A. (1971). *Selections from Prison Notebooks*. New York: International Publishers.

Gregg, P. (1969). *The Welfare State*. Amherst: University of Massachusetts Press.

Guest, D. (1981). *The Emergence of Social Security in Canada*. Vancouver: University of British Columbia Press.

Hanes, D. (1968). *The First British Workmen's Compensation Act*. New Haven: Yale University Press.

Haraway, D. (1988). "Situated knowledges: The science question in feminism and the privilege of partial perspective." *Feminist Studies* 14 (3):575-99.

Harding, S. (1986a). "The Instability of the Analytical Categories of Feminist Theory." *Signs: Journal of Women in Culture and Society* 11 (4):645-65.

Harding, S. (1986b). *The Science Question in Feminism*. Ithaca: Cornell University Press.

Hartsock, N. (1990a). "Postmodernism and Political Change: Issues for Feminist Theory." *Cultural Critique* 14:15-33.

Hartsock, N. (1990b). "Foucault on Power: A theory for Women?" In L. Nicholson (ed.), *Feminism/Postmodernism*. London: Routledge. 155-75.

Hartsock, N. (1987). "Rethinking Modernism: Minority vs. Majority Theories." *Cultural Critique* 7:187-206.

Hayek, F. (1972). *The Constitution of Liberty*. Chicago: University of Chicago Press.

Hayek, F. (1944). *The Road to Serfdom*. Chicago Press: University of Chicago Press.

Hewitt, M. (1983). "Foucault's account of Welfare." *Theory, Culture and Society* 2 (1):67-84.

Holloway, J., and S. Picciotto, eds. (1978). *State and Capital: A Marxist Debate*. London: E. Arnold.

Hopkins, A. (1986). "Class Bias in the Criminal Law." In S. Brickey and E. Comack (eds.), *The Social Basis of Law*. Toronto: Garamond. 127-36.

Horovitz, S. B. (1944). *Injury and Death under Workmen's Compensation laws*. Boston: Wright & Potter.

Ignatieff, M. (1978). *A Just Measure of Pain: The Penitentiary in the Industrial Revolution*. New York: Pantheon.

Ingman, T. (1978). "The Rise and Fall of the Doctrine of Common Employment." *Juridical Review* 23:106-25.

Jacobus, M., E.F. Keller, and S. Shuttleworth, eds. (1990). *Body/Politics: Women and the Discourse of Science.* New York: Routledge.

Jessop, B. (1980). "On Recent Marxist Theories of Law, the State and Juridico-Political Ideology." *International Journal of the Sociology of Law* 8:339-68.

Kaegi, E. (1978). *Asbestos-Related Disease: Implications for Occupational Health Practices in Alberta.* Edmonton.

Kaegi, E., and M. Baynton (n.d.) *Respiratory Disorders Associated with Coal Mining.* Edmonton.

Keller, E.F. (1992). *Secrets of Life: Secrets of Death.* New York: Routledge.

Kessler, H.K. (1941). *Accidental Injuries: The Medico-legal Aspects of Workmen's Compensation and Public Liability.* Philadelphia: Lea and Febiger.

Kuhn, T. (1962). *The Structure of Scientific Revolutions.* Chicago: University of Chicago Press.

Laclau, E., and C. Mouffe. (1987). "Post Marxism without Apologies." *New Left Review* 166:79-106.

Levine, D. (1991). "Punctuated Equilibrium: The Modernization of the Proletarian Family in the Age of Ascendant Capitalism." *International Labor and Working-Class History* 39 (Spring):3-20.

Leyton, E. (1978). "The Bureaucratization of Anguish: The Workmen's Compensation Board in an industrial disaster." In D. Handelman, D. and E. Leyton (eds.), *Bureaucracy and World View.* St. John's, NF: Institute of Social and Economic Research. 70-134.

Maclean, B., ed. (1986). *The Political Economy of Crime.* Scarborough, Ontario: Prentice Hall.

Mallalieu, W.C. (1950). "Joseph Chamberlain and Workmen's Compensation." *Journal of Economic History* 10:45-57.

Mandel, M. (1986). "Democracy, Class and Canadian Sentencing Law." In S. Brickey and E. Comack (eds.), *The Social Basis of Law.* Toronto: Garamond. 137-56.

Martin, B. (1982). "Feminism, Criticism, and Foucault." *New German Critique* 27:3-30.

Marx, K. (1967). *Capital, volume 1.* New York: International Publishers.

Marx, K., and F. Engels. (1967). "The German Ideology." In B.L. Easton and K.H. Guddat (trans. and ed.), *Writings of the Young Marx on Philosophy and Society.* Garden City, New York: Doubleday. (Original work published in 1846)

Meiksins, P., and E. Meiksins Wood. (1985). "Beyond Class? A reply to Chantal Mouffe." *Studies in Political Economy* 17:141-65.

Meyer, P. (1982). *The Child and the State.* Cambridge: Cambridge University Press.

Miliband, R. (1969). *The State in Capitalist Society.* New York: Basic Books.

Mine Workers' Union of Canada. (1927). Brief I. Submission *To the Special Committee appointed by the Government of the Province of Alberta, following resolution passed at recent session of Alberta Legislature, to consider the subject of workmen's compensation,* (Alberta Provincial Archives #64.11/126).

Mishra, R. (1977). *Society and Social Policy.* London: Macmillan.

Moscovitch, A., and G. Drover. (1987). "Social Expenditures and the Welfare State: The Canadian Experience in Historical Perspective." In A. Moscovitch and J. Albert (eds.), *The Benevolent State: The Growth of Welfare in Canada.* Toronto: Garamond. 13-43.

Mouffe, C. (1983). "Working-Class Hegemony and the Struggle for Socialism." *Studies in Political Economy* 12:7-26.

Navarro, V. (1986). *Crisis, Health and Medicine.* New York: Tavistock.

Navarro, V. (1980). "Work, Ideology and Science: The Case of Medicine." *International Journal of Health Services* 10 (4):523-50.

Navarro, V. (1978). *Class Struggle, the State and Medicine: An Historical and Contemporary Analysis of the Medical Sector in Great Britain*. London: Martin Robertson.

Neison, F. (1867). *Observations of Oddfellows and Friendly Societies*. London.

O'Connor, J. (1973). *The Fiscal Crisis of the State*. New York: St. Martin's Press.

Ogle, W. (1885). *Supplement to 45th Annual Report of Registrar-General for England and Wales*. London.

O'Neill, J. (1986). "The disciplinary society: from Weber to Foucault." *British Journal of Sociology* 37 (1):42-60.

Palmer, B. (1990). *Descent into Discourse*. Philadelphia: Temple University Press.

Panitch, L., ed. (1977). *The Canadian State: Political Economy and Political Power*. Toronto: University of Toronto Press.

Parliamentary Papers, (U.K.) (1887). *Report from the select committee on Employers' Liability*. 9.

Piva, M. (1975). "The Workmen's Compensation Movement in Ontario." *Ontario History* 67:39-56.

Poulantzas, N. (1978). *State, Power, Socialism*. London: NLB.

Poulantzas, N. (1973). *Political Power and Social Classes*. London: NLB.

Pritt, D. (1970). *Law, Class and Society, Book 1*. London: Lawrence and Wishart.

Ratcliffe, H. (1850). *Observations of the Rate of Mortality and Sickness existing among Friendly Societies, particularised for various Trades, Occupations and Localities with a series of Tables showing the Value of Annuities, Sick Gift, Assurance for Death, and Contributions to be paid Equivalent thereto, calculated from the Experience of the Members composing the Manchester Unity of the Independent Order of Oddfellows*. Manchester.

Ratner, R., J. McMullan, and B. Burtch. (1987). "The Problem of Relative Autonomy and Criminal Justice in the Canadian State." In R. Ratner and J. McMullan (eds.), *State Control: Criminal Justice Politics in Canada*. Vancouver: University of British Columbia Press. 85-125.

Raz, J. (1977). "The Rule of Law and its Virtue." *Law Quarterly Review* 93:195-211.

Reasons, C.E., L.L. Ross, and C. Paterson. (1981). *Assault on the Worker*. Toronto: Butterworths.

Risk, R.C.B. (1981). "This Nuisance of Litigation: The Origins of Workmen's Compensation Legislation in Ontario." In D. Flaherty (ed.), *Essays in the History of Canadian Law*, vol. 2. Toronto: University of Toronto Press. 418-91.

Rose, N. (1979). "The psychological complex: mental measurement and social administration." *Ideology and Consciousness* 5:5-68.

Sawicki, J. (1991). *Disciplining Foucault*. New York: Routledge.

Sawicki, J. (1986). "Foucault and Feminism: Toward a Politics of Difference." *Hypatia* 1 (2):23-36.

Sentes, R. (1981). *Hazards in the Workplace: The Responses and Recommendations of Alberta's Unionized Workers*. Edmonton.

Smart, B. (1982). "Foucault, Sociology, and the Problem of Human Agency." *Theory and Society* 11 (2):120-41.

Smart, C. (1989). *Feminism and the Power of Law*. London: Routledge.

Smith, B. (1981). "Black Lung: The Social Production of Disease." *International Journal of Health Services* 11 (3):343-59.

Smith, D.E. (1987). *The Everyday World as Problematic*. Toronto: University of Toronto Press.

Smith, D.E. (1981a). "On Sociological Description: A Method from Marx." *Human Studies* 4:313-37.

Smith, D.E. (1981b). *The Experienced World as Problematic: A Feminist Method*. University of Saskatchewan Sorokin Lectures, No. 12.

Smith, D.E. (1978). "K is Mentally Ill." *Sociology* 12 (1):25-53.

Smith, D.E. (1974a). "The Ideological Practices of Sociology." *Catalyst* 8 (Winter):39-54.

Smith, D.E. (1974b). "The Social Construction of Documentary Reality." *Sociological Inquiry* 44 (4):257-68.

Smith, D.E. (1974c). "Women's Perspective as a Radical Critique of Sociology." *Sociological Inquiry* 44 (1):7-13.

Somers, H., and A. Somers. (1954). *Workmen's Compensation.* New York: Wiley.

Swartz, D. (1977). "The Politics of Reform: Conflict and Accommodation in Canadian Health Policy." In L. Panitch (ed.), *The Canadian State: Political Economy and Political Power.* Toronto: University of Toronto Press. 311-43.

Thompson, E.P. (1975). *Whigs and Hunters.* London: Allen Lane.

Tucker, E. (1992). "Worker Participation in Health and Safety Regulation: Lessons from Sweden." *Studies in Political Economy* 37:95-127.

Tucker, E. (1984a). "The Law of Employers' Liability in Ontario 1861-1900: The Search for a Theory." *Osgoode Hall Law Journal* 22 (2):216-80.

Tucker, E. (1984b). "The Determination of Occupational Health and Safety Standards in Ontario, 1860-1982: From the Market to Politics to ...?" *McGill Law Journal* 29 (2):261-311.

United Mine Workers of America. (n.d.). *Submission of the United Mineworkers of America presented to the Premier, cabinet Ministers and M.L.A.'s Government of Alberta respecting Black Lung Disease (Coal Workers' Pneumoconiosis).* Edmonton, Alberta.

Walters, V. (1991). "Beyond Medical and Academic Agendas: Lay Perspectives and Priorities." *Atlantis* 17 (1):28-35.

Walters, V. (1988). "Workers' Perceptions, Knowledge and responses regarding occupational health and safety: A report on a Canadian study." *Social Science and Medicine* 27 (11):1189-96.

Walters, V. (1985). "The Politics of occupational health and safety: interviews with workers' health and safety representatives and company doctors." *Canadian Review of Sociology and Anthropology* 22 (1):57-79.

Walters, V. (1983). "Occupational Health and Safety Legislation in Ontario: An Analysis of its Origins and Content." *Canadian Review of Sociology and Anthropology* 20 (4):413-34.

Walters, V. (1982). "State, Capital and Labour: The Introduction of Federal-Provincial Insurance for Physician Care in Canada." *Canadian Review of Sociology and Anthropology* 19 (2):157-72.

Wiener, M. (1990). *Reconstructing the Criminal.* Cambridge: Cambridge University Press.

Wiener, M. (1987). "The March of Penal Progress?" *The Journal of British Studies* 26:83-96.

Workers' compensation Board, Alberta. (1983). *Guidelines for Assessment of Occupational Respiratory Disease.* Edmonton.

Workers' health safety and compensation, Alberta. (n.d.). *The Fibrosis Program* (brochure).

# 8

## Confronting the Construct of Child Neglect as Maternal Failure: In Search of Peacemaking Alternatives

### SANDRA WACHHOLZ

Like many social problems that befall families, there has been no shortage of "mother blaming" in the construction of the problem of child neglect (Wedenoja, 1991). A review of the literature reveals that the problem of child neglect has largely been defined and dealt with in an individualistic and gender-specific manner. It is a social problem which has generally been constructed, as Swift (1995) underscores, "as the failure of individual mothers to carry out their mothering responsibilities" (72). Posed behind this socially structured image of child neglect as maternal failure, however, is the human face of suffering. While the vast majority of those who have been accused of child neglect in Canada have been women, these individuals' lives have often been constrained and challenged by such problems as poverty, unemployment, and substandard, crowded housing. Studies have consistently identified a strong relationship between child neglect and various socioeconomic problems which produce conditions that make it difficult for mothers to care for their children (Kline, 1993; Krishnan and Morrison, 1995; Wolock and Horowitz, 1984).

The state's response to child neglect, however, fails to adequately address the material deprivation and socioeconomic oppression that is generally experienced by the women who come to the attention of the child welfare system. Essentially, the state has focused largely on punishing these women through the apprehension of their children or it has initiated treatment efforts in an attempt to "rehabilitate" or improve their mothering skills (Kamerman and Kahn, 1990). This narrow focus, which has generally been aimed at changing the behaviour of mothers rather than the socioeconomic conditions that are thought to give rise to neglect, has done little to ameliorate this problem and has served to obscure the complex realities of the poverty and poverty-related problems that often define the lives of the women who neglect their children (Kline, 1993).

The purpose of this chapter, then, is to present a critique of contemporary child-protection practices which have converged around the punishment and rehabilitation of those who are deemed to have failed in their maternal duties. Drawing on the peacemaking perspective in criminology recently advanced by Pepinsky and Quinney (1991), I will argue that rather than relying on the coercive force and social control mechanisms of child-protection mandates and the criminal justice system, more peaceful, socially just measures should be undertaken to address child neglect. Central to the peacemaking perspective is the belief that traditional "law and order" responses to crime and various other social problems have failed. For peacemakers, a reduction in crime and other forms of suffering will only occur through the introduction of policies that foster a more just, egalitarian sociopolitical order and, in turn, through the introduction of more caring, peaceful interpersonal relations among people. With this view in mind, in this chapter I explore a number of policy initiatives and directives that could be implemented to deal with the problem of child neglect in a less forceful and punitive manner. These options, which will be referred to as peacemaking alternatives, do not simply identify child neglect as a failure of maternal care, but rather locate the problem in social and economic inequality.

I begin with a succinct discussion of the nature, prevalence, and socioeconomic context of child neglect. I then review the gender-specific way in which child neglect has been constructed, which is followed by a critique of the state's traditional response to child neglect. Finally, I discuss the peacemaking perspective and a number of peacemaking responses to child neglect.

## Child Neglect: A Brief Introduction

While difficult to define precisely, child neglect can be thought of as the failure of a child's parent or guardian to provide minimally adequate care in such areas as supervision, housing, protection, education, affection, and health (Wolock and Horowitz, 1984; Swift, 1991). Although child neglect has often been dealt with as an appendage to the problem of child physical and sexual abuse, data reveal that child neglect is the most prevalent form of child maltreatment in Canada and that its physiological consequences can be as serious as those incurred by victims of physical abuse (Hepworth, 1985; Wolock and Horowitz, 1984).

Historically, interest in child neglect in Canada began to appear in the latter part of the nineteenth century. Concerned about the large number of working-class children who were experiencing homelessness and exploitation as a result of capitalist industrialization, social reformers initiated a movement to improve the living conditions of deprived children. The efforts of those involved in the movement facilitated the establishment of the first Children's Aid Society in 1891 and the first formative child protection statute introduced in Ontario in 1893 (Jones and Rutman, 1981; Swift, 1991).

Since that time, child protection statutes and mandates have broadened considerably. The duty of child protection has clearly emerged as a provincial responsibility. In each province, child protection-workers have the right to intervene in suspected or actual cases of neglect under the authority of provincial child-protection acts. While rarely used in cases of neglect because of their vagueness and punitive nature, criminal charges can also be laid against those who fail to meet the parental responsibilities that are specified in Section 197 of the Criminal Code of Canada (Callahan, 1985).

Notably, the vast majority of families in which child-protection workers intervene on grounds of neglect are those headed by very poor, single-parent women (Callahan, 1993). Although national figures on the socio-demographic profile of child welfare clients do not exist, provincial studies consistently indicate that female, single-parent families are the most likely to be involved in the child welfare system. A study in British Columbia (1988) indicated, for example, that the majority of the individuals whose children were coming into foster care were single-parent women on social assistance. Fully 72 per cent of these women received income assistance, and in well over half of the cases their children were apprehended on grounds of parental neglect (Campbell, 1991).

Poverty is, then, part of the socioeconomic reality of child neglect. Although a range of socioeconomic problems such as violence, drug and alcohol addictions, and poor mental health are associated with child neglect, research indicates that poverty is the variable that is most strongly correlated with the neglect of children (Pelton, 1994). This correlation, which will be discussed in the following section, is not adequately considered or addressed by the state in its response to child neglect.

## The Socioeconomic Context of Child Neglect: When Caring is Difficult

Although child neglect is a complex and multi-faceted phenomenon, research indicates that the most consistent socioeconomic correlate of this social problem is poverty. As Pelton (1994) underscores, "no other single factor has ever been found to be more strongly or as strongly related to child abuse and neglect than are poverty and low income" (27). Although most impoverished families do not neglect their children, low-income families are vastly over-represented in incidences of child neglect. As such, poverty has been identified as the context for neglect — a variable that increases the likelihood of neglect (Callahan, 1993; Pelton, 1994).

The strong correlation between child neglect and poverty has appeared overwhelmingly and consistently in a wide range of studies that have been conducted across different time periods (Jones, 1990; Pelton, 1994; Wolock and Horowitz, 1979, 1984; Zuravin, 1989). Notably, virtually every American national survey of officially reported incidents of neglect has indicated that the vast majority of cases involved families from the lowest socioeconomic class (AHA, 1988; Pelton, 1994). Various studies conducted in Canada have produced similar findings (Hepworth, 1985; Novick and Volpe, 1989). While precise figures are difficult to obtain, estimates from child-protection agencies suggest that in 1986 approximately 66-75 per cent of the Canadian children who came into care on grounds of neglect were from low-income families (Canadian Child Welfare Association, 1988).

The strong association between child neglect and poverty has also appeared in a variety of Canadian socio-demographic studies (Kirshnan and Morrison, 1995; Tousignant *et al.*, 1984). As a case in point, Chamberland *et al.* (1986) found a positive correlation between the poverty level and the rate of child neglect in various neighbourhoods in Montreal. Using census tract data and reports of child neglect that had been made to the city's child-protection agencies, the researchers studied 343 neighbourhoods over a six-month period and found that the number of poor, female-headed households in a given neighbourhood was the best predictor of a high rate of child neglect.

Importantly, studies of unreported cases of neglect have also found a strong correlation between child neglect and poverty (Sedlak, 1991). This association was found, for example, in two national studies of the incidence and prevalence of child abuse and neglect in the United States (U.S. Department of Health and Human Services, 1981, 1988). In both studies, survey data were gathered in 29 counties from professionals in various agencies (e.g., health departments, mental health facilities) and institutions (e.g., schools, day cares) about incidences of neglect that were unreported. The overwhelming majority of unreported cases in each study involved children from low-income families.

With respect to the correlation between child neglect and poverty that has been found both in studies of reported and unreported cases of neglect, it is important to indicate that various scholars have argued that this relationship is not simply an anomaly of reporting systems or of professional attitudes that are biased against the poor (Parton, 1985; Pelton, 1994). While researchers such as Pelton (1994), for example, do not deny the existence of some level of reporting bias in cases of neglect, Pelton does contend that there is substantial evidence to conclude that child neglect is strongly associated with poverty. According to him, statements implying that child neglect occurs without regard to socioeconomic class can be called into question on the following grounds: (1) far more cases of neglect are being reported due to new reporting laws and greater public awareness of the problem; and yet, the more vigilant public watch has not appreciably altered the socio-economic pattern of reports of neglect; and (2) studies indicate that even among the poor, child neglect is related to degrees of poverty. The highest incidence of neglect has been found to occur in families experiencing the most extreme level of poverty (Swift, 1991; Horowitz and Wolock, 1981). Pointing to the consistent finding in studies that the poorest children are at greatest risk of neglect and that the wealthiest children are at least risk, Pelton (1994) suggests that such findings "would be truly difficult to explain in terms of personal biases in the identification and reporting of child abuse and neglect; it is highly unlikely that prejudices are so fine tuned" (18).

Therefore, as various scholars have argued and as many studies suggest, it would appear that poverty is a critical factor in producing neglect. As various scholars note, poverty places children at risk of experiencing material neglect, which is one of the more common forms of neglect that come to the attention of child-welfare officials, as poor families frequently experience actual shortages of food, clothing, and household necessities (Parton, 1985; Pelton, 1994). Poverty is also thought to reduce the parental effectiveness and psychosocial functioning of those individuals who find it difficult to cope with the stress of the economic hardship associated with low income (Parton, 1985; Jones, 1990). As one woman who has been suspected of child neglect explained,

> It is difficult to take care of your kids when you are broke. I
> was just left sitting on welfare. I had to pay the rent, I had to
> pay the bills. This meant that I would often be without
> money, couldn't pay the rent, and we would have to move.
> We moved a lot. I was really stressed out all the time.
> Sometimes I would sit and cry all night. I found it really hard
> to care for my kids. I just wanted to lie on my bed. I didn't
> want to cook; I didn't want to clean. I knew that my kids
> should have come first, but I couldn't handle anything.[1]

In short, this woman, like many other women, found it difficult to care for
her children under difficult conditions.

## Holding Poor, Single-Parent Women
## Accountable for Child Neglect

Although a rather wide range of studies has demonstrated an association
between child neglect and such socioeconomic problems as poverty,
explanations of child neglect have generally focused on deficiencies in the
care-giving skills of women. In practice, this has meant that poor, single-
parent women have generally been held accountable for child neglect. As
discussed in the following section, the assumption that the locus of problem of child neglect rests in the realm of mothering is thought to be
linked, in large part, to patriarchal values and expectations about women's
responsibilities. These values and expectations have influenced the way in
which child neglect has been defined and understood, and they have done
much to structure the state's response to child neglect — punishing poor
women or rehabilitating their maternal skills.

## Patriarchal Views of Motherhood

Traditional gender-role expectations regarding motherhood, in combination with the liberal, capitalist value of individualism, are thought to play
an important role in engendering the belief that the locus of the problem
of child neglect rests in individual maternal care-giving deficiencies
(Breines and Gordon, 1983; Hutchison, 1992). In particular, this belief is
thought to be fuelled by the gender-role expectation that women are

largely responsible for the well-being of children (Fineman, 1991; Roberts, 1993). Traditionally, childcare has been allocated to women. It has been constructed as an obligation that is both natural and inevitable for most females. Although over the last decade men have also been identified as having an important role in child-rearing, women are still expected to be the primary care-givers to children (Boyd, 1989; Kline, 1993). It is still assumed that females will fulfil what Kline (1993) refers to as the "primary care requirement" (310). Thus, in the current patriarchal, capitalist, sociopolitical order that places a premium on individual rights and respon-sibilities, the well-being of children has largely fallen on the shoulders of women. The welfare of children is generally seen as an individual rather than a collective responsibility (Hutchison, 1992). Concomitant with the expectation that women are largely responsible for the welfare of children is the assumption that women will be "good" mothers regardless of the material conditions of their lives. It is presumed that women should be able to subordinate their own needs, to act unselfishly, regardless of whether they have sufficient support or financial resources to engage in care-giving (Hutchison, 1992). "Good mothering," as Kline (1993) argues, is an act that is presented as "natural, necessary and universal" for most women regardless of the realities of their lives (315).

Given this context, then, when children's needs have not been met it has generally been individual women and, in particular, those who are poor who have been held accountable for child neglect. In essence, child neglect has been treated as a gendered phenomenon rather than as a social problem that is intrinsically tied to socioeconomic inequality.

## Child Neglect as Maternal Failure

The tradition of identifying child neglect as an individual, gender-specific problem is readily apparent in the social-welfare research and in the child-protection legislation and social policies that have appeared since the social-reform period of the late nineteenth century, when child neglect first began to generate attention (Gordon, 1988). Both in the past and at present, child neglect has generally been constructed as a problem that originates from the failure of women to carry out their mothering duties.

Reflecting this pattern, a significant amount of the research that has emerged on the topic of child neglect over the last century has narrowly focused on women. A review of the literature reveals that many of the studies that have sought to identify the causal factors associated with neglect have centred on the personality characteristics and nurturing capacities of women. As Wolock and Horowitz (1984) note,

> Literally hundreds of studies — probably the bulk of investigations into the etiology of child maltreatment — have been concerned almost exclusively with psychological variables, i.e., with discovering distinctive personality characteristics or problems of abusing parents, or deficits in the nurturing or "mothering" provided to these parents when they were children (533).

Hence, the research that has been designed to examine maternal personality and care-giving deficiencies has substantially overshadowed the studies that have sought to examine the influence that socioeconomic conditions have on child neglect.

It is interesting to note that mothers have been identified as so central to the problem of neglect that various definitions of this social problem have incorporated references to women (Swift, 1995). Although some believe that child neglect should be defined in broad, sociological terms and that the definition should include references to societal and institutional neglect and abuse (Hutchison, 1990), scholars such as Gil (1970), for instance, have defined neglect as a "breakdown in the ability to mother" (243). The assumption that the personal traits and care-giving skills of mothers are the primary causal factors in cases of child neglect can also be found in several of the diagnostic tools that have been developed over time to detect neglect. As a case in point, Polansky *et al.* (1992) have created a complex scale which rates the adequacy of women's care-giving skills along a continuum of poor to excellent, with scores at the lower end suggesting neglect. The scale does not, however, incorporate any facet through which to examine how poverty and feelings of powerlessness affect an individual's capacity to mother (Callahan, 1993). Given its narrow focus, it is thought to reflect the individualistic and gender-specific way in which the problem of neglect has been conceptualized (Swift, 1991).

The mandates of child protection statutes, both in the past and in the present, are also thought to reflect the perception that child neglect stems from maternal care-giving shortcomings. Since the introduction of the first child-protection statute in Ontario in 1893, the legislation that has appeared in the various provinces and territories across Canada has directed child-protection workers to employ individual case investigations to assess the character, behaviour, and care-giving skills of those who have been suspected of neglecting their children. Child protection-legislation does not provide child-protection workers with an organizational or legal mandate to challenge or to change the conditions of poverty and deprivation that surround cases of neglect. Instead, it has narrowly focused on monitoring standards of parental care and, in particular, maternal care.

Therefore, as this succinct review has attempted to demonstrate, the care-giving skills of mothers have generally been identified as the locus of the problem of child neglect. Within this context, it is poor, single-parent women who have been held accountable for child neglect. These women, as the following section indicates, have generally been subjected to either "maternal punishment" or "maternal rehabilitation" for their neglectful behaviour.

## The State's Response to Child Neglect: Maternal Punishment and Maternal Rehabilitation

Although, as Callahan (1993) argues, the state should attempt to adequately address the poverty that many neglectful mothers encounter and should make such efforts "front and centre in their business," it does not (185). While child-protection agencies do offer certain resources to those who neglect their children as part of their approach to dealing with this problem, these support services are limited in scope. In general, the programs and resources offered by child-protection agencies or the community organizations to which an individual may be referred tend to be residual and tertiary in nature (Hutchison, 1992; Wharf, 1985). They are largely limited, for example, to skills training, educational resources, medical services, child care, and income vouchers. The provision of these resources is time-limited, and when an individual demonstrates progress, the services are typically withdrawn (Callahan, 1993). As one former child-protection worker lamented about these resources, "Usually these services are soft services like mental health or family counselling.... You pump in some resources or services into the home, but you don't provide them with a job or adequate housing — things that they really need."[2]

Essentially, the state relies primarily on the force of provincial child-protection legislation to encourage women to better carry out their maternal care-giving responsibilities. Drawing on a traditional "law and order" approach, the state has largely organized its response around punishing women by apprehending their children, or providing treatment initiatives to neglectful women. These responses appear to have been framed around the belief that neglect is primarily an individual, maternal problem that is best addressed through effective enforcement of the law.

### MATERNAL REHABILITATION

The state's most common response to child neglect has centred on the initiation of treatment programs which have been aimed at restoring or rehabilitating the maternal skills of women who have been identified as inadequate mothers (Kline, 1993; Swift, 1991). These treatment efforts are mounted by child-protection workers who, through provincial legislation, are directed to respond to the problematic parental care that comes to their attention.

One of the rehabilitative approaches that child-protection workers have encouraged neglectful mothers to undertake to improve the performance of their mothering role has been individual counselling. As various scholars argue, counselling has often been incorporated into the case plans for neglectful mothers as it is thought to be a means to address their emotional needs. The assumption is that if their emotional needs are met, mothers will be better able to care for their children (Wiehe, 1992). Programs that have focused on the improvement of parenting skills have also been a common "maternal rehabilitation" strategy. The literature is replete with a wide range of articles that discuss advances in parental training techniques designed for those who have been found to neglect their children (Crimmins *et al.*, 1984; Wiehe, 1992). Such techniques, along with, for example, stress reduction courses, assertiveness training programs, and basic life skill classes all reflect the multifaceted way in which the state has focused on aiding and treating mothers so that they can produce a higher, healthier level of mothering (Swift, 1991).

Indeed, it is important to indicate that while counselling and parental training initiatives can, at some level, increase individual competencies, the state's strong emphasis on treatment has been a source of debate and criticism. These treatment efforts, as Kamerman and Kahn (1990) argue, are particularly ineffective in meeting the complex socioeconomic needs of low-income, poor women. While they may provide individuals with a better ability to cope with their parenting obligations, they do not open up opportunities for decent housing, education, jobs or careers (Pelton, 1994).

Concern has also been expressed about the coercive nature of these treatment programs. While participation in them is generally voluntary, in essence it is not (Kamerman and Kahn, 1990). Child-protection workers, in what has been referred to as somewhat of a parajudicial position, wield a great deal of power (Tousignant *et al.*, 1982). As one social worker who was employed in child protection for approximately two years stated,

> Social workers, even with the best of intentions, by virtue of them just showing up on the door, without even necessarily even having said it, the threat is there that you could take away their kids. You can't get anymore coercive than that. I can't think of a more coercive situation, to get someone to behave in a certain way by implicitly or explicitly hanging over their heads the threat of removing their children. All you are really trying to do is control their behaviour and force a certain type of parenting or level of parenting on them that they don't have the resources to carry out.[3]

Although many provinces have sought to curb the discretionary power of social workers and have passed legislation which provides families with the right to least interference in their affairs, the discretionary power of social workers to "encourage" participation in treatment remains somewhat unchecked (Swift, 1991).

Finally, various scholars have also suggested that the state's strong focus on rehabilitating mothers tends, in essence, to exonerate it from blame. By treating child neglect as a disease that warrants individual treatment, attention is turned away from the structural inequality that is thought to play an important role in fostering child neglect (Parton, 1985; Pelton, 1994). By concentrating efforts on "dangerous people," as Parton (1985) laments, dangerous conditions are ignored.

MATERNAL PUNISHMENT

Another response of the state to child neglect has centred on the apprehension and placement of the children of neglectful parents into substitute care. Although over the last several years child protection agencies have made more of an attempt to provide protective services to children within their homes so as to avoid removing them from their families, apprehension is still an integral part of the state's response to child neglect (Hepworth, 1985). Indeed, while the underlying objective of apprehension is to protect children from adverse conditions and parental maltreatment, scholars such as Hepworth (1985) suggest that it is the ultimate sanction for those who neglect their children. Essentially, as one social worker who had worked in child protection stated, many neglectful parents view it as a form of punishment:

> I think that every parent, when the state is taking their kid, they are feeling like they are being punished. Some of them can understand it, but they still feel the sanction.[4]

However, First Nations women have been disproportionately subjected to this form of punishment. In 1986, approximately 20 per cent of the children in substitute care in the Canadian child welfare system were of First Nations origin, and yet First Nations children comprised only 2 per cent of the overall population of Canadian children at that time (Callahan, 1993; Wharf, 1986). The overrepresentation of First Nations children in the child welfare system is thought to be intrinsically tied to the centuries of colonialist oppression and racism to which First Nations women have been subjected. This oppression has produced widespread socioeconomic problems within First Nations communities that have made it difficult for some First Nations women to care for their children, who have consequently been taken into care on grounds of neglect. As one First Nations woman who is currently working in child protection on a reserve in New Brunswick stated in frustration,

> There has been a lot of injustice [associated with colonialism]. The identity of the people themselves; the identity of the human being was stripped. That is the ultimate robbery. I think that if you were to look at populations on reserves, you are going to see a lot of problems, a high unemployment rate — that's the true socioeconomic picture [of neglect]. I look at myself as a 220 pound Band-Aid, but major surgery is needed.[5]

Culture conflict, in turn, is also thought to account for part of the overrepresentation of First Nations children taken into protective care on grounds of neglect (Callahan, 1993; Kline, 1993). All too often, as Kline (1993) notes, First Nations women have been constructed as "bad mothers" by the courts, as their parenting norms have come into conflict with dominant cultural and middle-class expectations about parenting. This construction is thought to increase the chances of having their children being taken away on the basis of neglect (Kline, 1993).

Like "maternal rehabilitation," however, the state's approach of removing First Nations and non-First Nations children from their homes does little to address the underlying socioeconomic problems that often surround child neglect. In fact, as Callahan (1993) underscores, this approach often exacerbates the socioeconomic plight of poor women. When a child is removed from his or her family, the mother can become even poorer. Such women often experience a reduction in their income assistance allowance and the loss of their child tax benefit and their eligibility for subsidized housing. Essentially, these women have to adjust to being single. If or when their children are returned to them, they may have to start all over again (e.g., reinstate benefits, secure housing, etc.). Thus, the removal of children from their home presents many with not only emotional hardships, but also economic difficulties (Callahan, 1993).

It is important to stress that the children who are removed from their mothers' care on grounds of neglect obviously also encounter many difficulties in their lives. In child-protection cases, for example, the adversarial court procedure alone can serve to drive a wedge between children and their parents. After a court battle, as studies indicate, "losing" parents frequently withdraw from their children's lives even if the loss of custody is only temporary (Fanshel, 1975; Palmer, 1989; Taking Control Project, 1982). Moreover, for all too many children, this courtroom battle is an experience that can repeat itself many times. A recent study in British Columbia indicated that 70 per cent of the children who entered into care did so on grounds of neglect; furthermore, these children were much more likely to have more than one experience in substitute care than were those who entered care because of abuse (Campbell, 1991).

In short, "maternal punishment," like "maternal rehabilitation," is thought to have a number of substantial shortcomings. Both approaches have been identified by various scholars as problematic, shortsighted responses to child neglect. Essentially, they attempt to use the coercive power and social control functions of child-protection legislation to enforce a standard of parenting. Not surprisingly, they have done little to ameliorate the problem of child neglect. However, drawing on the peacemaking perspective, in the following section I discuss a number of policy and program initiatives which, as will be argued, are better solutions to the social problem of neglect. These peacemaking alternatives are designed to address more adequately the complex socioeconomic reality of child neglect in Canada.

## Criminology of Peacemaking

Over the last decade, a new perspective known as a "criminology of peacemaking" has appeared within the criminological literature. Standing in sharp contrast to the conservative-crime control agenda, peacemaking is characterized by its focus on humanism and social justice. Critical of the contemporary criminal justice system, which is identified as too deeply embedded in coercive power and punishment, peacemaking calls for the introduction of a more just, egalitarian sociopolitical order and for the development of more peaceful, interpersonal relations among people. These, it suggests, are the means to alleviate crime and other forms of human suffering (Pepinsky, 1999; Thomas and O'Maolchatha, 1989). As noted, this perspective informs the approaches to address child neglect identified in this chapter. Therefore, a discussion of the peacemaking perspective is presented in order to provide a conceptual understanding of the contribution that it can make toward dealing with child neglect in a more humane, effective manner.

### HISTORICAL DEVELOPMENT
### OF THE PEACEMAKING PERSPECTIVE

The peacemaking perspective has grown out of the disenchantment that several critical criminologists have felt about the traditional, "law and order" approach that underpins many industrialized countries' response to crime. Although many societies have recently formulated new laws, punished more offenders, built more prisons, and quantified greater amounts of knowledge about crime, peacemakers point out that this approach appears to have done little to ameliorate criminal behaviour and other forms of suffering such as child neglect (Pepinsky, 1999; Quinney and Wildeman, 1991). As Quinney, who is an advocate of the peacemaking perspective laments,

Let us begin with a fundamental realization: No amount of thinking and no amount of public policy have brought us any closer to understanding and solving the problem of crime. The more we have reacted to crime, the farther we have removed ourselves from any understanding and any reduction of the problem. (1991:3)

Sharing Quinney's belief, a growing number of criminologists now adhere to the peacemaking perspective. It is a radical alternative to traditional criminology that has been embraced by critical scholars from a broad range of traditions (e.g., humanism, anarchism, feminism, and Marxism).

The earliest and clearest articulation of the peacemaking perspective can be traced to the work of Harold Pepinsky (1988, 1991, 1999) and Richard Quinney (1988, 1991). Enriched by a year of study in Norway in the mid-1980s, Pepinsky published a paper in 1988 which is now identified as one of the first core discussions of the peacemaking perspective. Responding to an early draft of this paper, Quinney wrote to Pepinsky and indicated that "peacemaking was the direction criminology ought to move" (Pepinsky, 1991:299). Since that time, both have worked to develop the peacemaking perspective and, consequently, scholarship in this area has deepened and broadened. Peacemakers can now point with pride to the contributions that Quinney and Pepinsky have made to the study of crime and social justice.

## THE PEACEMAKING PERSPECTIVE

Central to the peacemaking perspective is the belief that oppression, domination, and structural inequality both sustain and foster violence and other forms of suffering such as child neglect, poverty, homelessness, pollution, and war. In essence, social injustice is thought to produce conditions that generate tension, conflict, and despair both among people and among nations. In this sense, peacemakers locate the problem of crime and other forms of maltreatment in deficient sociopolitical systems rather than simply in flawed individuals (Quinney and Wildeman, 1991; Pepinsky and Quinney, 1991; Pepinsky, 1999).

To address violence and other forms of suffering, then, peacemakers argue that it is necessary to introduce a more just, egalitarian sociopolitical order rather than harsh, controlling and punitive forms of punishment. For Quinney and Wildeman (1991), scholars who have written in the area of Marxist criminology, such a social order would strive to alleviate such structural problems as racism, sexism and classism, and it would be "based on cooperative social relations, [it would be] a communal society, ... a developing socialist society" (110). These peacemakers believe that it is important to introduce a democratic socialist political order for, as they state, "there can be no peace without justice" (Quinney and Wildeman, 1991:117).

Peacemakers contend, however, that it is not simply enough to introduce a more just sociopolitical order. To generate communities and societies that are more peaceful and less burdened by violence and other forms of suffering, individuals have to begin to act in a more peaceful, loving, compassionate manner as well. For peacemakers, social change is deeply interwoven with personal change (McDermott, 1994). As Quinney (1991) explains,

> Without peace of mind and heart, there can be no social peace between people and no peace in societies, nations and in the world.... The means cannot be different than the ends; peace can come only out of peace. (10)

To foster peace and compassion within oneself, peacemaking emphasizes an ethic of responsiveness. Simply put, this ethic calls upon individuals to explore their connection to other human beings, to the environment, and to the human suffering that exists within their personal lives and in the world around them. It is necessary to do this, according to the peacemaking perspective, for "social action comes out of the informed heart, out of the clear and enlightened mind" (Quinney, 1991:10).

Finally, along with the call for personal and political change, the peacemaking perspective also suggests that it is important to transform the criminal justice system. Given its reliance on force, control, and punishment, the criminal justice system is identified by the peacemaking perspective as an institution that is founded on violence. It is a system, as peacemakers lament, that assumes that violence can be overcome with violence. Therefore, the peacemaking perspective calls for the introduction of programs and policies within the criminal justice system that are thought to be more humane. These initiatives are identified as "peacemaking alternatives" and include such things as alternative dispute-resolution techniques, problem-oriented policing, abolition of facilities, community alternatives to prison, and drug treatment. They are not definitive solutions, but rather stepping stones that can be currently employed by societies as they move toward more peaceful relations. They offer, as Quinney (1991) indicates, "the concrete beginnings of a criminology of peacemaking" (11).

### PEACEMAKING: ITS APPLICATION
### TO THE PROBLEM OF CHILD NEGLECT

As the succinct review of the "criminology of peacemaking" has sought to demonstrate, this perspective adheres to the belief that social problems such as crime and child neglect have their origin in the social relationships of an unjust social order and that these social problems should be dealt with through personal, political, and institutional changes rather than through coercive laws and punishment. Drawing on this view, in this section I identify a number of alternative approaches that could be undertaken to address child neglect in a more humane and peaceful manner in Canada. These responses stand in sharp contrast to the state's traditional understanding and approach to child neglect which locates the problem of neglect in maternal care-giving deficiencies and which focuses on using the power and social control functions of the law to enforce a standard of maternal behaviour.

### PEACEMAKING ALTERNATIVES
### AT THE INTERPERSONAL LEVEL

Although there are a variety of initiatives that could be undertaken by the state to deal with child neglect cases in a more compassionate, humane manner, one viable peacemaking alternative would involve the introduction of mediation practices into child-protection procedures. Mediation is an alternative dispute-resolution technique that allows individuals who are involved in a conflict to work through differences with the support and aid of a third party (Palmer, 1989; Volpe, 1991).

Mediation has been identified as an attractive and useful dispute-resolution technique by peacemakers for a variety of reasons (Quinney and Wildeman, 1991; Pepinsky and Quinney, 1991). Importantly, mediation is thought to offer disputants the opportunity to explore the underlying concerns of a problem. It is also thought to provide the participants with a chance to collectively develop creative options to the conflict that is being addressed. As peacemakers suggest, these components of mediation can serve to empower disputants and, in turn, foster more peaceful inter-personal relations among them (Quinney and Wildeman, 1991; Volpe, 1991). Thus, although the utility of mediation has been called into question by some on the grounds that, for example, mediation may not effectively address the power imbalances that exist between parties and on the grounds that it may be difficult to encourage disputants to participate in mediation (Merry, 1989; Davis and Salem, 1984), peacemakers believe that in many situations it can function as a valuable peacemaking alternative (Volpe, 1991).

With respect to cases of neglect, it is not unreasonable to suggest that mediation, could serve a number of useful and important functions. Advocates of mediation such as Palmer (1989), suggest that it could be used to divert less serious cases of neglect from court proceedings. As noted earlier, the adversarial process involved in settling child-custody disputes may further exacerbate the crisis that victims of child neglect experience as it may drive an even deeper wedge between themselves and their parents. The adversarial process may also generate distress and despair among those charged with neglect. These individuals may come to feel alienated and refuse to accept further services from child protection agencies even when they only lose custody of their children temporarily (Palmer, 1989).

Mediation, however, may serve as a partial solution to some of the dilemmas that arise out of the adversarial process in child-neglect custody cases. The use of mediation to arrive at a childcare agreement may, for example, help to maintain more reasonable relations among parents and their children. Parents may feel less alienated by the mediation process and may be less likely to withdraw from the lives of their children. The environment that is established in the mediation conference may also provide the parents with an opportunity to express their views more directly and, therefore, a more sound child-care plan may emerge from the process. Finally, given that cooperative practices are central to the mediation process, the parents who are involved in the procedure may be less likely to feel as if they are being coerced and punished (Palmer, 1989; Volpe, 1991; Quinney, 1991). In short, mediation may introduce more humane and compassionate practices into child-protection procedures that would conceivably make the experience less hurtful for the poor, single-parent women who are most likely to be involved in this process.

PEACEMAKING ALTERNATIVES AT
THE STRUCTURAL LEVEL OF SOCIETY

According to the tenets of the peacemaking perspective, to address the problem of child neglect it is important not only to introduce more kind and caring programs and initiatives at the inter-personal level, but also to introduce policies and sociopolitical changes that would promote the development of a more just, egalitarian society — one that would focus less on such strategies as maternal punishment and maternal rehabilitation and more on addressing the socioeconomic needs of women and, in particular, the needs of poor, single-parent women.

Consistent with the peacemaking perspective, then, I argue that to provide a comprehensive, humane, and preventative response to the problem of child neglect, it is necessary to make major changes in the social and economic structure of the Canadian society. It is critical, in essence, to move beyond the current patriarchal, capitalist sociopolitical order toward an alternative vision of society that would be less deeply entrenched in such structural inequalities as racism, classism, and sexism. Although it is well beyond the scope of this chapter to articulate such a vision, in accordance with such peacemakers as Quinney and Wildeman (1991), this sociopolitical arrangement should be organized around the democratic socialist principles of solidarity, equality, and entitlement, which could be fostered through initiatives designed to redistribute power, income and societal, resources.

With such a sociopolitical arrangement in mind, in the following section I identify a number of "women policies" and "gender equity policies" which, from the perspective of various socialist feminists (Ferguson, 1988; Hernes, 1987), can be viewed as part of and consistent with a long-term strategy to organize society around democratic socialist principles. "Women policies," as Hernes (1987) explains, are social policies that involve welfare-income transfers and services aimed at increasing the quality of life for women and children. "Gender equity policies," in turn, are social policies that are concerned with increasing women's status and social power. While space does not allow for a comprehensive review of an agenda of such policies, I present an outline of some important policy initiatives in order to provide concrete examples of measures that can be taken to address child neglect in a more peaceful, caring, and compassionate manner. As preliminary steps toward structural change, the policies that are presented can be identified as being in accordance with the peacemaking perspective.

WOMEN POLICIES

Rather than relying on the traditional state policy of maternal punishment and maternal rehabilitation, various women's policies could be introduced to offer a more complete network of support to women in general and, in particular, to the women who come to the attention of child-welfare authorities. Included in this agenda could be, for example, a housing allowance policy. As noted earlier, studies indicate that substandard, crowded housing is often associated with the cases of child neglect that come to the attention of child-protection agencies (Wolock and Horowitz, 1984). The introduction of a housing allowance policy in Canada could provide such families with access to more suitable housing arrangements. Unlike the Canadian low-income housing programs that benefit only a small percentage of poor families, the housing allowance policies that appear in many industrialized countries are an essential component of comprehensive national family policies (Sidel, 1992). Simply stated, housing allowances are cash awards that assist families in their payment of rent, housing taxes, and other costs associated with housing. Given the high cost of housing in many parts of Canada and the growing problem of family homelessness, these allowances could be an important income supplement for low-income families with children (Kamerman, 1989).

A guaranteed child-support policy could also offer a more complete network of income support to women. As Evans (1991) emphasizes, lack of child support payments is one of the factors that make single-parent women vulnerable to poverty. To date, a high rate of default on child-support payments exists in Canada (Canadian Advisory Council on the Status of Women, 1987). Indeed, it is not unreasonable to assume that this problem contributes to the economic hardships of many single-parent families who are involved in the child welfare system. To address the dilemma of nonpayment of child support, however, a growing number of industrialized countries have introduced guaranteed child-support policies. These are policies in which a government guarantees to pay a minimum support payment to the custodial parent when the noncustodial parent fails to pay child support or fails to pay at an adequate level. In such cases, the government assumes responsibility for collecting the unpaid child support from the noncustodial parent. This policy has been identified as a means to reduce the need for welfare, and it has been heralded as an instrument that can help to alleviate the economic difficulties of single-parent families (Kamerman, 1989; Sidel, 1992).

The establishment of a national system of day care, in turn, is another policy option that would be beneficial to many women and, more specifically, to the low-income women who come to the attention of child protection authorities. One the greatest obstacles to employment for low- and moderate-income families is the lack of affordable, accessible, and flexible child-care options. Recognizing this dilemma, a substantial number of developing and industrialized countries have established national child-care policies; such policies tend to be jointly subsidized by municipal and national governments and are provided on an income-based fee to families. These policies are thought to highlight the importance of the economic value of child care and provide women with an opportunity to participate more fully in the paid labour force (Ferguson, 1988; Sidel, 1992; Spakes, 1992). As such, they are policy options that may serve to ease the economic strain that a substantial number of neglectful mothers endure.

Finally, while certainly not a definitive means of addressing the socio-economic oppression that many poor, single-parent women encounter, raising the rates of income assistance above the level of poverty is another policy that could be undertaken to improve the social safety net for women (Sidel, 1992). Across Canada, income-assistance rates do not adequately cover the costs of the basic necessities required to sustain a family. As the National Council of Welfare (1987) has noted, "In all the provinces, the definition of basic requirements is so stringent that the welfare benefit levels calculated according to these standards permit only an impoverished existence" (49). Indeed, the difficulties imposed by the low level of income assistance has, created economic crises for many families who are involved in the child welfare system. Raising income assistance to a level that would provide welfare recipients with a more adequate standard of living may serve as a more peaceful way of addressing the social problem of child neglect.

GENDER EQUITY POLICIES

To provide a humane and preventative response to child neglect, it is also critical to introduce policies which, as Hernes (1987) underscores, "[aim] at increasing women's political and social prestige and power in a more direct fashion" (26). What is needed, as various socialist feminists argue

(Ferguson, 1988), are policies designed to break down the patriarchy that women experience in the public and private spheres of their lives.

To that end, it is important to introduce, policies, for example, that are designed to increase women's access to and equality within the Canadian labour market. The gendered division of the labour market that has historically existed in Canada has segregated women into the lowest paid and least stable employment (Evans, 1991). As a starting point to counter this oppression, it is necessary to introduce pay equity policies that stress the value of work performed by women and introduce equal pay for work of equal value. These types of policies, in combination with initiatives that would encourage rearranging domestic and family responsibilities and increase women's access to education and training, could all be part of a larger agenda to generate social and economic independence for women.

Concomitantly, policies which would honour and encourage women's reproductive rights, new forms of family organizations, and greater access to and representation in decision-making arenas are all examples of initiatives that could serve to empower women. It is important to note, however, that by themselves these policies simply reform rather than transform society, but in conjunction with larger social movements to overcome the current patriarchal, capitalist sociopolitical order, they are consistent with the peacemaking perspective in criminology.

In summation, then, the policies and measures that have been discussed in this section can be identified as offering a more humane and compassionate response to the social problem of child neglect. In sharp contrast to the state's traditional response of maternal punishment and maternal rehabilitation, these initiatives more readily respond to the complex socioeconomic problems that are often associated with child neglect. Indeed, while these types of initiatives do not fit well into the current sociopolitical climate, this does not, as Neysmith (1991) argues, "designate them as unworkable or as naive idealism" (283). Many of the measures that have been discussed appear in various industrialized countries and, in particular, in Scandinavian social democracies. They reflect a commitment to social justice and to the belief that social problems are best addressed through measures that are designed to foster equality rather than through large investments in institutions (i.e., foster care, prisons, jails) which can only react to social problems once they have been created.

## Conclusion

As I have sought to demonstrate in this chapter, child neglect has largely been identified as a problem originating in maternal care-giving deficiencies. As such, it has generally been dealt with in an individualistic and gender-specific manner. Posed behind this socially structured image, however, is the human face of suffering. It is the face of women who live, in many instances, complex lives that are deeply challenged and constrained by socioeconomic problems that are the outgrowth of structural inequalities. It is, in essence, the face of individuals who find it difficult to engage in care giving under difficult conditions.

The state's response to child neglect has, nonetheless, largely ignored this reality. It has generally focused on identifying unacceptable parental behaviour and, upon such identification, has sought to enforce a standard of parental care. However, to more adequately address child neglect and the suffering that surrounds this social problem, it is necessary to move beyond the state's narrow approach of punishment and rehabilitation. It is simply not enough to try to protect children within their families; they and their caregivers should also be protected from the structural inequalities that affect families (Swift, 1991).

To address child neglect comprehensively, it is therefore necessary to recognize and respond to the suffering and despair of the families that come to the attention of child-protection authorities. From the perspective of peacemakers this would involve the development of more caring policies and personal initiatives and, in turn, the development of a more peaceful, egalitarian sociopolitical order for children and their parents — one that would identify child care as a collective rather than simply a maternal responsibility. It should no longer be acceptable to assume, as Hutchison (1992) suggests, "that children's needs can be met whether or not their caregivers [have] access to resources for providing sufficient care" (67).

## Notes

1. Semi-structured, in-depth interview with a female welfare client. Fredericton, N.B., April, 1995.
2. Semi-structured, in-depth interview with a male social worker. Fredericton, N.B., April, 1995.
3. Semi-structured, in-depth interview with a male social worker. Fredericton, N.B., April, 1995.

4. Semi-structured, in-depth interview with a male social worker. Fredericton, N.B., April, 1995.

5. Semi-structured, in-depth interview with a female, First Nation social worker. Fredericton, N.B., April, 1995.

# References

American Human Association (1988). *Highlights of official child neglect and abuse reporting: 1986.* Denver, CO: American Humane Association.

Boyd, S. (1989). "Child custody, ideologies, and employment." *Canadian Journal of Women and the Law* 3:111-33.

Breines, W., and L. Gordon (1983). "The new scholarship on family violence." *Signs: Journal of Women in Culture and Society*, 8:490-531.

Callahan, M. (1993). "Feminist approaches: Women recreate child welfare." In B. Wharf (ed.), *Rethinking child welfare in Canada.* Toronto: McClelland & Stewart.

Callahan, M. (1985). "Public apathy and government parsimony: A review of child welfare in Canada." In K. Levitt and B. Wharf (eds.), *The challenge of child welfare.* Vancouver: University of British Columbia Press.

Campbell, J. (1991). *An analysis of variables in child protection apprehensions and judicial dispositions in British Columbia child welfare practices.* M.S.W. Thesis, University of British Columbia.

Canadian Advisory Council on the Status of Women (1987). *Integration and participation: Women's work in the home and in the labour force.* Ottawa: CACSW.

Canadian Child Welfare Association (1988). *A choice of futures: Canada's commitment to its children.* Ottawa: Canadian Child Welfare Association.

Chamberland, C., *et al.* (1986). "Abusive and negligent treatment of children: Canadian and American realities." *Canadian Journal of Behavioral Science* 18:391-412.

Crimmins, D., *et al.* (1984). "A training technique for improving the parent-child interaction skills of an abusive neglectful mother." *Child Abuse and Neglect* 8:533-39.

Davis, A., and R. Salem (1984). "Dealing with power imbalances in the mediation of interpersonal disputes." *Mediation Quarterly* December:17-26.

Evans, P. (1991). "The sexual division of poverty: The consequences of gendered caring." In C. Baines *et al,* (eds.), *Women's Caring: Feminist Perspectives on Social Welfare.* Toronto: McClelland & Stewart.

Fanshel, D. (1975). "Parental visiting of children in foster care: Key to discharge?" *Social Service Review* 49:493-514.

Ferguson, E. (1988). "Liberal and socialist feminist perspectives on childcare." *Canadian Social Work Review* 5:44-64.

Fineman, M. (1991). "Images of mothers in poverty discourses." *Duke Law Journal* 2:271-95.

Gil, D. (1970). "Violence against children." Cambridge, MA: Harvard University Press.

Gordon, L. (1988). *Heroes of their own lives.* New York: Viking.

Hepworth, P. (1985). "Child neglect and abuse." In K. Levitt and B. Wharf (eds.), *The Challenge of Child Welfare.* Vancouver: University of British Columbia Press.

Hernes, H. (1987). *Welfare state and woman power.* Olso: Norwegian University Press.

Hutchison, E. (1992). "Child welfare as a woman's issue." *Families in Society: The Journal of Contemporary Human Services* 73:67-78.

Hutchison, E. (1990). "Child maltreatment: Can it be defined?" *Social Service Review* 64:60-78.

Jones, A., and L. Rutman (1981). *In the children's aid.* Toronto: University of Toronto Press.

Jones, L. (1990). "Unemployment and child abuse." *Families in Society: The Journal of Contemporary Human Services* 71:579-488.

Kamerman, S. (1989). "Toward a child policy decade." *Child Welfare* 68:371-90.

Kamerman, S., and A. Kahn (1990). "If CPS is driving child welfare — Where do we go from here?" *Public Welfare* 48:9-13.

Kline, M. (1993). "Complicating the ideology of motherhood: Child welfare and First Nation women." *Queen's Law Journal* 18:306-42.

Krishnan, V., and K. Morrison (1995). "An ecological model of child maltreatment in a Canadian province." *Child Abuse and Neglect* 19:101-13.

McDermott, J. (1994). "Criminology as peacemaking, feminist ethics and the victimization of women." *Women and Criminal Justice* 5:21-44.

Merry, S. (1989). "Myth and practice in the mediation process." In M. Wright and B. Galaway (eds.), *Mediation in the Criminal Justice System: Victims, Offenders and Community.* London: Sage.

National Council of Welfare (1987). *Welfare: The tangled safety net.* Ottawa: Supply and Services Canada.

Neysmith, S. (1991)."From community care to a social model of care." In C. Baines *et al*, (eds.), *Women's caring: Feminist perspectives on social welfare.* Toronto: McClelland & Stewart.

Novick, M., and R. Volpe (1989). *Perspectives on social practice: Children at risk project.* Toronto: Laidlaw Foundation.

Palmer, S. (1989). "Mediation in child protection cases: An alternative to the adversary system." *Child Welfare* 68:21-31.

Parton, N. (1985). *The politics of child abuse.* London: The Macmillan Press.

Pelton, L. (1994). "Is poverty a key contributor to child maltreatment?" In E. Gambrill and T. Stein (eds.), *Controversial issues in child welfare.* Boston: Allyn and Bacon.

Pepinsky, H. (1999). "Peacemaking primer." In B. Arrigo (ed.), *Social justice/criminal justice: The maturation of critical theory in law, crime and deviance.* Belmont, CA: West/Wadsworth.

Pepinsky, H. (1991). "Peacemaking in criminology and criminal justice." In H. Pepinsky and R. Quinney (eds.), *Criminology as Peacemaking.* Bloomington: Indiana University Press.

Pepinsky, H. (1988). "Violence as unresponsiveness: Toward a new conception of crime." *Justice Quarterly* 5:539-87.

Pepinsky, H. and R. Quinney. (1991). *"Criminology as peacemaking."* Bloomington: Indiana University Press.

Polansky, N., Gausin, J., and A. Kilpatrick. (1992). "The Maternal characteristics scale: A cross validation." *Child Welfare* 71:271-80.

Quinney, R. (1991). "The way of peace: On crime, suffering, and service." In H. Pepinsky and R. Quinney (eds.), *Criminology as Peacemaking.* Bloomington: Indiana University Press.

Quinney, R. (1988). "The theory and practice of peacemaking in the development of radical criminology." *The Critical Criminologist* 1:5.

Quinney, R., and R. Wildeman (1991). *The problem of crime: A peace and social justice perspective.* Mountain View: Mayfield Publishing.

Roberts, D. (1993). "Motherhood and crime." *Iowa Law Journal* 79:95-141.

Sedlak, A. (1991). *National incidence and prevalence of child abuse reporting: 1988; revised report.* Rockville, MD: Westat.

Sidel, R. (1992). *Women and children last: The plight of poor women in affluent America.* New York: Penguin Books.

Spakes, P. (1992). "National family policy — Sweden vs. the U.S." *Affilia* 7:44-60.

Swift, K. (1995). "An outrage to common decency: Historical perspectives on child neglect." *Child Welfare* 1:71-91.

Swift, K. (1991). "Contradictions in child welfare: Neglect and responsibility." In C. Baines *et al*, (eds.), *Women's caring: Feminist perspectives on social welfare*. Toronto: McClelland & Stewart.

Taking Control Project (1982). *Searching for my children*. (Videotape) Regina, Saskatchewan: University of Regina.

Thomas, J., and A. O'Maolchatha. (1989). "Reassessing the critical metaphor: An optimistic revisionist view." *Justice Quarterly* 6:143-72.

Tousignant, C. *et al*, (1984). "The downhill trends in prevention." *International Review of Community Development* 11:6-44.

U.S. Department of Health and Human Services (1988). *National study of the incidence and severity of child abuse and neglect*. Washington, D.C.: U.S. Department of Health and Human Services.

U.S. Department of Health and Human Services (1981). *National study of the incidence and severity of child abuse and neglect*. Washington, D.C.: U.S. Department of Health and Human Services.

Volpe, M. (1991). "Mediation in the criminal justice system." In H. Pepinsky, and R. Quinney (eds.), *Criminology as peacemaking*. Bloomington: Indiana University Press.

Wedenoja, M. (1991). "Mothers are not to blame: Confronting cultural biases in the area of serious mental illness." In M. Bricker-Jenkins *et al*. (eds.), *Feminist social work practice in clinical settings*. New Bury Park: Sage Publications.

Wharf, B. (1986). "Social welfare and the political system." In J. Turner and F. Turner (eds.), *Canadian social welfare*. Toronto: Collier Macmillan.

Wharf, B. (1985). "The challenge of child welfare." In K. Levitt and B. Wharf (eds.) *The challenge of child welfare*. Vancouver: University of British Columbia Press.

Wiehe, V. (1992). *Working with child abuse and neglect*. Itasca, Illinois: F.E. Peacock Publishers.

Wolock, I., and B. Horowitz. (1984). "Child maltreatment as a social problem: The neglect of neglect." *American Journal of Orthopsychiatry* 54:530-43.

Wolock, I. and B. Horowitz. (1979). "Child maltreatment and material deprivation among AFDC families." *Social Service Review* 53:175-94.

Zuravin, S. (1989). "The ecology of child abuse and neglect: Review of the literature and presentation of data." *Violence and Victims* 4:101-20.

# PART IV

*Social Location and Resistance to Law*

# 9

## Communities are Social:
## Locating Homeplace in the Sociology of Law

AUDREY SPRENGER

Legality is a durable and powerful structure because it is not exclusively legal. (Ewick and Silby, 1998)

In Margaret Laurence's *The Diviners*, a fictional autobiography, the answers to social identity rest in the last place protagonist Morag Gunn thinks to look — her homeplace, Manawaka, a small, rural town in the backwoods of Manitoba. However, it is in this revelation of place that Morag finds the possibilities for self-determination that such answers promise. As a girl growing up on Hill Street — among the poor and native — she longs to escape the filth and social stigma of her surroundings. However, although the lure of autonomy and mobility draw her to the city, none of the spoils of urban(e) life (education, marriage, sophistication) can obliterate the power of Manawaka, ever-present in her actions, words and imagination. Morag continues to travel with persistence, eventually residing as a Canadian expatriate, far and away from her childhood home; however, she ultimately finds herself reinventing the town and its inhabitants as an ancestral locale in stories spun for her daughter Pique. Like a diviner, who seeks running water beneath the earth in order to dig a well, Morag Gunn seeks the experiences beneath her memories of Manawaka, in order to sketch a cartography of nation, community, and self.

As Morag unravels the layers of experiences and conversations from her girlhood relationships — with her adoptive father, Christie Logan, the socially reviled town "scavenger" and his grotesquely fat, half-witted wife, Prin; members of the town's elite, who pity yet disparage her; her browbeaten and timid school friend Eva; Lazurus Tonnerre, a Métis Indian, head of the only family in Manawaka less respectable than her own; and perhaps most importantly, Lazurus' son, Jules Skinner Tonnerre, Morag's one true friend and love, as well as the father of Pique — she begins to expose the rigid and invasive social structure obscured behind Manawaka's public face of morality. Using scraps of hymns, patriotic rhymes and lessons learned from school books, tales told by Christie and songs written by Skinner, as well as excerpts from her own short stories and novels, Morag vividly captures the complicated and often conflicting ways in which different residents of Manawaka see themselves, their communities, and each other, particularly when recalling times past. She realizes that just as there is more than one way to experience and remember a shared homeplace, there is more than one way to understand the community identities linked to homeplace.

Laurence's metonymic use of Manawaka as the definitive core of Morag Gunn's social identity effectively combines the theoretical work of two schools of sociological thought with emphasis on the sociology of law — the Chicago School's field studies in social ecology (cf. Thomas and Znaniecki, 1927; Park 1925) and feminist epistemologies of home (cf. Thompson and Tyagi, 1996; Anzaldua, 1987; hooks, 1990; Martin and Mohonty, 1986; Pratt, 1984). Like the Chicago School, Laurence accounts for people's routine movement and activity to reveal how the mundane details of where they move and rest capture their social position in relationship to legal institutions (ranging from the streets to the police to social welfare agencies); and like feminist epistemologies of home, she accounts for people's bodies and imaginations to reveal how social experiences define the ways people see their place in the world as sociolegal subjects. Read as a "sociology homeplace," Laurence's *The Diviners* produces powerful sociological concepts that locate the tensions between people's actual experiences of "community" and institutionalized ideals of "work," "culture," and "family," and explains how sociologists can shatter, then reassemble, the "everyday/everynight" workings of legal institutions — or what Dorothy Smith (1987) would call "the relations of ruling."

In this chapter, I will re-interpret Laurence's analytical strategies as a mode of sociological inquiry to explore the very mutable relationship between "society" and "the law." Drawing from my experiences pursuing ethnographic field research in Southern Manitoba, not far from where Laurence envisioned Manawaka to be, I will employ the language of maps and narratives to show how people's ordinary experiences of home articulates the boundaries and extents of legality. This analysis is important to broader discussions about the social and legal status of "marginalized" communities, since settlement "out in the bush" is the homeplace of an "other Canada" often excluded or distorted in most forms of social discourse, including the sociology of law. "Other" not because it is somehow outside the Canadian social landscape, or culturally insignificant, but because homeplace "out in the bush" owes its existence, and often survival, to a long history of occupation and exploitation by the state, church, and forest industry. Therefore, by accounting for the experiences of people who reside in this homeplace I am able to offer a "situated" analysis of legality (Haraway, 1991) — one which is so explicitly marked by its social coordinates that it is actually locatable in the world.

## Sociology on the Skids

Seventy kilometres northeast of Winnipeg, at the intersection of Highway's 304 and 11, is a Mohawk filling station called Clark's Corner (MAP 1). The gas pumps are weakly lit by low wattage bulbs, and wired underneath the fuel prices is a hand painted sign for "fresh minnows," available at the grocery store inside. On most winter mornings the parking lot is filled with empty flat-bed logging trucks and brand new four-wheel drives — all left parked with the engine still running, blowing exhaust into the below-freezing air. In the doorway entrance to the cashier are stacked copies of the regional newspaper, "The Community Voice," as well as day-old copies of the "Winnipeg Free Press" and "Sun," brought in by bus from the city, and on the walls are tacked-up messages advertising snowmobiles for sale and high-school hockey games, Métis Association Board meetings and the annual Christmas pageant at L'Ecole Français. A Rothman's Cigarette clock ticks off at an hour ahead, left unchanged from daylight saving time, and underneath the cashier's counter is a glass case displaying Indian beaded belts and motor oil for sale. To the left is a grocery store with more highway goods, a magazine rack, and bathrooms. And to the right is a small restaurant that smells of fresh cigarette smoke and grease. The windows are steamed up in places from the heat and along the back wall is a lit-up Pepsi sign with black plastic letters listing off the choices of daily soups and pies.

By seven in the morning, all of the tables alongside the perimeter of the room are empty, but next to the kitchen a large group of men with woollen caps pushed back on their heads, and various layers of flannel clothing strewn on the floor below them, are sitting at four tables pushed together, with chairs jammed on either side. A waitress with two cardigans, one buttoned over the other, comes in and out of the kitchen with plates of eggs and sausages and toast. Every few minutes a man picks up his extra layers of clothes, and often a lunch box and thermos, and leaves the table, only to be replaced within minutes by another man coming into Clark's to join the crowd sitting next to the kitchen, smoking and eating breakfast.

Just porridge please for me Pat, and fast eh? Tell Marie not to scorch it today eh? Nothing black floating in the milk sweetie.

You hear that Marie? They're complaining about your porridge again. You're running late today Dave, eh? Shifts going to start without ya. Ann not get you up and fed on time to get to work or did they just call you in today because the machines were off last night? The mill is going to be backed up with all those logs eh? Good way to start a Monday.

Tell them to order some eggs then. You guys can afford it with all the dividends they got last week

You bring with you any of that ham you won at the Legion on Friday night, Dave? Give them that to serve with your eggs or did ya trade it in for beer tickets?

Been buying extra beer tickets instead of taking the ham, eh Dave? I'm sure Ann would appreciate that. Well, I guess it doesn't matter how much you're drinking at the Legion these nights eh? Not that you're allowed to drive anymore? Have the Queen's Cops still after ya, eh? The cops are after all of you guys in your new trucks.

Clark's stays empty until mid morning, when the parking lot becomes jammed with muddy and salt-covered school buses, and the restaurant with the women who drive them. One by one they come into the restaurant, wrapped warmly head to toe, with bright orange safety vests tied over their winter coats. Like the men who stopped off at Clark's Corner earlier in the morning, the school bus drivers sit clustered around the tables near the kitchen talking loudly, their voices carrying across the room.

Pat, can you believe the snow this morning? I couldn't find the kids along the road for all the drips. I can't believe we're getting snow like this already. It's going to be a bloody long winter.

I know, I know. They didn't come out and plough us out till this morning. I had to walk across the bridge to make it over here for work.

With that wind blowing? They're lucky to have you here, eh? You couldn't get some young thing up and out of bed, tramping across that bridge to open up. Not these days with the kids up all night in that bar.

The waitresses often sit with the school bus drivers, lighting cigarettes and drinking coffee, getting up only occasionally to take and serve an order for the few other patrons scattered across the room. Several empty tables away sit some men eating pie — the backs of their chairs each draped with a jacket, some marked "Sagkeeng First Nation," others "Indian Posse." Their conversations are spoken in low voices and periodically one of the men gets up from the table to fetch a coffee pot from the self-serve burners by the kitchen, and refills the others' cups. Right next to them are two elderly couples playing Cribbage, speaking to one another in French. Both the men and the elderly couples stay sitting in Clark's Corner long after the school bus drivers leave, and they remain through the noon-hour rush of office workers from the Mill and Band Office who have come in for lunch. By early afternoon every table in Clark's Corner is taken, many of them overflowing with bodies hunched over in conversation, an occasional voice rising above the din.

Hennesey, you son of a bitch! I told you we'd beat the hell out of you bastards! What kind of a fag Français have you got out there for a goalie?

Waitresses carry trays of food high over their heads, stepping over briefcases and kicked off boots. Every few minutes people push through the door, letting in gusts of freezing air, paying for gas and leaning past the cashier to scan the crowed tables, always shouting someone's name and often coming into the restaurant themselves to claim an empty seat. Not until after three o'clock when Clark's empties again and the second shift of waitresses start working, do the elderly couples pack up their cribbage board, kiss each other goodbye, and leave. Once gone, Clark's is empty except for two Mounties who sit by the windows, smoking and tapping the ashes from their cigarettes into the coffee creamer. Through the windows become visible packs of teenagers walking along the highway — girls with eye-shadowed and lip-glossed faces wearing unzipped ski jackets, and boys with hockey skates slung low over their shoulders. They dodge the heavy afternoon traffic of logging trucks coming in from the North, packed with fresh-cut timber. In groups of four and five they stop off at Clark's Corner, to linger in the grocery store, read magazines, and smoke cigarettes. Before dusk falls they are back walking along the highway, most of them headed west. A line of cars queues up along the gas pumps, and men wearing hockey jackets with "Abitibi Price Paper Company" embroidered over their breast pockets stand by their vehicles, stamping their feet, talking to one another.

> Not stopping by the Legion for a beer tonight?
> I'm half way home already.
> See you at the game tonight, then?
> If my wife lets me out of the house.

The line of cars at the gas pump slowly disappears, and as in the early morning trucks pull up, skidding sloppily into the few empty parking spots, the drivers young men in work clothes. They disappear into Clark's, then, one by one, reemerging with bags of take-out and Styrofoam cups, they climb back into their trucks, driving off in the direction of the mill.

Located just outside the provincial municipality of Powerview, Clark's Corner is an important stop in this industrial forest — from the Northern bush come truckers and loggers; from across the river, members of the Ojibway Band at Fort Alexander; from upriver Francophones living on old homesteads and family farms; and from downriver residents of Pine Falls — a privately owned and operated mill town. Like the governmental offices and grocery stores, schools, churches, and hockey arenas built up along Highway 11, Clark's Corner is one of the few places in the immediate area where people can stop off and congregate, since most sites of settlement in this industrial forest — sanctioned by industrial projects, Treaty Rights or language — are places that are closely surveyed, with restricted access.

Such settlements started around the early 1890s with the influx of Hudson Bay fur-traders, Catholic missionaries sent to assimilate the Ojibway, and Francophone farmers who moved their families from Quebec. Internal colonization continued with the construction of a pulp and paper mill, logging camps, and a hydroelectricity plant, which between 1926 and 1980 brought waves of mostly Anglophone migrants —

entire families from both Eastern and Western Canada seeking work, housing, schools, and healthcare in the company townsite of Pine Falls.

Residents of these different places remain socially bound by a shared dependence on forest resources — primarily on the jobs and revenue generated by the pulp and paper mill, although in a few cases, for sustainability. However, each residential enclave (including schools and churches), is physically segregated from the next by a few kilometres of highway, and each has legalistic restrictions with regards to daily traffic and permanent residence within it. Such restrictions were most recently reinforced by on-going sovereignty initiatives put forth by the Band on Fort Alexander; the re-opening late in 1992 of the Catholic Francophone School in East St. Georges, and the 1993 worker buy-out of the Abitibi Price pulp and paper mill, which included the corporate townsite at Pine Falls.

Built at the intersection of these physical and discursive borders, Clark's Corner "reflects" and "is reflective of" the sites of settlement that flank its every side. It is a place where colony intersects with industry; crown welfare meets corporate capitalism; native grates against white; French (accented with Ojibway) interrupts English (accented with French); Catholic sits next to Anglican; old crosses paths with young; man meets woman and woman meets man. It is a place where residents catch rides out to the bush camps or to the city; fuel up their trucks or pick up milk; post notices and get the newspaper; have breakfast; park their school bus; pass the time; greet one another; ignore one another; flirt and fight. But perhaps most importantly, Clark's Corner is one of the only places in this industrial forest where women can find paid employment as waitresses, and where people living on the reserve at Fort Alexander can sit down and drink a cup of coffee.

Roadside stops like Clark's Corner have long met the needs of forest dwellers, especially those who do not have free access to the everyday social provisions (such as housing, employment, utilities or a grocery store) located within residential settlements officially recognized by institutions like the state, the forest industry or the Francophone Catholic Church. Long before ground was even broken for the mill and company townsite at Pine Falls, Métis Indians who were denied treaty status by the federal government for being "too French" and jamming homesteads, and by the Francophone Catholic Church for being "too Indian," settled along the borders of Fort Alexander and St. Georges in "Bannock Town" — a small settlement of tents and shacks named for the fry bread eaten by the families who lived there.

After construction of the mill and company townsite of Pine Falls in 1926, "Bannock Town" swelled with the influx of workers lacking the requisite marital status or dependents for company housing, and continued to grow with the traffic of seasonal workers moving in and out of the bush, as well as with unmarried women, often with dependents. This small cluster of shacks, bar, and brothel — crowded tightly alongside Highway 11 — were distinguishable from the Métis settlement in "Bannock Town" only by their shiny tin roofs, and with the construction of a bilingual Catholic Church and public school (between 1939 and 1945), the two makeshift neighbourhoods continued to expand into one another, people settling farther and farther east toward St. Georges. However, after both the state and Catholic Chruch threatened to raze the Pinewood Beer Parlour and Shamrock Hotel (i.e., bordello) in 1948 — all part of broader national efforts to curtail alcohol consumption and prostitution among Treaty Indians — "Tin Town" merged with "Bannock Town" and these two shanty settlements incorporated as the village of Powerview. Once marked with this municipal address, the tavern became legal, the whorehouse officially ignored, and many families in "Bannock Town" eligible for some government-subsidized housing and welfare.

When I think of the activity in Clark's Corner, my memories are dominated by people in conversation, so dense with idiomatic expressions, shared memories, and in-jokes that waitresses would jump in and out of discussions without missing a beat — as if they'd heard it all before, as if they knew what would be said next. And although I quickly became familiar with the everyday routines and schedules of the people who moved through there, for a long time these conversations remained almost incomprehensible to me, a constantly shifting pattern of movement and voices, where seemingly obvious markers of community (such as tables of people divided by skin colour or the conversations and silences between different languages) were readily defied and often dissolved before my very eyes (like when fair-skinned men wore native gang jackets or Anglophone waitresses answered Ojibways in French). This sense of confusion persisted well beyond my first few field trips to the region and lasted long after I started my field research (which extended over several years and included more than six months of "permanent residency" there). Even after I myself was both a subject and practitioner of the daily rumours, gossip, and secrets passing through Clark's Corner, I was often overcome by feelings of unfamiliarity, caught between the fragmented and layered conversations of people who knew one another — as well as the activity swirling around them — intimately.

This sense of unfamiliarity that I felt marks that hard-to-grasp quality of community differentiating the residents of a place from those people just passing through. No matter how much time I spent in Clark's Corner — and no matter how much a part of the scene there I became — I was always an outsider, different from those who named the industrial forest home. At first, I was someone from the city, and later, after getting to know people, someone from the university, an expert writing about "local peoples' lives." However, regardless of either designation, it was the novelty of my presence that most defined my activities there, just as it was the routineness of forest dwellers' residency that most defined theirs — the distinction of "strangeness" versus "familiarity" being an identity marker and subjectivity far more salient than any other (i.e., class, gender, ethnicity, language). And yet, despite the power of this distinction, who and what make up a community are often difficult to capture, let alone describe, since indicators like "non-local" or "local" ("outsider" or "insider," "visitor" or "native") can easily become conflated with other identity markers, especially those indicators readily associated with traditional place designations like "the country" and "the city" — just like the people moving through Clark's Corner who, before my sociological gaze, turned into variables of "rurality" (such as "lumberjacks" and "their wives," "Indians," and "mill workers"), their bodies and voices different from my own "urbanity."

Therefore, acknowledging this distinction and understanding how it is linked to the mundane details of people's everyday lives are critical to any analysis of postindustrial community, since indicators of social identity and belongingness can easily be dismissed or misinterpreted, by those both familiar and unfamiliar with its discourse. For example, to the people who frequent Clark's Corner, the everyday activity and conversation moving through there are readily taken for granted and assumed. This is most obvious in the interactions (or lack thereof) between waitresses and different patrons, where the "subtle social rules" of community are sometimes loudly commented on, and other times silently practised (Goffman 1967; Bourdieu 1990). However, to the stranger passing through — especially one who stops off for a while to witness and record the on-going stir of everyday life — these same social rules either appear as a gross exaggeration or are curiously obscured from view — some hovering close to the surface (like the signs posted to announce community events) and others deeply embedded within local social discourse (like idiomatic references in conversation).

This observation about community identity and its relationship to place is hardly revelatory. Sociologists often employ "spatial metaphors" as an analytical way to capture the "messiness" (Stein 1960) of "community" — a very abstract and fluffily vague "social thing" (Lemert 1997) constantly subject to the dynamic processes of structural social change. This is especially true for sociologists of law, who often use "community" as a methodological concept and empirical category to track down the very dynamic relationship between "society" and "the law" (demonstrating, for example, how the law is variable and complex; how social networks, organizational resources, and local cultures shape both the written content and behavioural enactment of legality; how specific communities respond to particular situations and demand for legal services; how the law is shaped by extra-legal [i.e., social] factors; and how citizens initiate legal action outside the purview of official legal agents and without the invocations of formal legal doctrines).

However, while much of this work is useful in demonstrating that the law has no centre and little uniformity, I would suggest that such analyses need to be read with extreme caution, since in much of this work the "communities" that are studied and measured are assumed to be immediately recognizable and distinguishable from what is law. This assumption is revealed by an empirical focus on official legal institutions and their relationship to different communities. In much of this work, communities are recognized as "a part of the story of legality only when they engage as an 'official' legal actor," and as a result, many communities have been "theoretically interesting to sociologists only when they pass through the institutionalized legal boundaries to lodge their complaints, voice their grievances, or seek their legal rights" (Ewick and Silbey, 1998:20).

The most serious limitation of these analyses is that if one reckons the boundary of law to correspond neatly to formal institutional locations, the analytical power of community gets theoretically lost. By focusing their gaze on communities that "get across an institutionalized legal boundary," many sociologists fail to ask how communities "get to that hypothesized boundary in the first place," and exclude from observation that which needs to be explored and explained, such as "how, where and with what effect law is produced" in and through everyday, everynight social interactions within communities; how the law is impressed upon the people who produce community roles and statuses, relationships, obligations, prerogatives, responsibilities, and behaviours; how law does not only work to define social life and shape it, but to work through social life when "peo-

ple deliberately interpret and invoke the law's language, authority and procedures to organize their lives and manage their relationships" (Ewick and
Silbey, 1998:20).

This limitation of socio-legal research becomes most clear when we
consider how the "communities" in these analyses fall to one or another
analytical extreme. For example, in one instance, "communities" located
outside the city's centre (off the inner-city subway stops or suburban free-
way exits, or as in the case of Clark's Corner, some rural highway intersection) are held up as descriptive examples of the ways legal forces of
power have an impact upon ordinary people's lives (cf. Harper, 1992;
Duneier, 1991). However, in the next instance, these same legal forces of
power are argued to render the "subjecthood" of any place or any person
insignificant, or even obsolete, and claim to "better locate" postindustrial
communities within the specific institutions or epiphanal moments that
such forces of legal power define (cf. Duneier, 1999; Burowoy *et al.*, 1991).

Read alongside one another, these analyses seem divided over the question of whether "real-life" places and bodies matter or not. Such a question
of analytical ontology is often attributed to the different theoretical orientations of structuralism — which emphasizes "the real" (see Geertz, 1973;
Giddens, 1990), i.e., "community" is found in specific places, during specific times and circumstances — as opposed to post-structuralism, which
emphasizes "the imagined" or "the hyper-real" (see Foucault, 1973;
Baudrillard, 1975), i.e., "community" is an invented geopolitical location.
However, I would suggest that such extreme analyses are not so much the
result of a disciplinary struggle over two very different ways of knowing, but
rather the systematic failure of most sociologists to recognize that "community" is inextricably linked to "homeplace" — a social identity and subjectivity which is sometimes visible and sometimes not, but always situated
in the mundane experiences of people's everyday lives.

## Communities Are Social

Two kilometres west of Clark's Corner in the municipality of Powerview, a
"community social" (i.e., dance) is sponsored by a Catholic Women's
Church Group, to help raise money for a family whose house was burned
down by arson that past week (MAP 2). Many neighbours of the family
hitchhike across the Hydro Bridge to the other side of the River where the
"social" is taking place in the Powerview Ice Arena, six kilometres east of

the church — some of them first traveling ten kilometres west to the Beer and Liquor Mart in Pine Falls so they can buy bottles of rye and vodka to contribute to the charity tally, which will be made from alcohol sales.

Some men drive in for the dance from the bush camps, located 200 kilometres away, where they work as truckers and loggers; others drive less than a kilometre, their houses near, not only to the ice arena where the social is held, but to the pulp and paper mill where they are employed as unionized labour (both skilled and unskilled). School kids who live on the nearby Indian Reserve, Fort Alexander, as well as in the incorporated townships of St. Georges and Pine Falls, get rides to the social from siblings and friends home from university or with their fathers who are also employed at the mill site. Others walk along the soft shoulder, hitchhiking until a ride comes along, heading towards the ice arena as they are.

Outside the social in the parking lot of the arena, the Royal Canadian Mounted Police and Band Constables break up skirmishes between kids from rival high schools, some of them students at the public high school located next door to where the social is being held, others at nearby private high schools (one anglophone, one francophone Catholic, and one Anglo-Ojibway). Insults are shouted in English or French and then returned in Ojibway, and punches are thrown between cousins who attend different schools. One cop sells beer caps filled with hash oil to young men — most of them shift workers at the mill — who are hanging out in the parking lot in the heated cabs of their shiny, brand new pick-up trucks, long drunk on Molson's beer.

Eight dollars buys admission into the social, where beer and liquor tickets are sold at a table away from the make-shift bar — temporarily set up in the arena's concession stand, where during sports events and other school and church activities the same mothers and teenagers vend doughnuts and hot chocolate. Hockey pennants hang from the ceiling, lettered with the names of players long past, and hash burning through cigarette smoke comes in through the heating vents, from people lighting up in the basement, out of sight. At around 2:30 in the morning, after the nearby taverns close, people are still just starting to arrive, joining those who are already sitting at tables, talking, or congregated around the dance floor, watching young women in vinyl miniskirts and men in dark-green bush boots necking as they slow dance to the Spice Girls.

What's going on on this February night in Southern Manitoba where alcohol is sold for the purposes of welfare relief, state authorities break up fights and sell illegal drugs, and young bodies press up against old? Where is this "community social" held and for whose community is it held? Who attends this event and how do they get there? Who is welcomed and for what reasons? Who is turned away? Who dances together, drinks together, talks to one another, fights with one another? What happens in the early hours of the morning when everyone returns to their residences? Who is not there and for what reasons? And perhaps most importantly, if we unravel the different routes travelled to this "community social" and follow them back to where people came from, what can we can begin to reveal about the relationship between "society and the law"?

As I have previously mapped in my discussion of Clark's Corner, most places of residence in the industrial forest are heavily regulated by the state and forest industry, and alongside the bungalows and two-storey houses, bush barracks, and mobile homes come restricted places of employment, sites of health care and commerce, banks and government offices, education, and recreation — as well as the electricity, water, and people power to maintain and protect them. However, what this "community social" vividly reveals is how some residents of the industrial forest have different kinds of access to these institutionalized homeplaces and, in turn, to the different sites of everyday welfare provisions located within them. For example, for a family living on Louis Riel Boulevard — a small circle of cinder-block houses built right next to Fort Alexander, an Ojibway First Nations Indian Reserve — the only respite from an accidental house fire comes in the form of charity raised by a nearby Catholic Church located outside of Powerview; for the Catholic Church, located in Pine Falls, the fastest way to collect this charity money is to hold a community social at the public hockey arena down the highway in the neighbouring municipality of Powerview; and for residents of Powerview, as well as the neighbouring townships, trailer parks, concession roads, and bush camps — eight dollars' admission buys entry into one of the few places to go on a Saturday night in the middle of winter.

This "community social" is unquestionably a mode of resistance on the part of some forest dwellers who, marginalized (and often completely ostracized) by the state and forest industry, unearth subsistence and joy from the meagre resources that come their way. It dramatically reveals how some residents — all with limited access to the best (and often only) social resources in this industrial forest — are drawn together, whether as neighbours, allies, enemies or lovers. However, while it is important to recognize this "community social" as an act of resistance (or survival) in the face of deprivation, it is also important to raise questions about the real-life needs, camaraderie, violence, and sex that prompt such community activity in the first place: families lacking the most limited of social provisions, like native treaty status, employment, or a public place to gather; enough under-age men to cap the enrollment at three high schools, but too many to get lucrative shift work at the pulp and paper mill, located in Pine Falls, and most of them out to buy and sell hash or illegal beer to those under-age; men (workers long enough to be protected by a labour union) and women (barely over the driving age) meeting in a hockey arena to seduce one another.

What is the legal aspect of this "community social"? Might the fund-raising, confrontations, deals made, and dancing, even the arson on Louis Riel Boulevard itself, constitute in some sense a resistance strategy, a social decision to mine the homeplace "as almost a sole resource for everything that it can divulge, whether public resources or sexual play" (Thompson, 1990:278)? As I have previously pointed out in my discussion of Clark's Corner, on the rustic margins of postindustrialism, where the contradictions of rural development are mitigated by everyday social provisions tightly controlled by the state, multinationals, and the francophone Catholic Church, residents' everyday community activity constitutes a successful rebellion against the welfare and work imbalances embedded within these resources. Such expressions of community force forest dwellers — as a public — to provide a place and, in turn, social provisions for those residents systematically excluded by such institutions, and crack wide open the codes of cultural purity and familial morality embedded within the social provisions that these institutions provide.

However, like all symbolic inversions, this "community social" is temporary, marginal, and unstable and needs to be understood in the context of those forest dwellers who do not participate, as well as those who do. Very few residents of Fort Alexander, St. Georges or Pine Falls (except for some kids still in school or home from university) show up at the ice arena in Powerview, and their absence clearly demonstrates how even as some forest dwellers are drawn together as a community, others remain dramatically segregated, existing as communities apart. What does their absence mean in the context of this "community social," where forest dwellers come together across the physical and discursive borders that separate "Métis" from "francophones," "francophones" from "Natives," "Natives" from "mill workers," and "mill workers" from "women"? How do Fort Alexander and St. Georges become sites of familial and moral purity — differentiated by race, ethnicity or language — while Pine Falls remains culturally unmarked as a company town, its residents passively reaping the spoils of rural industrialism with social provisions and facilities far exceeding those found in either Fort Alexander or St. Georges? How do the stretches of highway cutting through these restricted sites of settlement become marked as a borderlands — to some forest dwellers, a site of social refuge, to others, a site of social refuse?

This "community social" — like the everyday activity and conversation moving through Clark's Corner—exists as an expression of community, because it is an act of resistance which generates its own survival. However, it also exists, I would suggest, because it is invisible to institutions like multinational corporations, the state or the church, and therefore is not expected to last very long. Such routine activity, embodying what Juan Flores (1993) would call the "power of the outrageous," is not recognized or accounted for by the signs that mark highways, nor by the grids of population density and depletion, that shift with changes in the going market price for paper, nor by Treaty Rights, the clergy at the francophone Catholic Church, or even the slow (but steady) growth of private businesses in Powerview. However, it is not only these institutionalized forces of power that fail to recognize and account for such activity. The place-based categories of community that sociologists use to study "society and the law" fall on the same "officially recognized" sites of settlement — provided they even consider such places on the rustic margins at all.

For example, most sociologists tracking institutionalized forms of legal power would target Pine Falls, Fort Alexander or St. Georges as postindustrial communities invented or built by these structural forces (such as the colonial state or global capitalism), capturing them without any reference to the borderlands these places create and from which they are segregated; and even analyses that build their definitions of community from field research at the most local level — or suggest that this is an important and neglected dimension of social scientific research — remain analytically bound by these same place-based definitions of community, looking for them in institutions of "work," "cultural difference," and "family." This has certainly been the case within sociological work on the "industrial forest," which, situated within the analytical boundaries of post-positivism, has produced a body of work on the "resource-dependent communities" found in "company towns," "Native territories," or family farms (cf. Bradwin, 1903; Robinson, 1962; Lucas, 1971). While these works include (or potentially include) some reference to people moving through or living on the peripheries of places "officially recognized," none of these analyses starts its discussion from the routine activity within these border-lands themselves, and therefore they all miss many of the important details of homeplace such as desperation, camaraderie, age, competition, ani-mosity, illegal activity, romance, and sex, which draw some people together into a community, and keep others segregated, in communities apart.

In this industrial forest, legalistic conditions infuse distinctions about racial and language purity, work and middle-class respectability, mas-culinity and sexual morality with distinct cartographic meaning about who belongs where in the industrial forest. However, despite the property rights and houses, as well as the communities of "workers," "Natives," and "Francophones" they divide, forest dwellers routinely move between these physical and discursive boundary lines and form a fourth community on their peripheries — what Gloria Anzaldua (1987) would call a "commu-nity of the borderlands." For many forest dwellers — unrecognized by the state, francophone Catholic Church or forest industry — this fourth com-munity is a site of struggle and resistance, offering a place of everyday social provisions like shelter and work, a school, and a church. However, for others — while providing some business services otherwise unavailable in the industrial forest (like a rooming house or Chinese restaurant, den-tist, bakery, or strip joint) — these borderlands are a social wasteland of cultural impurity and immoral activity, home only to families of mixed ancestry, single men home from the bush camps, and unmarried women with dependents.

Starting from different sites within these borderlands, then moving inwards toward the homeplace settlements they buffer — ranging from roadside stops to hockey arenas, to bush camps and sacred pow-wow grounds — this analysis captures the places forest dwellers move through regularly or rarely, mark as having "common" or "private" access, and describe as "dangerous" or "safe." Tracking this routine activity interrogates what homeplace in the industrial forest means politically, intellectually, and emotionally, and reveals how it operates as a marker of community identity, as well as a standpoint from which people see their place in the world. Best described as "ethnographic cartography," this analysis does not attempt to distil forest dwellers' daily experiential activity and conversations, subjective opinions, and autobiographical narratives into neat uni-dimen-sional categories of different community alliances and divisions.

Rather, it combines sketch maps with forest residents' personal narra-tives (both spoken and written, some of them publicized, some not) to cap-ture the complicated and often conflicting ways in which social identification is a process, produced through residents' routine movement and activity in a shared Someplace. This ethnographic cartography of homeplace in Southern Manitoba is different from the ideals of Canadian community repeated again and again in state legislation and law, popular song, speech, and press, which automatically equate Canadian identity with a "modernist" ethic (i.e., capitalism in the workplace, democracy in the government, science in culture, two-parent family in the home). In such dominant nationalistic discourses, "Canadian" identity is frozen into a social mosaic of racial, ethnic, and linguistic communities — what Arjun Appauduri (1996) would call a cultural "locality" or "ethnoscape" — where every contemporary or historical event is accounted for, sealed off, and closed to debate. This is certainly true for the industrial forest, so long a part of the legal, popular, and academic imagination in Canada that it has been categorically described as a social relic, rapidly disappearing in the context of postindustrialism. It is a decaying piece of Canadian heartland, where natural resources, including the workers who live there, are systematically exploited by global processes of rural industrialism, as well as an enduring site of Canadiana, a historic outpost for outcasts and outlaws (like Indians and the voyageurs), as well as heroic labourers (both the wealthy industrialists who built paper mills and the lumberjacks who felled timber for them). Within each of these representations there is an easy assumption that inhabitants of the industrial forest are essentially a resistant "other" — configurations commonly recurrent in most scholarly analyses, particularly the sociology of law.

However, in the industrial forest, like other exploited or oppositional places in Canada — e.g., from other resource-dependent places (like fishing villages and mining towns) to suburban enclaves to "inner-city" diasporas — the everyday activity of local residents stand as a kind of counter-map to these nationalistic promises of modernity. And I would suggest that recognizing and accounting for such daily, experiential activity maps these dominant nationalistic myths themselves and, in turn, the ways in which different groups and individuals are socially located and ranked by the ethics embedded in these myths. Therefore, this ethnographic cartography of homeplace in the Canadian "backwoods" is both a map of Canadian culture in the industrial forest, as well as an allegory for the possibilities of including this "other culture" in national discourse. Like most places "on the margins" of postindustrialism, — in Canada and around the world, the industrial forest in Southern Manitoba is a place that insists on the necessity of counter-mapping by local residents as a

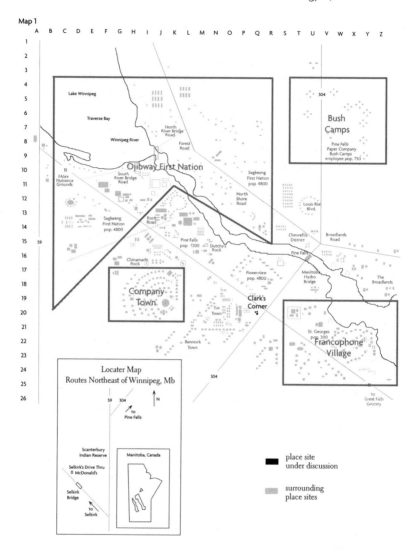

Map 1

means to name their homeplace, and to make these communities "real" on the landscape and in local discourse. Unlike a national identity of listed traits and abstract values, local residents' routine activity breathes life into the story of an "other Canada" in terms of identity dense with descriptions of everyday pleasures and sorrows. Always occupied and exploited, often deserted and betrayed, homeplace in the industrial forest is a site of Canadian culture where the contradictions of rural industrialism are left on the landscape, and where the story of Canada lives in everyday movement, conversation, and memory.

**Map 2**

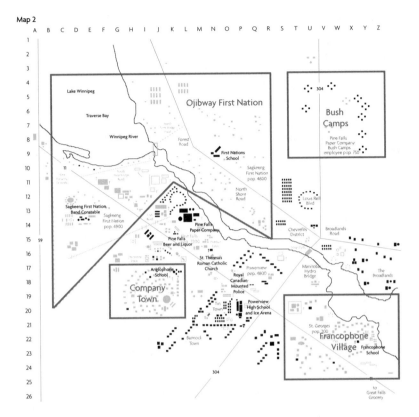

## References

Anzaldua, Gloria (1987). *Borderlands/La Frontera: The New Mestiza*. San Francisco: Spinsters/Aunt Lute Books.

Appauduri, Arjun (1996). *Modernity at Large: Cultural Dimensions of Globalizations*. Minneapolis: University of Minnesota Press.

Baudrillard, Jean (1975). *The Mirror of Production*. St. Louis: Telos Press.

Bourdieu, Pierre (1990). *The Logic of Practice*. Trans. Richard Nice. Stanford University Press.

Bulkin, Ellie, Minnie Bruce Pratt, and Barbara Smith (eds.) (1984). *Yours in Struggle: Three Feminist Perspectives on Anti-Semitism and Racism*. Brooklyn: Long Haul Press.

Burawoy, Michael, et al. (1991). *Ethnography Unbound. Power and Resistance in the Modern Metropolis*. Berkeley: University of California Press.

de Lauretis, Teresa (1984). *Alice Doesn't: Feminism, Semiotics, Cinema*. Bloomington: Indiana University Press.

Duneier, Mitchell (1999). *Sidewalk*. New York: Farrar, Straus and Giroux.

Duneier, Mitchell (1991). *Slim's Table. Race, Respectability and Masculinity*. Chicago: University of Chicago Press.

Ewick, Patricia, and Susan S. Silbey (1998). *The Common Place of Law. Stories From Everyday Life*. Chicago: The University of Chicago Press.

Flores, Juan (1993). *Dividend Borders: Essays on Puerto Rican Identity*. Houston: Arte Publico Press.

Foucault, Michel (1973). *The Order of Things: An Archeology of the Human Sciences*. New York: Vintage Books.

Geertz, Clifford (1973). *The Interpretation of Cultures*. New York: Basic Books.

Giddens, Anthony (1990). *The Consequences of Modernity*. Stanford: Stanford University Press.

Ginsburg, Faye, and Anna Lowenhaupt Tsing (1990). *Uncertain Terms: Negotiating gender in American Culture*. Boston: Beacon Press.

Goffman, Erving (1967). *Interaction Ritual*. Garden City, NY: Anchor Books.

Haraway, Donna (1991). *Simians, Cyborgs and Women: The Reinvention of Nature*. New York: Routledge.

Harper, Douglas (1992). *Working Knowledge: Skill and Community in a Small Shop*. Berkeley: University of California Press.

hooks, bell (1990). *Yearning: Race, Gender and Cultural Politics*. Boston: South End Press.

Laurence, Margaret (1974). *The Diviners*. New York: Knopf.

Lemert, Charles (1997). *Social Things. An Introduction to the Sociological Life*. Boston: Rowman and Littlefield.

Lucas, Rex (1974). *Minetown, Milltown, Railtown: Life in Canadian Communities of Single Industries*. Toronto: University of Toronto Press.

Martin, Biddy, and Chandra Mohonty (1984). "*Feminist Politics: What's Home Got To Do With It?*" In de Lauretis (see above).

Mihn-Ha, Trinh T. (1989) *Woman-Native-Other: Writing, Postcoloniality, and Feminism*. Bloomington: Indiana University Press.

Park, Robert E. (1925). *Human Communities*. New York: The Free Press of Glencoe.

Pratt, Minnie Bruce (1984). "*Identity: Skin, Blood*." In Bulkin, Pratt and Smith (see above).

Robinson, I.M. (1962). *New Industrial Towns on Canada's Resource Frontier*. Chicago: University of Chicago.

Smith, Dorothy (1987). *The Everyday World As Problematic: A Feminist Sociology*. Boston: Northeastern University Press.

Stein, Maurice R. (1960). *The Eclipse of Community: An Interpretation of American Studies*. New York: Harper Torchbooks.

Thomas, William I., and Florian Znaniecki (1927). *The Polish Peasant in Europe and America*, 2nd. ed. New York: Knopf.

Thompson, Becky W., and Sangeeta Tyagi (eds.) (1996). *Names We Call Home: Autobiography on Racial Identity*. New York: Routledge.

Thompson, Sharon (1990). "'*Drastic Entertainment*': *Teenage Mothers, Signifying Narratives*." In Ginsburg and Tsing (see above).

# 10

## The Crown Owns All the Land?
## The Mi'gmaq of Listuguj Resist

MELINDA MARTIN

"The Crown owns all the land." This statement, made during a first-year property law course, had one aboriginal student reeling. That student was a Mohawk woman who later went on to teach law: Patricia Monture-Angus. She recounted the time she was a student, sitting in a first-year property law class and first being introduced to the concept that "The Crown owns all the land." She said she felt as though the ceiling was crashing down on her, yet her classmates seemed unaffected as they continued to scribble in their notebooks. As a Mi'gmaq[1] woman, I know how she felt. When I was in my first-year property law class, I could not make sense of the concept of property. That statement, that simple concept "the Crown owns all the land," put everything into perspective for me. I finally understood how the Mi'gmaq could be dispossessed of their ancestral land.

### Terra Nullius

When the Newcomers arrived, they met the original inhabitants of this country, my ancestors. They encountered peoples with whom they did not share the same language, values or concepts, and who were not the original inhabitants of the "Christian World Order" (Prins, 1996:56). According to the doctrine of *Terra Nullius*,[2] "proprietary rights could only exist within the framework of law enacted by an organized state; the land of prestate people without such law was therefore legally vacant" (Green and Dickason, 1989:235). The Newcomers concluded that for the purposes of international law, indigenously occupied territories can be regarded as

*Terra Nullius*, that is, lands without a recognized owner and available for occupation by a "civilized" member of the Western family of nations.

Under the principles of European laws, the Newcomers claimed the Doctrine of First Discovery, which gave the discoverers the "exclusive right to extinguish the Indian title of occupancy, either by purchase or conquest" (Williams, 1990:666). "For five hundred years this doctrine and its discourse of diminished indigenous legal status and rights has been relied on by European and European derived settler states to regulate and legitimate their colonial activities in indigenous peoples' territories ... Those legal practices of denying native tribes full title or sovereign rights in the territories they occupied was adopted by Spain, Great Britain and all the major European colonizing nations as the law of 'civilized' nations in their dealings with indigenous peoples whose territories they invaded."[3] It is this doctrine that begets the concept that "the Crown owns all the land." It assumes that the Crown has jurisdiction over all the land and its resources in what is now known as Canada. This concept disregards aboriginal title existing prior to contact. However, the Mi'gmaq have resisted the concept that "the Crown owns all the land" since contact. Today, the people of my community, the Mi'gmaq of Listuguj,[4] maintain that they have sovereignty and jurisdiction over their traditional territory because they never sold, ceded or surrendered the land. To understand the resistance movement taking place in Listuguj, some background on the struggle to date is needed.

## Pre-Contact Mi'gmaq

Since time immemorial, the Mi'gmaq have inhabited what is now known as Maritime Atlantic Canada.[5] Prior to the arrival of the Newcomers, the Mi'gmaq were a sovereign nation with Mi'gmaq social, economic, and political structures. They were a migratory nation that hunted, fished, and gathered what nature provided along the coast during the summer and moved inland during the winters, practising conservation measures with respect to hunting and fishing.

Traditionally, the basic social unit consisted of an extended-family structure. This loosely structured unit would usually be headed by a *Sagamaw*, whose power and authority were only as strong as the support he received from his extended family. While the rank as *Sagamaw* was hereditary, displays of exemplary leadership qualities of honesty, wisdom and courage were sought; otherwise, advice would not be heeded (Dorey, 1994). Individual Mi'gmaq typically maintained a large measure of autonomy and freedom, while disputes over hunting and fishing were referred to the local *Sagamaw* for resolution. Extended families formed part of the larger kin groups or bands who typically got together when there was enough to support large gatherings. The leaders would gather for councils on band and regional levels to deal with both internal and external affairs. Held as the need arose, the councils allocated hunting territories, settled internal disputes and decided on participation in wars (Dorey, 1994:8; Nietfield, cited in Prins, 1996:34). According to Prins,

> With the essential self-sufficiency of each family unit and general lack of resources specialization among the widely scattered and migratory Mi'gmaq, there was no place for a formal political hierarchy to organize labour and redistribute on a regular basis. Instead a traditional Mi'gmaq political pattern included a loosely structured organization, participatory decision making, voluntary association, minimalized institutionalization, and situational (as-needed) political leadership based on consensus instead of coercion. (Thwaites, cited in Prins, 1996:33)

Much of what we know about the traditional way of life of the Mi'gmaq comes from the accounts recorded by traders and missionaries shortly after contact. Many Mi'gmaq today attest that their traditional political structure was hierarchical in nature, with a centralized system of leadership. They also maintain that when the Newcomers first arrived, the land was divided into seven districts, each district represented by a regional band chief. They assert that prior to contact there existed a grand council, consisting of a chief from each district, and the Mi'gmaq saw that the grand council was headed by a grand chief. The community of Listuguj is located in the most northerly district of the Mi'gmaq, the Gespegewaqi district. This district encompasses parts of the Gaspé peninsula and parts of northern New Brunswick.

Historians however, state that the historical documentation on the existence of a pre-contact political structure better known as the Grand Council is inconclusive. While it may be that the exact structures of the political entities prior to contact are unknown, we do know that the Mi'gmaq were an autonomous people prior to contact.

## The Newcomers Arrive

The first Newcomers arrived in the territory in the 1500s. By the early 1600s the Mi'gmaq were entering into economic relations with the Newcomers, initially providing them with furs in exchange for manufactured goods. The Mi'gmaq way of life was slowly turning away from self-sufficiency to reliance on the trade demands of the Newcomers. However, contact with the Newcomers also exposed the Mi'gmaq to a variety of foreign diseases (such as smallpox, measles, cholera, and the bubonic plague). It is hard to determine exactly how many thousands of Mi'gmaq perished as a result of the exposure to these diseases, but what is known is that the arrival of the Newcomers brought other changes to the Mi'gmaq that would alter their way of life forever.

By the late 1600s the Newcomers had started to move into traditional Mi'gmaq territory in larger numbers, subjecting the Mi'gmaq to further colonial influences. To combat this expansion by the Newcomers, the Mi'gmaq allied themselves with the Maliseet, Passamaquoddy, Penobscot, and the more remote Abenaki communities.

The Mi'gmaq entered into treaties with the Newcomers. For example, in 1752, "a treaty was entered into for the benefit of both the British Crown and the Micmac people, to maintain peace and order as well as to recognize and confirm the existing hunting and fishing rights of the Micmac."[6] A number of similar Peace and Friendship treaties were entered into between the Mi'gmaq and the Crown. These treaties emphasized peace and friendship between the parties which, in the Mi'gmaq view, clearly recognized the sovereignty of the Mi'gmaq. The Newcomers conducted themselves in a manner consistent with the Doctrine of Discovery. In effect, while they interpreted the treaties in such a way as to give themselves access to and control of the traditional territories of the Mi'gmaq, it is important to note that none of the Maritime treaties of the eighteenth century ceded any land.[7]

Aboriginal rights were recognized and re-affirmed by the Newcomers' government in the Royal Proclamation of 1763, which confirmed that the aboriginal people could not be molested or disturbed by the Newcomers' governments, their courts or their citizens, at least not upon "any Lands whatever" which were "not ceded to or purchased by" the Crown. In an unpublished article *St. John River Society and the Dispossession of the Maliseet people*, Andrea Bear Nicholas documents how land along the St. John River was distributed during the 1760s. She relates how the Maliseet people along the St. John River were dispossessed of their lands, showing how the authorities of the day failed to obtain the proper surrender of lands from the original inhabitants prior to issuing certified land deeds to new settlers, as set out in the Royal Proclamation. The method by which the Mi'gmaq were dispossessed of their lands was not unlike the experience of the Maliseet people. A strong correlation can be drawn between the Maliseet and Mi'gmaq, as it was the same governing body that controlled the distribution of the land inhabited by the Maliseet and the Mi'gmaq. As constitutional expert Bruce Clark writes,

> Among the first illegal settlers trespassing upon Indian lands were the Newcomers' lawyers, judges and police. They made it safe for, and then invited in, the rest of the settlers. When the Indians complained about this blatant breach of existing law, the trespassing lawyers, judges and police employed their stolen monopoly over the legal process in the Indian territories to protect the illegal settlements. (Clark, 1996)

Title to the lands along the St. John River was, in effect, illegally secured because it was the authorities themselves who were engaging in these practices. Although such practices were prohibited, no one was charged. The effect of such practices is that such lands were illegally settled. Judges, lawyers, and police, who initiated the invasion of the Indian lands, are now able to maintain control over these lands through their monopoly over the legal institutions.

## Jurisdiction Divided

By 1867, four provinces joined together to form the Dominion of Canada. Sections 91 and 92 of the *Constitution Act, 1867* divided jurisdiction solely between the federal government and the provinces. In a speech, Indian Commissioner J.A.N. Provencher explained the beliefs and goals of the Canadian government in 1873: "treaties may be made with them simply with a view to the extinction of their rights, by agreeing to pay them a sum and afterwards abandon them to themselves" (De Brou and Waiser, 1992:95).

Previous legislation concerning the original inhabitants was amalgamated in 1876 into the *Indian Act*, which was created to regulate "Indians and the land reserved for Indians" (*Indian Act*, s.c. 1876, c.18). This legislation incorporated the Mi'gmaq into the term "Indians," and thus the Mi'gmaq and other "Indians" became subjects under federal jurisdiction. The *Indian Act*, as it still stands today, includes but is not limited to provisions about band membership, housing, education, and land transfers. The authority of band government is subject to the ultimate authority of the federal government through its Department of Indian Affairs. According to the Act, Indians were childlike wards who were to be protected from corrupting outside influences while at the same time controlled by the government and its designated officials. The Act confirmed the mid-nineteenth century government policy of trying to remake Indians into Europeans. The Peace and Friendship treaties have provided some protection from provincial regulation, with respect to hunting and fishing; in time, however, most aspects of an Indian's life are subject to provincial and federal legislation.

In 1924, the federal government delegated administrative authority over fisheries to Quebec. The province of Quebec has enacted a number of restrictive fishing regulations since. These regulations have included restrictions on allowable species, methods of fishing, maximum number of fishing days per season, maximum number and size of fish caught, licensing requirements, and sanctions for violating these regulations. Prior to the 1960s, a small number of the Mi'gmaq of Listuguj still engaged in salmon fishing as a livelihood for some time. According to Mi'gmaq fisherman Isaac Metallic a verbal agreement existed between the government and the Mi'gmaq offering the Mi'gmaq jobs if they did not fish. During the first half of the century very few employment opportunities in the area were available for the Mi'gmaq of Listuguj. Work was largely limited to logging camps, as guides on the nearby Matapedia and Kedgwick rivers, at the Champoux sawmill located at the nearby Church point, or on river drives. However, guiding and working the river runs were very dangerous occupations, and many Mi'gmaq died on the job: "those jobs held by Indians were lucrative for when an Indian died he was not replaced by another Mi'gmaq. However, when an Indian died he was not replaced by another Indian, he was replaced by a non-Indian" (Isaac Metallic, personal interview, 1996). As employment opportunities diminished many Mi'gmaq began covertly resorting to fishing in the dark of night. These fishermen were occasionally intimidated and harassed by provincial fishing wardens, yet they were neither arrested nor charged as a result of their fishing activities. When employment was available the Mi'gmaq fished less. Despite the regulations in force at the time fishing wardens seemed to turn a blind eye to the Mi'gmaq who continued to fish.

## The Fishing Agreements

Author David Long cites how the Canadian state attempts to garner Native consent which includes political co-optation of key Native leaders, by the 1970s "specialized funding into specialized programs that support community development projects" (Long, 1992:128). The government offered annual agreements to the Mi'gmaq; in exchange, the Mi'gmaq were to abide by the quotas set out in the agreements.

In 1974, the Mi'gmaq of Listuguj first entered into an agreement with the Quebec government over the on-reserve management and utilization of fish resources. The Mi'gmaq would restrict salmon fishing along the Restigouche River, and in return the provincial government funded various projects on the reserve. According to Isaac Metallic,

> the modern written agreements, signed in the seventies were used like blackmail, as a creation for employment. The agreements were signed behind closed doors, between the provincial government and the chief and council, without consultation with the people. The chief would get a percentage, telling people he's creating work. D.F.O.(Department of Fisheries and Oceans) gave $400,000 in exchange for an agreement. That's not enough to employ two thousand people. It can only employ ten to fifteen people. (Isaac Metallic, personal interview, 1996)

This signing of fishing agreements by Mi'gmaq leaders constitutes a clear example of the co-optation of leaders by the state. In was indeed only after band leaders began co-operating with the Newcomer government by signing fisheries agreements that Mi'gmaq were charged for fishing illegally by provincial authorities.

In the spring of 1981, Listuguj representatives and officials of the Quebec provincial ministry of wildlife and fisheries (Ministère de Loisirs, Chasse et Pèche — MLCP) were in the process of negotiating the terms of their annual bi-partite salmon-fishing agreement. Both parties agreed on a host of issues, but they could not agree on the number of days for the salmon season. Quebec wanted the Mi'gmaq to fish for only three consecutive days of twenty-four hours. After consulting with the fishermen of Listuguj, the chief asserted that his people wanted to fish for six days a week, for twelve hours each day. Although both proposals totalled the same number of hours, the two sides were unable to reach an agreement and broke off negotiations on June 8, 1981.

On June 9, M.L.C.P. minister Lucien Lessard issued a directive to "ensure that band members removed all nets from the estuary within 36 hours or by midnight June 10, 1981 or face the full rigour of the law" (National Indian Brotherhood, 1981:17). The response of the Mi'gmaq fishermen was to continue fishing without an agreement. They kept their nets in the water, in direct contravention of the provincial directive. On June 11, Minister Lessard followed through with his threat. According to a National Indian Brotherhood report, "riot-equipped Quebec provincial police and Quebec fisheries wardens staged a simultaneous land, air, and sea incursion of the Restigouche River. At the time six or seven salmons nets were still on the river" (National Indian Brotherhood, 1981:6).

All the exits to the reserve were blocked and the Mi'gmaq people were prevented from circulating freely. They were terrified by the number of riot-clad police and fisheries wardens that descended on the community. The Quebec Provincial Police searched boats, garages, and backyards for fishing nets. Several nets in the river and in backyards were confiscated or destroyed. In the process, several Mi'gmaq men were physically assaulted by the Q.P.P. The police had low regard for the people; one officer was overheard saying, "I used to be afraid of Indians when I was stationed in Matapedia [a community located 20 km from Listuguj] but I'm not scared today."[8]

Rene Martin recalled his experience that day: "I ran into the water. I stayed in the water until one of the choppers came towards me. I said, 'I'm gonna give up now.' There was one Q.P.P. that grabbed me by the hair. They brought me up the hill and they threw me on the ground and stomped on me. They put cuffs on me then picked me up by the hair. Once we got to the van, they stopped. The guy that was on the other side pulled me up by the hair again and punched my face."[9] Then band councillor, Michael Isaac Sr. noted the lasting impact of the behaviour of some Q.P.P. officers: "Looking out the window and seeing Q.P.P.s urinating in front of our women and children ... and can't do anything about it ... I wouldn't want that feeling again" (Isaac Metallic, personal interview, 1996).

Following the June 11 raid, the Q.P.P. began to conduct extra patrols along the highway intersecting the reserve. They performed lengthy and detailed searches of cars seeking to enter the reserve and set up a road-block on the New Brunswick side of the interprovincial bridge and fired tear gas onto the nearby wharf where a few Mi'gmaq people were standing. Fortunately no one was injured. In spite of these tactics, some fishermen continued to fish without an agreement signed by the band, and predictably the Q.P.P. raided the reserve once again. "On June 20, 1981 an undetermined number of provincial fisheries wardens appeared again on the Restigouche river. They seized approximately twelve dozen salmon nets, using one speed boat and one large armoured tug" (National Indian Brotherhood, 1981:6).

The Mi'gmaq responded by setting up their own blockade on reserve land just off the provincial highway. This short-term strategy was to prevent the Q.P.P. from conducting any more raids on the reserve. Fishermen, band council members, and concerned citizens manned the blockades, while aboriginal peoples from across Canada came to Listuguj to help the Mi'gmaq defend their fishing rights. The Chief told those manning the barricades, "If they use force, we'll retaliate; if they trespass or if anyone gets hurt, shoot 'em" (Isaac Metallic, personal interview, 1996). Frantz Fanon, anti-colonialist and author of *The Wretched of the Earth* (Fanon, 1963), writes that "Violence is the tool of the oppressor." In this case the Mi'gmaq were prepared to use violence, only in self-defence, if violence was directed at them. Isaac Metallic recalls that some of the vehicles at the blockade contained guns and rifles, although guns were not visible. It was the Quebec government that used force in arresting the fishermen during the raid. By having guns present (albeit hidden) the Mi'gmaq were merely responding to the oppression of the Quebec government and its armed Q.P.P.

The Mi'gmaq manned the barricades around the clock following the second raid, but negotiations between the town of Campbellton, New Brunswick and the Mi'gmaq saw both sides take down the barricades. On June 23, Minister Lessard contacted Chief Alphonse Metallic to re-open negotiations. The Chief made it clear that the Mi'gmaq would not negotiate with the Quebec government because of the armed intervention of June 11. When Minister Lessard unilaterally issued a fishing permit for Listuguj, Metallic rejected it, reiterating his intention to deal exclusively with the federal government on jurisdictional matters. The Mi'gmaq continued to fish in accordance with band council by-laws, in direct contravention of provincial regulations.

When the Mi'gmaq went to court for the charges arising from the raids, their lawyer arranged for them to plead guilty. Most of them were fined $25 with a suspended sentence. Two chose to plead not guilty: "We weren't doing anything wrong. We were just fishing."[10] Three witnesses, including a photographer, attested that the defendants had not resisted arrest; however, the provincial-court judge decided that he did not believe the witnesses or the photographs taken. The judge added that the defendants must have planned to do something that day if they had arranged for their personal photographer to take pictures. The judge stated that he wanted to make an example of the defendants, one in particular: Donald Germain was found guilty, fined $250, and placed on one-year probation. But, Germain appealed to the Court of Appeal, which ruled that the lower-court judge had made errors in fact and law. The conviction was overturned and the defendant was acquitted.

Following the raids of 1981, the fishermen insisted that the band council include them in future salmon-fishing negotiations. However, the next band election in 1982 brought a change in the band administration. The new administration did not continue the resistance against provincial jurisdiction over fishing; instead the new chief signed the salmon-fishing agreement without consulting the fishermen. Between 1982 and 1992, agreements between the Chief and the provincial government continued to be negotiated. The band received money for signing the agreements and in return band members were required to adhere to fishing limitations set out in the agreements. At the same time, many Mi'gmaq who continued to fish contrary to the agreements were routinely charged by provincial fish and game wardens. Brenda Gideon-Miller was elected chief of the band council in 1992. She reflected on the actions of the fishermen.

> Fishing is an important factor in the history of our people. The fishermen have been doing what our ancestors have been doing forever. Back in 81 we made a physical statement. They (the fishermen) fought to fish, they had the guts and the foresight and regrouped and organized. It took a long time to manifest itself into something long-term. We wanted long term solutions. We had to revitalize systems that have always been there. (Gideon-Miller, personal interview, 1996)

As Nnu Sagamaw[11] Gideon-Miller notified the Quebec government that they would no longer negotiate salmon-fishing agreements.

## Tribal Council Revived

Tired of being charged with violations of provincial regulations, the fishermen were in the process of re-establishing a fishermen's association. They asked Gary Metallic Sr., fisherman and hereditary chief in the Mi'gmaq Grand Council, to join their association. Gary Metallic Sr. holds the title of *Keptin* of the tribal council, a hereditary position delegated to him by the sons of the former *Keptin* of the seventh district, Alphonse Metallic. Gary Metallic Sr. agreed that such an association was needed, but at the same time he considered it to be a reflection and pawn of the federal government. In the end he agreed to join the organization only if it were structured and represented a traditional tribal council.

At a community meeting of fishermen, elders and band councillors, and interested band members, the idea of the tribal council was discussed. All agreed that it should be a non-political, traditional body. They called it the Listuguj Overseers Tribal Council (L.O.T.C. ). In Gary Metallic's words, "We're no longer recognizing the state's authority with respect to fishing. We have authority by virtue of our existence" (Gary Metallic Sr., personal interview, 1996). Initially, the tribal council was reinvigorated as an organization of fishermen, it evolved to include traditionally-minded individuals interested in conservation and the management of the rivers and forests (Isaac Metallic, personal interview, 1996).

## Mi'gmaq Devise Their Own Conservation Plan

For the next two and a half years, the tribal council and the band conducted public consultations on fishing. Community members were encouraged to provide their input on the conservation management plans for the Mi'gmaq and were involved in the consultation and decision-making process. After many public consultations, the community finally agreed to a conservation management plan that was adopted by the L.O.T.C.. Although there are no quotas, to date most fishermen are abiding by the conservation agreement. They do so because they themselves have helped develop the conservation management plan. Biologists agree that the Mi'gmaq have developed a good conservation plan and, ironically, in 1996 the province of Quebec recognized Listuguj with an award for its conservation plan.

To ensure that the conservation management plan is maintained, Listuguj trains its own conservation officers to patrol the water. It has also negotiated a service contract with the provincial department of fisheries for monitoring the river. In the words of Gary Metallic Sr., "We let the feds pay for the services we provide" (Gary Metallic Sr., personal interview, 1996).

## Mi'gmaq Assert Jurisdiction

The Mi'gmaq of Listuguj maintain that they are a sovereign nation since traditional Mi'gmaq territory has not yet been ceded or purchased by the Crown. They continue to assert that they have jurisdiction beyond the current boundaries of the Listuguj reserve, insisting that their jurisdiction spans the traditional Mi'gmaq territory, the Gespegewaqi District. As a sovereign nation, the Mi'gmaq of Listuguj assert that their traditional territory is under Mi'gmaq jurisdiction and not subject to the jurisdiction of federal or provincial governments or courts: "If we're going to set up our own institutions and government structures, policing is an important aspect of public security and controlling society" (Gary Metallic Sr., personal interview, 1996). To move toward their goals, the Mi'gmaq found it imperative to take control of policing in the community. Prior to 1993, policing in Listuguj was externally controlled, by the provincial government. Public security was provided by the Amerindian police, who received their mandate from the Quebec Provincial Police. Listuguj now has its own independent police department.

As the Mi'gmaq assert their sovereignty, they are interested in getting their jurisdiction recognized. The Mi'gmaq maintain that jurisdiction over their traditional and unsurrendered lands lies with them and not with the provincial or federal government. Consistent with this assertion they have applied to the Supreme Court as intervenors in the reference regarding the constitutionality of Quebec's right to secede from Canada. In the Mi'gmaq application for intervenor status in that reference they assert that if Quebec were to secede, it would not include the traditional territory of the Mi'gmaq because those lands were never ceded, surrendered or sold by the Mi'gmaq. Comments made by band councillor Michael Isaac Sr.

during the 1981 raids are still applicable today: "Here's a government crying about sovereignty ... about being discriminated against by the rest of Canada. Here's the same government doing the same thing — talking about what English Canada is doing to them, only worse they're using guns."[12]

Reasserting control over traditional Mi'gmaq territory has generated serious conflicts over jurisdiction. Director of Public Security in Listuguj, Henry Mitchell notes that he is "under conflicting orders from two sources, both of which claim the exclusive jurisdiction to legislate in respect of the definition of my duty as a peace officer. On the one hand, the federal Crown and the provincial Crown purport to have jurisdiction under Crown right. On the other hand, the Mi'gmaq Nation at Listuguj purports to have jurisdiction under Native Right."[13]

Rather than waiting for governments to dictate what powers the Mi'gmaq can exercise, they have revived their traditional tribal council, chosen to expand their jurisdiction and are taking control over, more and more issues. Essentially the strategy used to regain control over salmon fishing is now being applied in more areas in the reassertion of Mi'gmaq sovereignty.

Originally the tribal council dealt only with the protection of fishing rights, but their role was recently expanded to include child welfare. In 1996, the tribal council was approached by the state of Washington to intervene in an adoption case. The minor was a child of a band member of Listuguj, and was being placed for adoption in the state of Washington. Before proceeding with the adoption Washington state requested a court order from the tribal court to approve the adoption. The American federal statute *Indian Child Welfare Act* (1978) requires state courts and agencies to give notice to the tribe where the child is from, that the child is in foster care or is being considered for adoption. Until the time of this case, the revived tribal council of Listuguj had not yet made any decisions regarding child welfare. However, they reasoned that as a council/government they could also act as a court, because traditionally there was no delineation between government and court. Disputes were traditionally resolved within the nation. As a tribal council/court of the Mi'gmaq territory, they agreed to examine the issue.

In this decision, the Listuguj tribal council/court determined that the Mi'gmaq father should have custody over the child, but later the father found himself unable to care for the child. The tribal court then decided that it would be in the best interest of the child to stay with their non-aboriginal grandmother. The Washington court accepted the decision of the tribal council/court, and agreed to keep the council abreast of the situation.

In a second child-welfare case dealt with by LOTC, a band member residing in the U.S. had divorced her non-aboriginal husband. A Californian court gave the father primary custody of the two children from that union. The mother vehemently disagreed with the decision and immediately returned to Listuguj with her children. The father then obtained a court order from a nearby Quebec family court, which issued a court order to apprehend the mother and the children. Under normal circumstances, the Listuguj police would be obliged to carry out the court order to apprehend the mother and her children; however in this case the mother approached the tribal council for assistance.

The tribal council/court met again to decide their second child-welfare case. The father and his legal counsel were invited to appear before the tribal council/court but declined the offer. Based on the information before them, the tribal council/court decided that it would be in the best interest of the children if the mother and her children remained in the community with their extended family, rather than return to the father. To accomplish this end, the LOTC issued its own court order (Gary Metallic Sr., personal interview, 1996). It ordered the Listuguj police not to apprehend the mother and her children, which essentially rendered the Quebec court order unenforceable in Listuguj. However, if they should require hospitalization, they risk being apprehended by outside police authorities, as the court order issued by the provincial court is enforceable once they leave the reserve. To date, the father has suspended all legal actions.

As a result of their intervention in the second child-welfare case, the director of public security and the spokesperson of the tribal council are being charged for contempt of court. Their defence has been that Quebec does not have jurisdiction over Mi'gmaq territory, just as it was when they asserted jurisdiction over fishing. If the provincial court wants to challenge the issue of jurisdiction, the Mi'gmaq are prepared to make their case.

Today the *Indian Act* continues to regulate the life of an Indian. For example, the Department of Indian Affairs and Northern Development (DIAND) allocates program dollars to each federally recognized band. DIAND further provides the band with funds for such things as training, education, and infrastructure. Currently the *Indian Act* band council of Listuguj relies heavily on the DIAND for funding. The Mi'gmaq of Listuguj risk losing their funding from Indian Affairs, as DIAND does not recognize political bodies other than the *Indian Act* band councils.

DIAND thus controls the actions and purse strings of the band council since DIAND reserves the right to review most band council resolutions.

To break from this dependency on the federal government, the people are taking action. The Mi'gmaq have revitalized their traditional tribal council. In contrast to the Indian Act band council, the tribal council abides by traditional values and receives no core funding from either Canada or Quebec. Gary Metallic notes that "the price to pay for sovereignty is economic pressures." He goes on "We're getting resistance from our own people because this (asserting jurisdiction) involves change." It is this economic pressure, the risk of losing government funding that concerns other Mi'gmaq. "If we don't lose sight of our goals, we'll be better off at the end of the road. We believe the benefits that we gain will far outweigh the present system" (Gary Metallic Sr., personal interview, 1996). More control over the land and resources would reduce the reliance on government funding. Equitable resolution to outstanding land claims could provide the Mi'gmaq people with some financial security. These solutions require action on behalf of the Crown in right of Canada and the Crown in right of the province; however, the governments do not wish to acknowledge that they may not own all the land, since to do so would risk losing control over the land and its resources.

As the Mi'gmaq try to revive their traditional form of government, they are also involved in rekindling traditional alliances. The Mi'gmaq are members of the Wabanaki Confederacy, a relationship that dates back to the 1700s. The Wabanaki Confederacy represents a united body of Aboriginal peoples that first assembled to fight a common enemy, the Newcomer's government. The first Wabanaki Confederacy meeting in over two hundred years took place in 1992, and although it was primarily social in nature, it represented a first step toward reviving past alliances and reuniting the Wabanaki Confederacy member nations.

To reassert jurisdiction on a larger scale, the Mi'gmaq of Listuguj have joined the Passamaquoddy to initiate a Confederated Native Court. Its members include the members of the Wabanaki Confederacy as well as members of the Algonkian-speaking nations. To date, they have the support of representatives from the Mi'gmaq, Algonquin, Passamaquoddy, Maliseet. and Mohegan nations. These members have launched court interventions on behalf of the traditional tribal councils on a variety of issues surrounding aboriginal jurisdiction in both Canada and the United States. The Passamaquoddy, for example, are reasserting jurisdiction over their traditional territory, which includes the town of St. Andrews, New

Brunswick. The Mohegans are reasserting jurisdiction over their traditional territory, which includes Staten Island, New York. The Mi'gmaq of Listuguj are reasserting jurisdiction in their traditional territory, which includes parts of northern New Brunswick and parts of the Gaspé Peninsula in Quebec. In each case, the aboriginal people are questioning the validity of the Newcomers' jurisdiction over traditional territory inhabited by aboriginal peoples. Collectively, the Aboriginal peoples are seeking to have their jurisdiction recognized internationally.

Previous Mi'gmaq strategies have included trying to get treaties enforced in the Newcomers' courts. But victories for the Mi'gmaq have been rare or marginal at best, and there has only been a minimal recognition of Mi'gmaq rights. This is not surprising, since it is always the Newcomers' courts, not the courts of the Mi'gmaq, which sit in judgement in disputes between the Newcomers and the original inhabitants. It is the Newcomers' courts that get to determine the rights that they accord to the Mi'gmaq.

Not long ago I heard a Passamaquoddy man say "governments can't give sovereignty but they sure can take it away."[4] Another Passamaquoddy man, Fred Moore, said "As it stands, the government can legislate me in and out of existence."[5] The same holds true for all aboriginal peoples. As long as Aboriginal peoples allow the Newcomers to restrict or define the terms of Aboriginal sovereignty, the government can legislate all Aboriginal peoples out of existence.

The Mi'gmaq are resisting the legal and social structures that were forced upon them when the first Newcomers came to this land, challenging the economic and political powers that usurped their jurisdiction when the Newcomers claimed the Doctrine of Discovery. The Mi'gmaq want a nation-to-nation relationship with Canada and to move toward this they are attempting to use past structures to deal with present-day realities. This represents a dramatic redefining of their legal relationship with the world. Asserting jurisdiction is more in line with the actions of my sovereign ancestors. It speaks to the fact that jurisdiction is derivative. If the Newcomers wanted to assert jurisdiction, they first needed to acquire ownership of the land from the original inhabitants. To date the Crown has not demonstrated that it has gained legitimate title to the land. Until the Rule of Law prevails, the Crown does not own all the land.

# Notes

1. The term "Mi'gmaq" represents the English term "Micmac." It is the spelling adopted by the Listuguj First Nation.

2. *Terra Nullius* is the Latin term for land with people.

3. The Doctrine of Discovery was extended in the 1823 U.S. Supreme Court decision of *Johnson v. M'Intosh* 21 U.S. 543 (U.S. III., 1823). Chief Justice John Marshall's opinion is considered an important and influential elaboration of the Doctrine of Discovery. It has been cited many times in Canadian cases dealing with Aboriginal rights and Aboriginal title.

4. Listuguj, formerly known as Restigouche, is a Mi'gmaq community located on the Gaspé peninsula in the province of Quebec. An interprovincial bridge connect the community to New Brunswick.

5. The Mi'gmaq have inhabited all of PEI, Nova Scotia, the coast of New Brunswick, northern Maine, and the Gaspé coast. The Maliseet inhabit the lands along the Saint John River and the Beothucks lived primarily in Newfoundland.

6. *R. v. Simon* [1985] 2 S.C.R. 387.

7. *R. v. Simon* [1985] 2 S.C.R. 395.

8. Chief Alphonse Metallic, quoted in the National Film Board film *Incident at Restigouche*.

9. Robert Barnaby, quoted in the National Film Board film *Incident at Restigouche*.

10. Robert Barnaby, quoted in the National Film Board film *Incident at Restigouche*.

11. The title of chief was changed to the Mi'gmaq term *Nnu Sagamaw*.

12. Michael Isaac Sr., quoted in the National Film Board film *Incident at Restigouche*.

13. Excerpt of correspondence from Henry Mitchell, Director of Public Security, to Hon. Paul Bégin, Minister of Justice for Quebec, dated July 17, 1996. This letter was included in the Mi'gmaq of Gespegewaqi application for intervenor status in the matter of succession of Quebec file: 25506.

14. Anonymous man at Pleasant Point, Maine, meeting regarding the sovereignty of the Mi'gmaq and Passamaquoddy nations, January 25, 1997.

15. Fred Moore, Passamaquoddy representative, at Pleasant Point meeting (see note 14).

# References

Clark, Bruce (1996). "Eclipse and Enlightenment: a legal opinion." Listuguj, QC, Sept. 4.

De Brou, Dave, and Bill Waiser (1992). *Documents Canada: A History of Modern Canada in Documents*. Saskatoon: Fifth House.

Dorey, D.A. (1994). "Aboriginal Self-Government for the MiKma'ki People of Nova Scotia." Native Council of Nova Scotia.

Fanon, Frantz (1963). *Wretched of the Earth*. New York: Grove Press.

Gideon-Miller, Brenda (1996). Personal Interview, Listuguj, QC, Nov. 15.

Green, L.C., and Olive P. Dickason (1989). *The Law of Nations and the New World*. Edmonton: University of Alberta Press.

*Incident at Restigouche* (1984). National Film Board of Canada.

Long, David (1992). "Cultural Ideology and Militancy: The Movement of Native Indians in Canada, 1969-1991." In William K. Carol (ed.), *Organizing Dissent: Contemporary Social Movements in Theory and Practice*. Toronto: Garamond.

Metallic, Gary, Sr. (1996). District Keptin, Seventh district, spokesperson for the Listuguj Overseers Tribal Council. Personal Interview, Listuguj, QC, Nov. 17.

Metallic, Isaac (1996). Fisherman and member of the Listuguj Overseers Tribal Council. Personal Interview, Listuguj, QC, Oct. 10; Nov. 15.

Monture-Angus, Patricia (1997). "Identity and Aboriginal Women." Presentation at St. Thomas University, Frederiction, NB, Jan. 15.

National Indian Brotherhood (1981). "Inquiry into the Invasion of Restigouche; Preliminary Report, July 15, 1981." Ottawa.

Prins, Harald (1996). *The Mi'kmaq: Resistance, Accommodation and Cultural Survival.* Orlando, FL: Harcourt Brace Publishers.

Williams, Robert A. (1990, Sept.). "Encounters on the Frontiers of International Human Rights Law: Redefining the Terms of Indigenous Peoples' Survival in the World." *Duke Law Journal* (4): 600-704.

# 11

## The Persuasive Cartographer: Sexual Assault and Legal Discourse in R. v. Ewanchuk

### Rebecca Johnson

> The power exerted by a legal regime consists less in the force
> that it can bring to bear against violators of its rules than in its
> capacity to persuade people that the world described in its
> images and categories is the only attainable world in which a
> sane person would want to live. (Gordon, 1984:109)

In recent years, scholars have explored the terrain of the intersecting disciplines of law and geography (Pue, 1990; Wije, 1990). Cartography — the making of maps — has emerged as a recurrent theme. Certainly, legal scholars have made effective use of the techniques of mapmaking: they have documented differential rates of crime across the country (Canadian Centre for Justice Statistics, 1996; Sacco and Johnson, 1990), revealed gaps in the provision of legal services (Economides and Blacksell, 1987; Economides, 1996), documented the ongoing prevalence of racism (Kobayashi, 1990), and demonstrated the links between race, class, and poverty in urban centres (Kirschenman and Neckerman, 1991; Squires *et al.*, 1987; Dunn, 1994). Interestingly, scholars have also increasingly used cartography in a figurative sense, evoking mental maps. Such maps emerge as metaphors for depicting, interpreting, describing, evoking and explaining the subject matter of study (Twining, 1999).

In this essay, I follow the latter practice and suggest that in judicial reasons — the heart of legal discourse — one can see judges engaging in "cartography." In the reasons they give in legal cases, judges use images and categories to sketch out the contours of very concrete "maps" of the world. Making reference to these metaphoric maps, judges seek to persuade us of the necessity (indeed the inevitability) of the reasons they give. They seek to persuade us, as Gordon argues in the epigraph above, that the world they describe in their images and categories "is the only attainable world in which a sane person would want to live." To the extent that the cartography of legal discourse produces not simply a map but indeed a blueprint, the question is this: to what extent is legal discourse an effort to persuade us to act in such a way as to bring its imagined world into existence? To paraphrase *Star Trek's* Jean-Luc Picard, to what extent does legal discourse persuade us to "make it so"?

I will explore this question in the context of sexual assault law, using the Alberta Court of Appeal reasons in *R. v. Ewanchuk*.[1] I begin my cartographic exploration in Part I with a discussion of maps and blueprints. In Part II, I review the history of current *Criminal Code* provisions relating to sexual assault, and then compare the very different "maps of the world" embedded in the reasons for judgment of Justices Fraser and McClung in *Ewanchuk*. In Part III, I discuss the ways in which metaphors of maps and blueprints can provide a means for legal audiences to accept a greater degree of ownership for their participatory roles in the processes of legal world-making.

## Part I: Maps and Blueprints

### A PRELIMINARY DIGRESSION

I begin this discussion with an admission that I suffer a fascination with maps and blueprints. Indeed, a map and a blueprint were two of the sacred and mystical documents of my childhood. As a child, I was bundled off every summer to spend my school-free days at my grandfather's cabin in B.C.'s Okanagan Valley. There, I had my first experiences with the mysterious worlds of cartography and construction. My grandfather would remove from a container a large roll of paper: a detailed map of the area. Captured in its whispery lines was the world around us, the world that was, or rather, very nearly the world that was. My grandfather told us the secret: there was a lost lake that had not been found and mapped by the cartographer. The summer before I turned 6, my uncles took the family on a quest to find the lost lake. Armed with sack lunches, we headed off into the forest and hills. Although we found the lake and returned home safely, venturing into the unknown without a complete map of the world was an experience in terror for me. What if we were to become lost? How would we find our way back without an accurate map to show us the way home?

My father also had a scroll of paper that he would lay out on the table before us. This time, the lines on the paper were blue and powdery. It was a blueprint for our very own summer cabin, the home he would build for us. Pointing to lines and angles on the paper, he painted in our imaginations the vision of something real. He took us to the spot in the woods where the house would stand. We walked among the trees and ferns through what would be the kitchen and living room, we peered up into what would be the attic, and sat down on the forest floor, imagining the window through which we would be able to see through the cedars to the hills across the lake. But, in all the summers of my childhood, the cabin remained in the world of the imaginary. The dream of a home did not escape the powdery blue confines of the paper. The cabin was not brought into the world of the real.

I digress into stories of my childhood to link together maps and blueprints, to draw out their similarities. Blueprint and map: both scrolls of paper troubled me. I lacked fluency in their languages. How was I to translate my teeming world of fern, cedar, sun-speckled growth, and colour-drenched sunset to a monochrome trace of thin and wavy lines? How was I to mentally twist curve and angle to create an image of a home with a warm fireplace, sheltering me from torrential summer thundershowers? But I was troubled not only by a lack of literacy. Both documents left me with additional pressing worries. I feared the potential inaccuracy of the map, feared that in using it, I could be lost in an unmarked world, unable to find my way back to the safety of paths I knew. How could I know the map could be trusted? The blueprint raised different fears. What if the dream remained only a dream? How could the home be brought into existence? How would I be able to participate in making the dream a reality? How was one to gather the resources and people necessary to actually create the thing?

Both scrolls contained narratives rich with the promise of adventure, stories of inclusion and exclusion, of threat and danger, of new beginnings and safe returns. But there did seem to be some significant differences in these narratives. The blueprint was a story of possibility, a story that contained a vision of what might be and an implied set of imperatives — commands to be followed ("Do *this* if you wish to create this home"). Even as a child, I understood the imperative contained in the blueprint. Only action would bring the vision into existence. The map, on the other hand, seemed to be a representation of something which already existed. If the map also contained a set of imperatives, they were more along the lines of "follow the marked paths if you wish to return home safely," or "watch here for danger." For the literate, the map held the promise of valuable advice on how to negotiate one's way through existing and solid territory. It was a guide for locating oneself in the world. The map required only fluency in the language of maps, and trust in the map maker. While the blueprint carried an explicit agenda, the map seemed to be neutral — a marker of what *was*, not simply the tantalizing promise of what *might be* if I were to bring my actions in line with the drafter's vision.

### NEUTRALITY QUESTIONED: MAPMAKING AS WORLDMAKING

The assumption of neutrality in mapping has been displaced over the years, with knowledge of how the practices of mapping are themselves contested (Monmonier, 1991). Indeed, cartographers have acknowledged that "maps work by serving interests" (Wood, 1992:4). Donna Haraway, in her discussions of the Human Genome Project with its attempt to map the human gene, suggests that "mapmaking is world making," saying that "maps are models of worlds crafted through and for specific practices of intervening and particular ways of life" (Haraway, 1997:135). Maps are not simply descriptions of reality; they are a set of instructions to imagine the world in a certain way. To help us imagine the world as the cartographer imagines it, we are given a map which is selective in the details it offers us. Maps work as much by obscuring as by revealing; indeed, the obscuring is necessary for the map to work.

For example, the famous map of the London underground system works by removing from our attention all the multitudinous details of London city life, focusing our attention exclusively on the process of getting from one subterranean location to another. A sea chart removes information about what is above water level, and focuses on the variable depths of the land under the water, providing the sea captain with information to help him or her avoid rocky shoals and pass safely through the seas. By reducing detail, the map-maker enables the map-user to see things and make connections that would otherwise be difficult to see. And since maps serve interests, it is exactly these connections that the cartographer seeks to make present.

It is worth emphasizing that while maps must exclude and obscure, a map that neglects certain essential elements will not serve its function.

Some maps are simply inaccurate, and it is necessary to continually verify the accuracy of the maps being presented for our approval and consent. Indeed, there are occasions when inaccuracy in a map can have fatal consequences. It is important to attend to the difference between exclusion that is designed to reveal certain connections, and exclusion that is the result of error or mistake.

In the two examples above, the purpose of the map seems clear: to help a person move from one geographical location to another. But maps also encourage movement along political spectra, by encouraging the viewer to see different sorts of relationships between themselves and the world around them, to make connections between phenomena not usually placed together. For example, consider a map that documents the increase in unemployment among the upper, lower, and middle classes over the past decade, or a map illustrating the ratio of teachers to soldiers in countries around the globe, and then a map with dots indicating the incidence of housing discrimination as reported to the Michigan Civil Rights Commission. Such maps, by obscuring some details, make other details visible, and indeed seek to encourage a change in the way the viewer sees the world and its threats.

Further, maps do not only show what *is*. They sometimes make projections into the future, as a way of encouraging action in the present. For example, imagine an animated map showing the diffusion of the AIDS virus over time. The map not only shows the documented increase, but also makes projections into the future on the basis of current data. This projection, one that paints a pandemic future, is designed to create fear, which will mobilize current action (which, depending on the interests of the map user, might be to encourage funding for AIDS research, or to encourage strict quarantine laws). Similarly, in the struggles over the proposed casino in Vancouver, activists created a map of Vancouver showing a speculative vision of the skyline with the casino in place (Blomley, 1998). The map showed how the view would be destroyed by the megalith casino. Again, the map-maker drew what might be in the future, as a way of mobilizing present action against the casino.

Maps, then, are made for many different purposes: to help people negotiate rocky shoals; to make connections between their lives and different social phenomena; to see new threats in the world; to encourage political activity. Articulated thus, the distinction between maps and blueprints begins to blur: both may encourage action, both work by reducing detail, and neither is neutral. Despite these connections, maps and blueprints, as understood in popular culture and discourse, continue to be experienced as quite distinct, filling very different functions. Blueprints have explicit agendas. They direct attention to imagined worlds, and articulate the action that is required in order to bring the imagined out of the realm of the possible and into the realm of the concrete. Maps, on the other hand, *appear* less political, seeming to focus attention on tracing the contours of a world *that already exists*. I will return to this distinction later, but for now, I wish to examine what these maps might look like in the world of law.

How does the legal regime create its maps of the moral and social world? Through the tools of traditional legal method. Working in much the same manner as the cartographer of the physical, law directs our attention to certain details while concealing, obscuring, and erasing those dimensions of the world that are not relevant to a given legal vision of the world (Mossman, 1986). Using the tools of legal method, the selection of facts, the notions of relevancy and precedent, the legal regime creates its maps. Through the processes of attention and blindness, legal discourse, like the more familiar discourse of geographic cartography, reveals to us a specific world, documents the threats present in that world, and suggests appropriate avenues for people to mobilize against those threats.

For a map to be successful, to serve the interest that gave it birth — be it constructed with the tools of traditional or of legal cartography — the potential map user must be persuaded of the value of the map, of the map's success at capturing reality. This persuasive task is all the more difficult in situations where there is more than one map. Such situations raise the very issue which troubled me in my early encounters with my grandfather's map: accuracy. What if the map being relied upon is inaccurate, or fails to mark the presence of dangers or threats? Where two maps describe the world in different ways, how does one decide which map to rely upon? In the section that follows, I consider the conflicting maps of the world of sexuality and assault that emerged in *Ewanchuk*.

## Part II: Sexual Assault: Mapping the World in *Ewanchuk*

### THE LAW OF SEXUAL ASSAULT

The law has long acknowledged the persistence of sexual violence, and has crafted legal responses to this violence. However, the legal responses have often been very problematic from the point of view of the victims of such violence.[2] In Canada, for example, the crime of rape was long defined in such a manner as to render invisible a host of sexual violations by focusing on whether or not there had been penile-vaginal intercourse. Further, the possibility of spousal rape was a definitional impossibility, since the crime required proof of sexual intercourse by a man with a woman who was not his wife. Proof of rape was also often dependent on evidentiary standards not required for other offences.

Over the past twenty years, Canadian legislators have attempted to redraft the criminal law relating to sexual violence. As part of a large scale reform effort in the early 1980s, the law of "rape" was replaced by the law of "sexual assault." The doctrines of recent complaint and corroboration were repealed, and a "rape shield" law was put in place to protect complainants from questions about their moral character or past sexual history.[3] Though the rape shield was found to be unconstitutional by the Supreme Court of Canada in *R. v. Seaboyer*,[4] the Court did state that evidence of the moral character of the complainant in general was not relevant, and that even in the absence of a rape-shield law, the vast majority of such evidence should properly be excluded by judges. But the courts (and the victims of sexual assault) continued to face difficulties in the treatment of sexual assault. Some of these difficulties can be explained against the language of the law itself. The primary assault section reads as follows:

**265 (1) Assault** — A person commits an "assault" when

(a) without the consent of another person, he applies force intentionally to that other person, directly or indirectly;

(b) he attempts or threatens, by an act or a gesture, to apply force to another person, if he has, or causes that other person to believe on reasonable grounds that he has, present ability to effect his purpose; or

(c) while openly wearing or carrying a weapon or an imitation thereof, he accosts or impedes another person or begs.

**265 (2) Application** — This section applies to all forms of assault, including sexual assault, sexual assault with a weapon, threats to a third party or causing bodily harm and aggravated sexual assault.

**265 (3) Consent** — For the purposes of this section, no consent is obtained where the complainant submits or does not resist by reason of

(a) the application of force to the complainant or to a person other than the complainant;

(b) threats or fear of the application of force to the complainant or to a person other than the complainant;

(c) fraud; or

(d) the exercise of authority

Clearly, the question of consent is pivotal to the question of assault (MacKinnon, 1989: Pateman, 1980). Sexual contact that is consensual does not come within the world of criminal sexual assault law. But the law has not had a simple time dealing with the world of consent. In particular, how is one to know whether or not a given encounter was consensual? Particularly, what is a judge to do when there is a dispute about consent?

A central case dealing with this question is *R. v. Pappajohn*.[5] The woman in question asserted that she had been bound and assaulted by the accused. He, on the other hand, asserted that the encounter, though a bit rough and tumble, was consensual. While the Supreme Court sustained the man's conviction, the majority did accept the possibility that situations could exist where a judge would accept two quite disparate versions of events: a woman may not have consented; a man may have believed the woman to be consenting. Since the issue in a sexual assault trial was the *accused's* criminal guilt, it was the *accused's* belief that was most pressing. To the extent that he had an honest, albeit mistaken, belief in consent, he would not be guilty of sexual assault.[6] The problem is striking. One can have a sexual assault, but have no sexual assaulter. From the point of view of the victim of sexual assault, the Court seemed to sustain an approach that focused on the belief of the person instigating the sexual contact, rather than on that of the person subjected to that contact. Indeed, in the context of sexual assault in particular, the law had often presumed consent in the absence of evidence to the contrary. So, for example, to the extent that a woman failed to raise a "hue and cry," she risked a finding that she had consented. To the extent that a woman was unable to show the physical signs of her resistance (bruises, broken bones, ripped or torn clothing), an inference of consent might be drawn.

Partly in response to public outrage over the issue of mistaken belief in consent, the government adopted new provisions in 1992, sometimes referred to as the "no means no" provisions. In these provisions, the government sought to reverse the burden, and ensure that the person asserting the presence of consent provide some evidence of that consent. The provisions read as follows:

**273.1 (1) Meaning of "consent"** — [For the purposes of the sexual assault provisions], "consent" means ... the voluntary agreement of the complainant to engage in the sexual activity in question.

**273.1 (2) Where no consent obtained** — No consent is obtained, [for the purposes of the sexual assault provisions] ... where

(a) the agreement is expressed by the words of conduct of a person other than the complainant;

(b) the complainant is incapable of consenting to the activity;

(c) the complainant expresses, by words or conduct, a lack of agreement to engage in the activity; or

(d) the complainant, having consented to engage in sexual activity, expresses, by words or conduct, a lack of agreement to continue to engage in the activity.

**273.2 Where belief in consent not a defence** — It is not a defence to a charge [of sexual assault] that the accused believed that the complainant consented to the activity that forms the subject-matter of the charge, when

(a) the accused's belief arose from the accused's

(i) self-induced intoxication, or

(ii) recklessness or wilful blindness; or

(b) the accused did not take reasonable steps, in the circumstances known to the accused at the time, to ascertain that the complainant was consenting.

In these provisions, the government attempted to establish new rules to deal with arguments about implied consent, and about mistaken belief in consent. The new rules required an accused who wished to raise this defence to show that he or she had taken reasonable steps to ensure that they had the voluntary agreement of the other person. Questions about these new rules arose in the context of *Ewanchuk*.

THE CASE[7]

In this case, the 17-year-old complainant had gone to a job interview with the 30-year-old accused. The accused arranged for them to meet in the parking lot of a mall, where the accused had his car and trailer. The complainant asked if they could talk inside the mall. The accused preferred to stay near the trailer. The interview began in the car, but then the accused suggested they move to the trailer. When they entered the trailer, the complainant heard what sounded like the accused locking the door behind him. She became afraid that she would be attacked or killed, and, having just seen a T.V. program on strategies to survive such attack, tried to maintain outward composure and hide her fear. The accused had the complainant sit on the floor, and over the next two and a half hours, he instigated sexual activity on three occasions. On each occasion she asked him to stop, and he complied temporarily, but on each occasion proceeded to a more intimate form of contact. Finally she asked to leave, and the two left the trailer. She asked him to write his name for her on one of his brochures, and he offered her a $100 bill. She left, and promptly reported the assault. The trial judge, having heard the evidence, said the following:

> B [the complainant] is a credible witness, and I know that she was afraid. All of B's thoughts, emotions, and speculations were very real for her. However, she successfully kept all her thoughts, emotions, and speculations deep within herself. She did not communicate most of her thoughts, emotions, and speculations. She did clearly communicate with the one word "no" on three separate occasions, and on each occasion A [the accused] stopped.
>
> B says that she did not want to let A know that she was afraid. Like a good actor, she projected an outer image that did not reflect her inner self. B did not communicate to A by words, gestures, or facial expressions that she was "frozen" by a fear of force. B did not communicate that she was frozen to the spot, and that fear prevented her from getting up off the floor and walking out of the trailer.
>
> The Crown must prove lack of consent (and A's knowledge of the lack of consent) beyond a reasonable doubt. Consent may be implied or expressed, and clearly in this case we are dealing with implied consent.... In any event, the onus is not on the accused to prove implied consent. The onus is on the Crown to prove beyond a reasonable doubt that there was an absence of consent. The Crown has not proven its case, and I acquit the accused. (para 2, p. 86-87)

In coming to this conclusion, the trial judge made reference to some of the factors that presumably led him to conclude that an absence of consent had not been proved. He pointed out that the encounter took place in the middle of the day, that there were windows on both sides of the trailer and that other cars and people were in the parking lot, that there was no evidence that the door of the trailer actually had been locked, that the accused gave the complainant a brochure for his business which gave his address, and that he spelled his name for the complainant to write on the brochure as well as giving her his phone number. Also, having earlier been told that she had a young baby and that money was tight, he gave her a $100 bill when she left.

The Crown asserted that the trial judge had misunderstood the law, and appealed to the Alberta Court of Appeal. There, Justice McClung (supported in the result by Justice Foisy) concluded that the trial judge had applied the correct test in law, and that the acquittal should stand. Chief Justice Fraser, in dissent, came to a quite different conclusion. In her view the trial judge misapprehended the test concerning consent, and thus the acquittal could not be sustained, nor should there be a retrial. Rather, she found that, on the facts found by the trial judge, a conviction could properly be entered on the sexual assault charge. The Supreme Court of Canada eventually adopted a position similar to that expressed in the dissent of Justice Fraser. However, in this discussion, I focus not on the answer provided by the Supreme Court, but on the reasons given by Justices McClung and Fraser. In these reasons, we can more clearly compare the presence of two different maps of the world. At issue in these reasons is not just the meaning of the law of consent, but the map of the world in which this law is embedded.

JUSTICE McCLUNG'S MAP OF THE WORLD

In both sets of reasons, the judges begin by painting a picture of the relevant facts. There is, obviously, a process of selection here, and in the process of selecting relevant facts, the judges begin the process of creating a map of reality. Justice McClung begins by invoking the fear of appellate courts acting beyond their powers. Trial courts see witnesses and hear evidence. They are in the best position to make determinations about facts. Appeal courts do not make findings of fact. They are there to review errors of law. According to McClung, the Court of Appeal is being asked to overturn the findings of fact of the trial judge. An appeal court, he cautions, simply has no jurisdiction to upset trial findings of fact that have evidentiary support: "A Court of Appeal improperly substitutes its own view of the facts of a case when it seeks for whatever reason to replace those made by the trial judge" (para 1).

With this introduction, McClung foregrounds the threat of a renegade court, acting against the dictates of the rule of law. He goes on to emphasize the importance of the facts in the case. After including an extended passage from the reasons of the trial judge, McClung says, "The facts revealed by the record establish that the accused had no proven intention of forcibly pursuing his way with the complainant" (para 3). Though there were age and size disparities between the two, he does not find these significant. He instead emphasizes that both parties were of the age of consent: "the record does not reveal that size or age disparities were in any way determinative of what took place here between two persons who were both over the age of consent" (para 5). Indeed, in a much-quoted statement, he goes further:

> The Chief Justice's concerns [about age and size disparities] aside, it must be pointed out that the complainant did not present herself to Ewanchuk or enter his trailer in a bonnet and crinolines. She told Ewanchuk that she was the mother of a six-month old baby and that, along with her boyfriend, she shared an apartment with another couple. (para 4)

McClung adds that, in pointing out these aspects of the trial record, he has no intention of denigrating the complainant or lessening the legal protection to which she is entitled. Though she was not sexually naive, he concedes that she was nonetheless afraid. However, he adds, the facts suggest that her concerns about the possibility of force "were misplaced":

> ... during each of three clumsy passes by Ewanchuk, when she said "No!" he promptly backed off, while assuring her at least once, that he was "not that kind of person" and "that she needn't worry" and that he was a man of restraint. When she finally said she wanted to leave the vehicle he neither argued against it or materially obstructed her, delaying her exit. Again her wishes prevailed. (para 5)

In this description of the world, the two appear somewhat as equals in power. McClung paints a portrait of a clumsy man, but nonetheless a man of restraint, a man who essentially respected the wishes of the complainant, a complainant suffering from honest but fundamentally mis-placed fears. Her fears, he argues, are not the basis upon which one should construct a theory of criminal guilt. Whether or not *she* subjectively believed she was at risk, the central legal issue should be whether or not *he* subjectively believed she was consenting. The question of consent, McClung notes, cannot be resolved simply by reference to the mental state of the complainant, particularly one whose fears (as he has con-cluded) were misplaced:

> trial judges or juries are not obliged to assume that the reso-lution of the issue of consent or its absence in these cases becomes a completely internal and subjective exercise reserved to the complainant alone — an exercise that is ret-rospective, optional and silent, and one perhaps in contra-vention of the objective facts underlying the case. To exclude the belief of the accused from any contribution to the consent issue (and quite possibly his own fate) cuts across enshrined Canadian criminal law precepts and renders the law uncer-tain, inconsistent and resented. Every right-minded Canadian, male or female, deplores violence against women. But even the pursuit of a violence-free society must not be allowed to repudiate, or even dilute, the entrenched and statutory safeguards of our jurisprudence which have long and fairly protected those accused of serious crime. (para 7)

Now the map of the world reveals threats and dangers. Attention to the internal state of mind of the complainant creates a risk that long-entrenched safeguards will be diluted or repudiated. In this map, the issue is not violence against women. That is accepted as deplorable. But, as the facts have been painted by McClung, that is not the situation at hand in this case. The complainant's fears were misplaced. Her fears, however, have created the risk of an unjust conviction.

He goes on to describe the sexual activity in language that minimizes any suggestion of violence, and indeed, minimizes the sexual nature of the contacts:

> Three overtures were made by Ewanchuk. The first two were marginally identifiable, if at all, as sexual in nature. They involved mutual body massages which, while they neared her

> sexual organs, were not in contact with them. Nonetheless, the last was a clearly sexual activity; a deliberate exposure of his sexual anatomy as he rubbed himself against her clothed pelvic area. This performance...would hardly raise Ewanchuk's stature in the pantheon of chivalric behaviour, but it did take place in private and following her protest — "No!" — led to nothing. (para 11)

Again, he does not condone the behaviour in question, but in this map of the world, this behaviour is something to turn one's nose at, not something that should lead us to the untoward step of overturning our long-established safeguards on innocence and guilt. In this map, McClung again emphasizes the seriousness of sexual assault:

> It is right that we be constantly reminded that sexual assault can intractably erode the present and future integrity of its victims. Clearly this is so. Yet we must also remain aware that nothing can destroy a life so utterly as an extended term of imprisonment following a precipitately decided sexual assault conviction. (para 12)

McClung returns to his initial assertion that the facts must reign supreme. There was, he says, no finding that Ewanchuk pursued a sexual touching "in the face of an obvious lack of consent from his partner" (para 18). His assertion here again paints the threat of renegade appellate judges acting outside the boundaries of the law: "No beguiling or emotive restatement of the evidence can convert that fact finding to an error of law in order to erect a Crown appeal which otherwise does not lie" (para 18). This language of "beguiling and emotive" restatement is evocative of mythic language about Eve in the garden, being tempted to take the apple that will lead to expulsion. He encourages us to resist such language, to remain focused on justice. Referring to slogans used in a variety of feminist campaigns against violence, he says:

> In the search for proof of guilt, sloganeering such as "No means No!", "Zero Tolerance!", and "Take back the night!" which, while they marshall desired social ideals, are no safe substitute for the orderly and objective judicial application of Canada's criminal statutes. (para 12)

In phrases like these, McClung suggests that *that* is what was going on in the case. In this mapping, feminist sloganeering is evoked as the real threat to the criminal justice system.

Rape itself is identified as a threat, but the accused is not described in ways that identify him as a rapist. Ewanchuk is presented not as particularly sympathetic, but as a buffoon deserving of perhaps our pity, maybe even a slight degree of contempt, but certainly not of fear or danger. Indeed, he concludes:

> Ewanchuk's advances to the complainant were far less criminal than hormonal. In a less litigious age going too far in the boyfriend's car was better dealt with on site — a well-chosen expletive, a slap in the face or, if necessary, a well directed knee. What this accused tried to initiate hardly qualifies him for the lasting stigma of a conviction for sexual assault and Alberta's current bullet-train removal to the penitentiary for prolonged shrift. (para 21)

Again, in this map of the world, the real threat is unjust conviction. The complainant over-reacted with a sexual assault charge, perhaps because of her inappropriate under-reaction when in the trailer. A slap, or expletive, or knee was the appropriate response to clumsy hormonal advances. The solution is not to decentre the fundamental precepts of guilt.

A COMPETING MAP OF THE WORLD: JUSTICE FRASER

The map of the world in Chief Justice Fraser's judgment is framed by her decision to place the question of consent front and centre. The trial judge, she argues, erred in law as to the meaning of consent. Referring to the history of sexual-assault legislation reviewed above, she argues that the approaches of both the trial judge and Justice McClung reflect an approach to sexual assault that the government had made no less than three legislative attempts to overcome. The law, she argues, places the focus of attention on the person seeking to instigate a sexual experience, not on the recipient of those sexual attentions: "the new focus is on the culpability inherent in the accused's failure to take reasonable steps to determine if the act he is about to engage in is in fact mutual and consensual" (para 57). Recall that McClung had commented that the complainant had failed to communicate her fears to the accused, emphasizing *her* responsibility in the matter. Fraser asserts that such a view reflects an inversion of the approach set out in the *Criminal Code* provisions:

> these amendments represent further legislative steps to over-
> come the apparent unwillingness by some to let go of the
> debunked notion that unless a complainant physically resis-
> ted or expressed verbal opposition to sexual activity, an
> accused was entitled to assume that consent existed. Instead,
> the amendments place the responsibility to ascertain the *pres-
> ence of consent* to sexual activity precisely where it belongs —
> on the person, male or female, who wishes to initiate sexual
> contact with another person. (para 58)

While both McClung and Fraser focus on the problem of consent, they paint pictures of quite different threats. In McClung's map of the world, the threat is that the subjective internal experience of a complainant will be given priority, resulting in the precipitous conviction of an accused in the absence of any evidence that the accused had known that the other person wasn't consenting. In Fraser's map of the world, the threat is that a notion of implied consent creates the conditions for the victimization of those who are the recipients of unwanted sexual attention, by presuming them to consent in the absence of active resistence on their parts. She says:

> it is wrong in law to assume that a woman gives her "implied
> consent" to sexual activity unless and until she overtly signals
> her non-consent.... Parliament ... recognized that to presume
> that such "implied consent" exists denies women's sexual
> autonomy, not to mention their *Charter* equality rights.
> Women in Canada are not walking around this country in a
> state of constant consent to sexual activity unless and until
> they say "No" or offer resistance to anyone who targets them
> for sexual activity. (para 67)

An "implied consent" approach, in her map of the world, poses a threat to personal autonomy, and to equality rights. With this threat foregrounded, she returns to the facts, to sketch in the details of the map. Did Ewanchuk, she queries, take reasonable steps to determine if the acts he wanted to engage in were mutual and consensual? She first explores the issue of age and size, sketching a picture of the two people involved in the case: the complainant — 17 years old, 5'1" tall and about 105 lbs; the accused — in his 30s, over 6' tall and 2 to 3 times the size of the complainant. She says:

> It has been suggested that these facts are somehow irrelevant. I do not agree. They bear upon a number of issues, including whether the complainant submitted out of fear and also whether, in these circumstances — a job interview between two people who had no prior relationship with each other — Ewanchuk took reasonable steps to ascertain consent. (para 30)

While McClung had emphasized the relative power balance between them, Fraser paints a different picture, one which focuses not only on size, but also on context. The context, she asserts, is a job interview, and the power dynamics in such a context should alert an employer to an even heightened sense of responsibility with respect to issues of consent to sexual activity.

McClung had agreed that the complainant was afraid, but had argued that her fear was misplaced. Fraser, on the other hand, focuses not on whether or not the complainant's fear was misplaced, but rather on the accused. What did the accused actually *do* to ensure that consent had been given? The evidence, she argues, reveals that he in fact made *no* relevant inquiries about consent. In stating that the complainant had not entered the trailer in bonnet and crinolines, McClung seemed to assert that she was not so sexually naive as to have been unaware of the sexual dynamics in the situation. Fraser disputes the legitimacy of a conclusion that relies upon the traditional wisdom that girls who go into men's rooms are asking for it, saying that "Neither the complainant's agreeing to enter the trailer nor her agreeing that she was a friendly, open and affectionate person meets the "reasonable steps" threshold especially given the context here, a job interview" (para 114).

Indeed, in a bid to shift the construction of the complainant as having "asked for it," Fraser returns to the facts to more fully explore the context in which the complainant entered the trailer. In this telling of the facts, she maps a world in which the complainant told the accused that she preferred to have the interview in a more public place, but where, through a series of interactions, he actively moved the interview in the direction of the closed trailer. If Ewanchuk was blind to his responsibilities to ensure that he had consent, Fraser argues, that blindness could only have been wilful at best. In support of this conclusion, Fraser refers to the testimony of the complainant at trial:

Q. Did he ask you if you wanted him to lie on top of you before you [sic] did?

A. No.

Q. Did you want him to lie on top of you?

A. No.

Q. When he laid on top of you, what were you doing?

A. I was just laying there. I was — I didn't say anything. I didn't move.

Q. Was he saying anything to you?

A. Yeah. He was moving his pelvic area, and he was telling me that he could get me so horny so that I would want it so bad, and he wouldn't give it to me because he had self-control and because he wouldn't want to give it to me.

Q. Before that happened, had there been any discussion between the two of you about having any kind of sexual activity?

A. Not at all.

Q. What happened after he started moving his pelvic area against your pelvic area?

A. He asked me to put my hands across his back and touch his back, and I didn't.

Q. And how did ... [the pelvic grinding] stop?

A. I asked him to stop. I said, Just please stop. And so he stopped, and he got up to look at me, didn't get completely up off me, and he then just said, It's Okay. I won't hurt you. Don't be afraid. (para 38)

In this segment, Fraser uses the complainant's testimony to paint the portrait of a man busy constructing the complainant in accordance with his own imagined desires rather than attending to reality. We see Ewanchuk projecting his own desires onto the girl, telling her that it was she who desired the contact, and that he (as the self-controlled man) was going to withhold sexual pleasure from her until she was begging for it. Again, one can see the facts mapped very differently in the majority and dissenting judgment. While McClung had emphasized that Ewanchuk had stopped in response to the complainant's request, Fraser emphasizes that Ewanchuk stopped only to continue. In Fraser's map, Ewanchuk heard the complainant say "No, stop" but chose to reinterpret it as "please continue what you are doing, but first assure me that you won't hurt me when you are doing what I secretly desire you to do."

Fraser returns to the question of fear. In McClung's mapping of the world, the complainant's misplaced fears remained entirely subjective and uncommunicated. Fraser's review of the trial testimony suggests that, in spite of her attempts to hide her fear, the complainant's fear had in fact been very clearly communicated. In this mapping, Ewanchuk, wilfully blind, proceeded with his own agenda in the face of clear evidence that the complainant was not a willing participant, and further, was very fearful:

> Q. At the time he said to you, Don't be afraid, were you afraid?
> A. Very afraid. He said to me, I had you worried, didn't I? You were scared, weren't you? And I said, Yes I was very scared. And I had been holding myself from crying, and I knew that the expression on my face was fearful, and I did have tears in my eyes, and then he just said. It's okay. And he went to hug me, and he just laid on top of me again and continued what he was doing.
> Q. ... did he ask you if you wanted him to continue the sexual activity that had started?
> A. No, he just continued any ways, and he kept on telling me again and again not to worry, that he wouldn't hurt me, that he had self control, and that even though I was so horny, he wasn't.
> Q. Had you ever said anything to him to indicate to him that you were enjoying the sexual activity?
> A. This whole time I barely said anything except for the times that I said, No, stop. (para 38)

In his map, McClung had focused on the accused's assurances to the complainant "that she needn't worry." In his vision, the accused is portrayed as a clumsy man, but a man of restraint. Fraser, again using the complainant's voice from the trial transcript, suggests a quite different interpretation of the situation. Indeed, in her mapping, the assurances of the accused "not to worry" take on a more ominous tone, suggesting that there *is* something to be fearful of. Indeed, the complainant appears to have interpreted Ewanchuk's comments in just such a fashion:

> A. ... he then just said, Its okay. I won't hurt you. Don't be afraid. And he said, Do you trust that I won't hurt you. And I said, Yes, I trust that you won't hurt me.
> Q. Why did you say that you trusted he wouldn't hurt you?

> A. I was scared that if I said, No, I don't trust you, get off me
> or if I made a struggle, that he would force me to do some-
> thing worse or he would force himself on me more. (para 38)

Given that Ewanchuk continued in the face of tears, the admission that she was scared, and explicit demands to stop, Fraser argues that the accused can hardly be seen to have taken reasonable steps to assure that the complainant was complying. There was no express consent, and these facts hardly seem to illustrate consent through action, unless one presumes that consent exists. Fraser argues, "the emphasis is not on whether an accused got a 'No' or its equivalent (a kick in the groin, a poke in the eye, etc.) but whether he got a 'Yes' or its equivalent" (para 110). Ewanchuk, she says, "had no right to presume this consent absent some positive indication from the complainant that what she was interested in was sexual activity with him and not the job he purported to offer." (para 71) And indeed, she notes, the complainant did say "no," and said "no" on three occasions:

> Once the complainant said "No," Ewanchuk was then on
> notice that the complainant objected to what he was doing.
> This was supposed to be a job interview. And yet Ewanchuk
> persisted in his unwanted sexual activities, lying on top of her,
> grinding his pelvic area into hers, and then exposing his penis
> and rubbing it into her pelvic area. (para 92)

It is noteworthy also the difference in how the "unwanted sexual activities" are described in the two judgments. In McClung's language, the issue was "clumsy passes," two "overtures" which were "marginally identifiable if at all as sexual in nature," and a third overture which did involve the "exposure of his sexual anatomy"[8] in a manner that would not raise his stature in the "pantheon of chivalric behaviour," but which "led to nothing." The language in Fraser's judgment emphasizes a greater degree of control by Ewanchuk, and threat. She recounts a number of instances where he told the girl "I won't hurt you." He massaged her upper body and attempted to touch her breasts. She is more graphic in her description of him "grinding his pelvic area" into the complainant's, and "exposing his penis and rubbing it into her pelvic area."

## Part III: Legal Discourse as Worldmaking: Returning to the Metaphor of the Blueprint

Focusing on the metaphor of maps, one can see the debates about the *Ewanchuk* case in a certain light. Earlier, I posed the question, "how does one know which map is the authoritative one?" The easy answer in law is to rely on the principle of *stare decisis*. This principle states that lower courts are bound by the reasons given by higher courts. Thus, the problem can, it seems, be resolved quickly and with ease. Look to the Supreme Court. The Supreme Court adopted an approach similar to that taken by Chief Justice Fraser, and concluded that *Ewanchuk* had failed to show he had taken any reasonable steps to ensure that consent was present. McClung's map of the world, one might conclude, was simply missing too much information to be valuable as a guide in the world.

But to truly understand the ways in which legal discourse operates in the world, it is helpful to think about cases using not only metaphors of maps, but also of blueprints. Where the dominant metaphor is one of mapping, legal debates focus on whether or not the map presented in a given case is "accurate" — an adequate description of the world. The value of the metaphor of a blueprint is that it brings attention back to the issue of construction. In a blueprint, the issue is not "world-describing," but "world-making." While maps purport to represent an existing reality, blueprints capture a vision of a reality that might be — a vision that can be brought into existence only through the participation of others. The blueprint makes explicit both the agenda of the drafter, and the necessity of the reader's co-participation. It asks of the reader: Is this something you wish to bring into reality? If so, act as follows. This formulation indeed places participation front and centre.

What things in legal discourse become visible when we think about cases in terms of the blueprint metaphor? Let us return to *Ewanchuk*. In the two judgments, there are not simply two different maps of the world, but also two different blueprints; and action on the basis of either map will inevitably bring into existence very different worlds. How so? The map in McClung's world encourages a view where men are understood to right-fully rely on certain assumptions about consent. One of these is the assumption that responsibility for consent falls on the shoulders of women. It is women, in this view, who determine the course of sexual encounters by either conceding or withholding consent. Women are required to make their internal subjective worlds visible by, where appropriate, demonstrating lack of consent through expletives, slaps, or knees to the groin. Men are not required to actively seek evidence of consent. Indeed, men are presumed to be always willing, and women are the gatekeepers who determine whether or not things will proceed. This vision of the world, to the extent that people rely on it, holds in place a regime where sexual autonomy is at risk, and where indeed the promise of truly consensual action is hardly possible.

In Fraser's vision, the blueprint tells all those interested in participating in sexual activity to take responsibility for ensuring consent. This view encourages a quite different view of sexual behaviour. It not only requires men to take active steps to determine if there is consent, but does the same of women. That is, it encourages a view of sexual activity centred on the equivalent ability of men and women to make active choices and to enter into the world of dialogue. Rather than relying on myths and stereotypes about male and female sexuality, people are required to seek information, to check, to verify. Fraser's blueprint requires a greater degree of communication between people about the boundaries of potential sexual encounters.

For men and women, the *Ewanchuk* case presents two different visions about action in the world. McClung's vision, I would argue, purports to protect men not only from vengeful, lying women, but also from the inner subjective experience of wrongfully fearful girls who mistakenly keep their concerns to themselves. McClung's vision not only leaves such women at risk of rape by a man who is not a rapist; it also deprives men of the set of skills needed to ensure that they are involved in mutually desired activity. Fraser's view presumes that the average man is not interested in pursuing an activity that is not desired by both parties. The blueprint in her vision provides a mechanism for men to protect themselves not simply from the threat of wrongful accusation, but also from the possibility of finding themselves involved in an experience which is the result of fear rather than desire. Surely Fraser's imagined world is more appealing to men than McClung's, which protects them against unjust conviction, but not against the possibility of finding themselves involved in an experience based not on mutual desire and consent, but upon fear and coercion.

In the persuasive cartography of judicial decision-making, we can see that the maps of legal discourse are woven tightly with a number of blueprints. While there is value in uncovering and examining the detail in these maps, it is also crucial to attend to the embedded blueprints. In treating these maps as if they were simply descriptions of the world, map-users may find themselves acting in ways which (unwittingly) bring an imagined world into existence. To be persuaded of the accuracy of a map is to govern oneself according to the contours of that map. However, where the lines traced on the document are more akin to instructions than to descriptions, those who govern themselves according to the document participate in the creation of the world imagined therein. If we fail to understand the ways in which legal discourse is not simply description, but also a set of instructions about the appropriate way to act in the world, we may also fail to see that — to the extent that we uncritically accept law's "maps" of the world — we may participate in making those maps real.

## Addendum

A while ago, a vacation took me to Chicago. While there, I met up with a friend from a small American town. So, on a warm sunny day, we strolled down a lakeside avenue, laughing and chatting. But the sense of holiday atmosphere was abruptly broken. A black man passing us from the other direction suddenly started screaming and cursing at us. His violent verbal outburst was clearly directed at us, and it sent my adrenaline racing: Which way should I run? Where should I hide? But nothing further happened. The man kept walking in the other direction, directing a further string of verbal and gestural insults at us as he went. I was totally taken aback. As my heartbeat slowly returned to a normal rate, I racked my brains for an explanation. I could only come up with two: mental illness, or drugs.

I turned to my friend and started expressing my shock at the interaction. Why had the man directed such anger and fury at us? Here, my friend, looking somewhat sheepish, filled in the details I had missed. As we had been walking down the street, my friend had seen the black man approaching. It was clear that the black man would pass us on the right-hand side of my friend. My friend knew his wallet was in his right-hand pocket, and decided it wasn't safe enough there. So, he reached into his pocket, removed his wallet, and moved it to the comparative safety of his left-hand pocket. The black man approaching us had seen this action. He had also, it seems, correctly interpreted the reason for the decision to move the wallet. He understood that, in my friend's eyes, he had been constructed as a potential pick-pocket or thief, and that this construction had probably been on the basis that he was a black man.

What had happened? My friend, from a small American town, was simply acting on the basis of one specific "map" of the world. It is a map we all know, a map that suggests that cities are dangerous places, and that black men — particularly young black men — are threatening, and potentially violent.[9] Believing in the accuracy of the map, my friend was taking what he saw as the necessary steps to protect himself from the threats inscribed on that map.

We could use the metaphor of mapping here, and the metaphor would suggest certain questions for discussion. For example, a person might argue that my friend's map was inaccurate, pointing out that people are more likely to be the victims of intra- than of inter-racial violence, or that black men are more threatened than threatening. Such discussions, while useful, involve debates about reality. But attention to the metaphor of blueprint raises questions not simply about an existing reality, but about the ways in which individuals participate in the process of creating reality.

The blueprint metaphor highlights this second important dimension in my story. Acting on the basis of what he thought was a world map, my friend believed he was simply navigating his way through a pre-existing world. However, and whatever his intentions were, his actions played a part in bringing into reality a world in which race makes a profound difference — a world in which race is the marker for threat, and in which white people are justified in taking special measures to protect themselves from the racial other. His actions could be seen as reinforcing the view that white people are incapable of treating black people with the degree of respect reserved for other whites. Like most liberal-minded white people, my friend is committed to the notion of equality. However, that day on the streets of Chicago, his actions reproduced the blueprint of racial hierarchy, helping to bring into existence a world based on racial inequality.

It is here that map and blueprint merge. As Haraway argues, "Life is constituted and connected by recursive, repeating strands of information" (1997:135). When one absorbs and accepts as world maps strands of information that contour the black man as threatening, one acts accordingly. And when one absorbs and accepts strands of information that contour men as always sexually willing, and women as responsible for making express any denial of consent, one also acts accordingly. But action on the basis of a blueprint wrongly understood as a map participates in the very creation of this reality. Such behaviour "makes it so."

# Notes

1. *R. v. Ewanchuk* (1998), 212 A.R. 81.

2. Under some ancient Middle Assyrian laws, for example, if a married man raped a virgin living in her father's house, he would be required to marry the woman, while the innocent wife of the rapist would be given to the father of the raped woman to be dishonoured (made a prostitute). Here, the "victim" of the crime is the father, rather than the woman who had been raped. Certainly, one can imagine the devastating impact of the prospect of an indissoluble marriage to one's rapist. See Lerner (1986:116). While modern laws have reconceptualized the victim as the woman herself, rather than as the father or husband of the raped woman, the legal responses have remained problematic, and conviction rates have remained low. For a thoroughgoing discussion of the situation in Canada up through the early 1980s, see Stanley (1985, 1987).

3. There is a significant body of literature documenting the role such information plays in sexual assault cases. Some studies have shown the tendency of juries, in crimes with victims, to weight the conduct of the victim in judging the guilt of the defendant (see Kalven and Zeisel [1966]; Hans and Vidmar [1986]). In jury simulations tests, it appeared that any information implying that the victim had a prior sex history had the effect of reducing the perceived guilt of the accused regardless of whether this information was verified (see Catton [1975]). Another jury simulation test showed that those who received information of the prior third party sexual relations of the complainant were more likely than those who did not to infer consent, infer more responsibility to the victim, and became more reluctant to convict the accused (see Borgida [1981]).

4. *R. v. Seaboyer* (1992), 66 C.C.C. (3d) 321.

5. *R. v. Pappajohn* (1980), 52 C.C.C. (2d) 481.

6. In *R v. Sansregret* (1985), 18 C.C.C. (3d) 223, the Court added that this honest belief cannot be the result of wilful blindness. In that case, the accused broke into the house of his estranged girlfriend, forced her to strip at knife point, and threatened to kill her. In an attempt to survive, she focused on convincing him that reconciliation was possible, and agreed to have sex with him. Despite the fact that the accused believed the woman to be consenting, the Court concluded that such a belief could only have been maintained through wilful blindness to the context. No defence to the charge was available, and the accused was found guilty of sexual assault.

7. Here, all citations are to the Alberta Report version of the case, (see n. 1). I will use the paragraph number to identify quotations, and supplement the citation by adding the page number where a paragraph extends over more than one page.

8. McClung in fact repeats the trial judge's recounting of the final episode: "Later on A took his soft penis out of his shorts and placed it on the outside of B's clothes in her pelvic area" (para 2, p. 86 ). I can't help but wonder if the significance of the reference to a soft penis doesn't serve to emphasize the fact that this was not 'really' a sexual assault. That is, a soft penis cannot be a threat. Further, the emphasis to placing it 'outside her clothes in the pelvic area' also serves to neutralize the power and threat in the act.

9. For a discussion of the ways in which black men are portrayed in popular cultural media, see, for example, Giroux (1996), hooks (1992), Rivers (1996).

# References

Blomley, Nicholas (1998). "Landscapes of Property." *Law and Society Review* 32 (3):567-612.
Borgida, E. (1981). "Legal Reform of Rape Laws." *Applied Social Psychology Annual* 2:211-41.

Canadian Centre for Justice Statistics (1996). *A Graphical Overview of Crime and the Administration of Criminal Justice in Canada.*

Catton, Katherine (1975). "Evidence Regarding the Prior Sexual History of an Alleged Rape Victim: Its effect on the Perceived Guilt of the Accused." *University of Toronto Faculty of Law Review.* 165

Dunn, Seamus, ed. (1994). *Managing Divided Cities.* Keele: Ryburn Publishing.

Economides, Kim (1996). "Law and Geography: New Frontiers." In P.A. Thomas (ed.), *Legal Frontiers.* Aldershot: Dartmouth.

Economides, Kim, and Mark Blacksell (1987). "Access to Justice in Rural Britain: Final Report." *Anglo-American Law Review* 16 (4):353-75.

Giroux, Henry A. (1996). *"Fugitive Cultures: Race, Violence, and Youth."* New York: Routledge.

Gordon, Robert (1984). "Critical Legal Histories." *Stanford Law Review* 36:57.

Hans, Valerie P., and N. Vidmar (1986). "Juror's Views of Rape." *Judging the Jury.* New York: Plenum Press. 199-217.

Haraway, Donna J. (1997). *Modest_Witness@Second_Millennium.FemaleMan©_Meets_Onco-Mouse™.* New York: Routledge.

hooks, bell (1992). "Reconstructing Black Masculinity." In *Black Looks: Race and Representation.* Boston: South End Press.

Kalven, Harry, Jr., and H. Zeisel (1966). *The American Jury.* Boston: Little, Brown. 243

Kobayashi, Audrey (1990). "Racism and the Law in Canada: A Geographical Perspective." *Urban Geography* 11:447-73.

Lerner, Gerda (1986). *The Creation of Patriarchy.* New York: Oxford University Press.

MacKinnon, Catherine (1989). *Towards A Feminist Theory of the State.* Cambridge, MA: Harvard University Press.

Monmonier, Mark (1991). *How to Lie with Maps.* Chicago: University of Chicago Press.

Mossman, Mary Jane (1986). "Feminism and Legal Method: The Difference it Makes." *Australian Journal of Law and Society* 3:30.

Kirschenman, Joleen, and Kathryn M. Neckerman (1991). "'We'd Love to Hire Them, But...': The Meaning of Race for Employers." In C. Jencks and P.E. Peterson (eds.), *The Urban Underclass.* Washington: The Brookings Institution.

Pateman, Carol (1980). "Women and Consent." *Political Theory* 8:149.

Pue, W. Wesley (1990). "Wrestling With Law: (Geographical) specificity vs. (Legal) Abstraction." *Urban Geography* 11 (6):566-85.

Rivers, Caryl (1996). *Slick Spins and Fractured Facts: How Cultural Myths Distort the News.* New York: Columbia University Press.

Sacco, Vincent F., and Holly Johnson (1990). *Patterns of Criminal Victimization in Canada.*

Squires, Gregory D., Larry Bennett, Kathleen McCourt, and Philip Nyden (1987). *Chicago: Race, Class, and the Response to Urban Decline.* Philadelphia: Temple University Press.

Stanley, Marilyn (1985). *Sexual Assault Legislation in Canada: An Evaluation.* Ottawa: Department of Justice.

Stanley, Marilyn (1987). *The Experience of the Rape Victim with the Criminal Justice System Prior to Bill C-127.* Ottawa: Communications and Public Affairs, Department of Justice.

Twining, William (1999). "Mapping Law: The MacDermott Lecture." *Northern Ireland Legal Quarterly* 50 (1):12-49.

Wije, Chand (1990). "Applied Law and Applied Geography." *The Operational Geographer* 8 (1):27-31.

Wood, Denis (1992). *The Power of Maps.* New York: Guilford Press.

# Contributors

**Lori G. Beaman** is assistant professor in the department of sociology at the University of Lethbridge. Her primary research focus is the exploration of law as discourse, with specific attention to access to justice. Her current research examines the ways in which religious freedom is translated by the courts, particularly in relation to religious minorities. She lives in Lethbridge during the school year, and returns to the east coast to rehydrate and write in the summers.

**Chris 'Nob' Doran** is associated with the department of social science and the Centre for Criminal Justice Studies at the University of New Brunswick, Saint John. His work has appeared in a variety of edited books and scholarly journals, including: *Social and Legal Studies, Journal of Historical Sociology, Canadian Review of Sociology and Anthropology, Women and Criminal Justice, Canadian Journal of Sociology, Canadian Journal of Political and Social Theory,* and *Social Studies of Science.* Currently, he is working on the development of a formal theory of "incorporation."

**Patricia Hughes** currently holds the Mary Louise Lynch Chair in Women and Law in the Faculty of Law at the University of New Brunswick. She earned a doctorate in political theory at the University of Toronto in 1975, with a thesis on John Stuart Mill entitled "Women, Property and the State: Reconciling Irreconcilables" and subsequently taught political science until taking a law degree at Osgoode Hall Law School in 1982. She has been variously an adjudicator, university professor, and candidate for Parliament.

**Rebecca Johnson** is an assistant professor in the Faculty of Law at the University of New Brunswick. In her life before law, she studied music and management. She now teaches constitutional law, criminal law, feminist advocacy, and a course on representations of women and law in popular culture. Her recently completed doctoral dissertation (Michigan, 2000) explores the ways that women's lives are marked by different combinations of privilege and disadvantage through the intersection of gender with race, class, and sexual orientation.

**Gayle MacDonald** is an associate professor of sociology at St. Thomas University. Her areas of expertise include sociology of law, feminist jurisprudence, and criminological theory. In addition to this collection, she has edited a *Critical Issues in Corrections* text, which is also coming to press. MacDonald's current work is in the area of sexuality and law, and she is conducting research on the sex trade in the Maritimes.

**Susan Machum**, a native-born New Brunswicker, holds a doctoral degree in sociology from the University of Edinburgh. Her M.A. in sociology is from Dalhousie University and her Honours B.A. is from St. Thomas University. She has been a sessional professor at Mount Allison University and St. Thomas University, and a part-time lecturer at St. Thomas and the University of New Brunswick in Fredericton. Her interests are women's work, social change, the transformation of rural areas, political economy, inequality, and environmentally sustainable development.

**Melinda Martin** is a Mi'gmaq woman and member of the Listuguj First Nation. She graduated from the University of Ottawa with a law degree (Common Law) in June 2000. This followed a B.A. (Native Studies) received from St. Thomas University in 1997. Melinda returned to the University of Ottawa in the fall of 2000 to pursue a Civil Law degree. As a student representative of the Indigenous Bar Association (IBA), Melinda testified in November 1999 before the Fisheries and Oceans Parliamentary Standing Committee concerning *R. v. Marshall*.

**Sheila Noonan** is associate professor in the Faculty of Law, Queen's University, Kingston. Her work has always been decidedly feminist, critical and caring. She has written extensively in areas of feminist jurisprudence, on children's rights, on abortion, and in this volume, the history of mid-wifery, witchcraft, and medicine. She is currently on disability leave from Queen's, enjoying what the universe has to offer.

**Audrey Sprenger** is a lecturer in the department of sociology and women's studies at the University of Wisconsin-Madison. She is currently working on a community study and epistemological critique of ethnography called "Place Maps: The Sociology of Home" and an ethnographic atlas of work on the Canadian Prairies focusing on non-resource-dependent labour. She is also working on a textual analysis of Canadian forest policy and law from the 1900s to the present, examining how sentimental tropes of "home" have been used to build and develop the Canadian industrial forest.

**Sandra Wachholz** is currently teaching in the criminology department at the University of Southern Maine. She received her Ph.D. from Sam Houston State University in Huntsville, Texas. Her research and publications address the relationship between structural oppression and violence against women. She was a Fulbright Scholar at the University of Stockholm, Sweden.

# Index

# Index of Court Cases

This book is composed
in Electra. Considered a
landmark of Early Modern
type design in the United
States, Electra was created
by the Boston typographer
William Addison Dwiggins
in 1935.